D0531444

ETHICS AND EDUCATION

BY R. S. PETERS

Brett's History of Psychology
Hobbes
The Concept of Motivation
Authority, Responsibility and Education
Social Principles and the Democratic State
(with S. I. Benn)

ETHICS AND EDUCATION

R. S. PETERS

Professor of The Philosophy of Education
University of London Institute of Education

London
GEORGE ALLEN & UNWIN LTD
RUSKIN HOUSE MUSEUM STREET

FIRST PUBLISHED IN 1966
SECOND IMPRESSION 1967
THIRD IMPRESSION 1967
FOURTH IMPRESSION 1968
FIFTH IMPRESSION 1968
SIXTH IMPRESSION 1969

FIRST PUBLISHED IN THIS EDITION 1970
SECOND IMPRESSION 1971

This book is copyright under the Berne Convention. All rights are reserved. Apart from any fair dealing for the purpose of private study, research, criticism or review, as permitted under the Copyright Act, 1956, no part of this publication may be reproduced, stored in a retrieval system, or transmitted, in any form or by any means, electronic, electrical, chemical, mechanical, optical, photocopying, recording or otherwise, without the prior permission of the copyright owner. Enquiries should be addressed to the Publishers.

© *George Allen & Unwin Ltd, 1966*

ISBN 0 04 370011 X *Cased*
ISBN 0 04 370032 2 *Paper*

PRINTED BY PHOTOLITHOGRAPHY
IN GREAT BRITAIN
BY ALDEN AND MOWBRAY, OXFORD

PREFACE

This book is designed to serve two functions. Firstly it is meant to serve as an introductory textbook in the philosophy of education in the field of ethics and social philosophy; secondly it presents a distinctive point of view both about education and about ethical theory. It is hoped, therefore, that it will be of interest both to teachers and to students of philosophy.

The very nature of the book is bound to expose it to criticisms from some of the two types of reader for whom it is intended. On the one hand hard-headed teachers will complain that it is too abstract, that it does not get down sufficiently to the concrete substantive problems of the class-room. On the other hand some students of philosophy will complain that many of the philosophical points are not argued in enough detail. The reply to the first type of criticism is that this book is as concrete as it can be without abandoning its claim to be a philosophical work. To expect it to be any more concrete, or to provide answers to substantive questions, is to fail to understand what sort of inquiry philosophy is and the part which it can play as a contributory element in educational theory. The reply to the second sort of criticism is to admit that the treatment of philosophical issues is simplified, as it must be in work of this nature, but to express the hope that it is not superficial. In other words philosophical positions are put forward which could be and, in some cases, have been defended elsewhere in more detail in publications designed exclusively for students of philosophy. Those who work in areas such as political philosophy, and the philosophy of education, where philosophical issues are very much 'immersed in matter', have to learn to live with criticisms of this sort which are an occupational hazard. If sensitivity to such criticisms prevents them from committing their views to print in a form in which they are intelligible to non-specialists, both political and educational theory will remain in the state in which they have been for so long—an undifferentiated mush, uninformed by the basic disciplines which, logically speaking, must contribute to them.

A more valid criticism of this book is that it has been written too soon and too quickly. It should have taken five years instead of the three years which it has actually taken. The author's views on many issues have taken shape as the work has proceeded; new points have kept on presenting themselves which need further following up. There has been the excitement of charting a comparatively unexplored region where there are almost no signposts. But this is one of the main reasons for publishing a book somewhat prematurely. The point is to provide a few signposts for others and to map the contours of the field for others to explore in a more leisurely and detailed manner. The important thing in the philosophy of education is that something should be there to indicate what it is and to provide a determinate structure on which students can train their critical faculties. The philosophy of education is in too undeveloped a state to delay much longer the publication of such a work. It will only develop as a rigorous field of study if a few philosophers are prepared to plough premature furrows which run more or less in the right direction.

Philosophy is essentially a co-operative enterprise. Advances are made when two or three are gathered together who speak more or less the same language and can meet frequently for the purpose of hitting each other politely on the head. Under such conditions it is difficult to state precisely one's indebtedness to others on particular points. I am very conscious of my indebtedness to Stanley Benn, for instance, with whom I worked for five years previously on our *Social Principles and the Democratic State*. Many of the ideas which are worked out in Part Three of this book originated in discussions I had with him during that period. He has also been kind enough to send comments on Part Two from his new post at the Australian National University.

Many other ideas, especially on ethics and philosophy of mind, date back to those halcyon days at Birkbeck College when I worked with Ruth Saw, David Hamlyn and A. Phillips Griffiths. My indebtedness to Griffiths, especially in respect of the elaboration of the transcendental arguments advanced in Part Two of the book, is considerable. We were in continuous discussion about ethical issues over a period of years and wrote a joint article for *Mind* on 'The Autonomy of Prudence', which proved to be the jumping-off place for Chapter V on *Worth-while Activities*. Griffiths is now Professor of Philosophy at the University of Warwick and has been good enough to comment in detail on Part Two. Professor Hamlyn has also been kind enough to comment on Chapter VIII on *Respect for Persons*, which gave me more trouble than any other chapter in the book.

On more strictly educational matters I am most indebted to Paul Hirst, who has just been appointed to the Chair of Education at King's College, who has been my colleague during my three years at the Institute. I have had vigorous discussions with him over this period on most issues raised in Part One of this book. I have also learnt much from Basil Bernstein, also of the Institute of Education, with whom I have discussed many sociological issues. He was kind enough to make detailed comments on Chapter IX. My thanks are also due to Lionel Elvin, Director of the Institute, for his comments on Chapter IV. I am also indebted to Professor Israel Scheffler, of the Harvard Graduate School of Education, for his comments on an early version of Part One of the book.

I would like also to thank Professor A. C. F. Beales of King's College, Professor W. R. Niblett, Dean of the Institute of Education, and Professor L. A. Reid, my predecessor in the Chair of the Philosophy of Education at the Institute, for their kindness in commenting on the completed manuscript before it was dispatched to the publisher. This book, as I started off by saying, has taken shape in process of being written. This has been exciting for the author, but exasperating for anyone who has had to decipher the manuscript and reproduce it in legible form. My thanks are therefore finally due to my secretary, Stella Worsfold, for the patience, good humour and precision with which she has carried out this unenviable task.

University of London Institute of Education   *R. S. Peters*
October 1965

CONTENTS

11

CONTENTS

CONTENTS

INTRODUCTION

There was a time when it was taken for granted that the philosophy of education consisted in the formulation of high-level directives which would guide educational practice and shape the organization of schools and universities. These expectations of philosophy still persist in ordinary language. They are as implicit in the question 'What is his philosophy of education?' as they are in the question 'What is his philosophy of life?' Professional philosophers, however, are embarrassed by such expectations. For during the twentieth century, philosophy has been undergoing a revolution,[1] which has consisted largely in an increasing awareness of what philosophy is and is not. Few professional philosophers would now think that it is their function to provide such high-level directives for education or for life; indeed one of their main preoccupations has been to lay bare such aristocratic pronouncements under the analytic guillotine. They cast themselves in the more mundane Lockian role of underlabourers in the garden of knowledge. The disciplined demarcation of concepts, the patient explication of the grounds of knowledge and of the presuppositions of different forms of discourse, has become their stock-in-trade. There is, as a matter of fact, not much new in this. Socrates, Kant, and Aristotle did much the same. What is new is an increased awareness of the nature of the enterprise.

It is understandable that it should be thought incumbent on the philosopher to produce high-level directives; for the questions he asks have a high-level or second-order character. Plato rather grandiloquently described the philosopher as the spectator of all time and all existence, thereby putting the second-order character of philosophical questions in a cosmic setting. The image of the spectator is an appropriate one; for just as a spectator, to a certain extent, detaches himself from the activities of which he is a spectator in order to watch and comment on them, so also does a philosopher detachedly ponder upon and probe into activities and forms of discourse in which he and others engage. But not all those who adopt the stance of a spectator to human affairs are philosophers; for journalists, chroniclers, and sociologists could adopt a similarly reflective and detached stance without ever asking a philosophical question. What distinguishes the philosopher is the type of

[1] See Ryle, G. (Ed.), *The Revolution in Philosophy* (London, Macmillan, 1956).

second-order questions which he asks. These are basically the same questions asked by Socrates at the beginning—the questions 'What do you mean?' and 'How do you know?'

Such questions, of course, did not arise in a social vacuum. Athens was a great trading centre and with the merchandise came travellers with diverse beliefs and customs. Under conditions such as these the habit of a people to rely on its traditional stock of beliefs and customs is disrupted. For reflective people begin to wonder whether there is some truth in what others say and whether there is some virtue in their customs. To ask such questions is one thing, but to answer them is quite another; for it is only possible to decide between competing beliefs and standards if criteria emerge by reference to which they can be assessed. The search for such criteria is the kernel of philosophical inquiry. Philosophers make explicit the conceptual schemes which such beliefs and standards presuppose; they examine their consistency and search for criteria for their justification. This does not imply that philosophers can only produce an abstract rationale of what is in existence, like a high-level projection of the plan of a house. For inquiry at this level can develop with some degree of autonomy. Presuppositions can be drastically criticized and revised; grounds for belief can be challenged and new ones suggested; conceptual schemes can be shown to be radically inconsistent or inapplicable; new categorizations can be constructed. The philosopher is not entirely the prisoner of the presuppositions of his age.

As philosophy developed its various branches became differentiated in accordance with the different realms of knowledge such as mathematics, science, and morals which gradually emerged out of an amalgam of undifferentiated assumptions. Indeed the asking of philosophical questions was itself part of the process by means of which such distinct realms became differentiated. A scientific question, for instance, is one that can, in principle, be answered by certain kinds of procedures in which observation and experiment play a crucial part. But the clarification and discussion of the concepts used and of how they have meaning, and of the procedures by means of which these questions are answered, is a philosophical inquiry. Bacon's *Novum Organum*, for instance, was both an abstract from the actual practice of scientists, and a potent catalyst in the differentiation of science as a distinct realm of knowledge. His work provided inspiration for the founding of the Royal Society as well as a rationale of the practice of its precursors.

Thus the development of the philosophy of different activities and realms of discourse has proceeded *pari passu* with the differentiation of the types of concepts and procedures distinctive of them. Moral philosophy or ethics, with which much of this book will be concerned, developed *pari passu* with the separation of morality as a code of conduct, conceived of as being distinct from custom and law. Moral philosophers such as Hobbes and Kant did much to establish this differentiation. What is distinctive of ethics as a branch of philosophy is that it is concerned with the analysis and justification of answers to practical questions where 'practical' is contrasted with 'theoretical'. Questions can arise about what the moon is made of, when Stalin died, or why swallows migrate at the end of the summer. These are all theoretical questions in that no issue of doing anything or changing anything is settled by answering them. The issue is about what is the case or why it is so or when something happened. Practical questions, on the other hand, are concerned with what ought to be the case, with reasons for action. To consider whether a man ought to be killed is different from wondering whether he is dead; to deliberate whether it is right to smoke is different from speculating about the causes of smoking. This realm of discourse has its own distinctive concepts such as 'ought', 'right', 'desirable', 'worth-while', and 'good' as well as its own distinctive procedures for answering questions which are raised. Practical questions cannot be answered by tests in the laboratory any more than scientific questions can be answered by moralizing. Men have laboriously learnt to distinguish what they demand of the world from how things are. The development of such a differentiated consciousness is a major achievement of the human race. To this development philosophy has contributed much.

In some realms of discourse, however, the different types of questions so far distinguished are necessarily intermingled. By this is meant that the issues raised necessarily require the answering of both theoretical and practical questions before they can be settled. Educational issues are of this nature; for any proposals about education involve judgments about worth-while things which are to be transmitted. They therefore have assumptions built into them both about what is worth while and about how they can be transmitted. The philosopher's task is therefore a complex one; to discharge it he has to apply analyses of concepts and theories of justification developed in the various branches of philosophy —especially in ethics, social philosophy, epistemology and philosophical psychology. For, as can readily be inferred from the foregoing analysis, education raises no philosophical problems that are *sui generis*; it is a field, like politics, where several of the basic branches of philosophy have application. This inference needs to be spelt out in a bit more detail; for the philosophy of education has not been rigorously explored since the 'revolution in philosophy' because, to a large extent, there has been a widespread misunderstanding about what it is. Philosophers, on the other hand, treat it with mild contempt either because they assume that its exponents regard it as a *sui generis* branch of philosophy or because their bent is to pursue fundamental questions in ways dictated by the history of the discipline itself and not as they arise from concrete issues; educators, on the other hand, formulate principles in ignorance of the detailed discussion by philosophers of the fundamental assumptions presupposed by their principles. The result has been that, since the passing of John Dewey and the type of philosophy which he represented, there has been little done in which the grasp of the concrete has been illuminated by philosophical thinking of a rigorous type. What then are the main issues with which the philosophy of education is concerned?

(i) There is, first of all, the analysis of concepts specific to education —such as 'education', 'teaching', 'training', and 'university', and 'school'. This falls under philosophical psychology on the one hand and social philosophy on the other; for the concepts belong to the families of concepts concerned with learning and with social institutions.

(ii) The application of ethics and social philosophy to education should be obvious enough. There are assumptions about worth-while content which require justification; there are also assumptions about the desirability of the procedures by means of which this is to be transmitted. Problems of content raise the age-old issue of the desirability of poetry rather than of push-pin; problems of procedure raise ethical issues to do with liberty, equality, authority and punishment.

(iii) Assumptions about transmission also raise not only low-level empirical questions about learning and motivation but also fundamental problems in philosophical psychology about the conceptual schemes employed by educational psychologists and the types of procedures by means of which their assumptions can be tested—e.g. Freudian assumptions about 'the unconscious'—which are particular problems in the philosophy of science.

(iv) Finally there are all sorts of philosophical problems connected with the curriculum. In so far as education involves the transmission of differentiated forms of thought such as science, history, morals and mathematics, the philosophy of these forms of thought is obviously relevant. For a discussion of their transmission cannot proceed adequately without a clear grasp of what is distinctive about their content. There is then the problem of how the logical aspects of these forms of thought are related to the psychology of learning. There are questions, too, about the relation of school subjects to forms of thought, about what could be meant by 'the integration of the curriculum', and how it contributes to moral and aesthetic education.

At least three books would have to be written to deal adequately with the problems indicated in this brief sketch of a programme for the philosophy of education. This book will not attempt to compress three books into one. It will deal only with the application of ethics and social philosophy to problems of education. To do this there must be a preliminary, if brief, treatment of the concept of 'education'. For it would be precipitate to plunge into fundamental ethical issues involved in education without a precise notion of what education is and of the types of value-judgment that it exemplifies. The analysis of the concept of 'education' will therefore be tailored to the issues of justification and of moral education which are to be raised in later parts of the book.

Such a curtailment of conceptual analysis is not just required by limitations of space. It can also be defended by the plea of pertinence; for the exploration of concepts can be conducted with varying degrees of minuteness and along manifold dimensions. There is little point in such an exploration unless something depends on what is made explicit. To fail to make necessary distinctions is a cardinal philosophical sin; but it is equally sinful to make distinctions which are never used. This sin, which is characteristic of the pathology of philosophy, can only be avoided if conceptual analysis is linked with some other issue such as that of the justification of beliefs. It is hoped, therefore, that the preliminary analysis of 'education' will shine with virtue in that its detail and depth will be determined mainly by the use to which it will be put in later sections of the book.

PART ONE

THE CONCEPT OF 'EDUCATION'

CHAPTER I

CRITERIA OF 'EDUCATION'

I. THE CONCEPT OF 'EDUCATION'

It might be thought that the obvious way of beginning a study in the philosophy of education would be to formulate a definition of 'education' and to see whether this would fit all examples of it. After all, did not Socrates do just this when he tried to clarify concepts such as 'justice' or 'courage'? Did not G. E. Moore proceed like this in his *Principia Ethica* when conducting what he called a 'typically ethical inquiry' into 'good'? To proceed in this way, in the middle of the twentieth century, would reveal a certain insensitivity to one of the main contentions of the recent 'revolution in philosophy'. For Wittgenstein, one of the leaders of this revolution, argued with great subtlety that philosophers from Socrates to Moore had been mistaken in thinking that a formula could be found which would encompass the different uses of words like 'justice' or 'knowledge' in which they were interested. The uses of a word are not always related by falling under a definition as in geometry where definitions are provided for terms such as 'triangle'. Rather they often form a 'family' united 'by a complicated network of similarities overlapping and criss-crossing; sometimes overall similarities, sometimes similarities of detail'.[1] This is particularly true of the sorts of terms in which philosophers are interested; for they are usually very general terms, which have developed a life of their own in a variety of contexts. They have seldom been consciously erected to perform a limited function in a confined system. The Greek words αἰτία (cause) and λόγος (reason), for instance, developed a very rich and ubiquitous life of their own. It would be as difficult to give a precise definition of them as it would be to pin down the concept of 'love' with a formula.

'Education' is a concept of this sort, though it is not as difficult to get a grip on it as it is on more abstract concepts such as 'cause' or 'truth'. Nevertheless there are usages of the *term* 'education' which it would be difficult to encompass in any precise definition. For instance, people often say things like 'It was a real education to have to travel

---

[1] Wittgenstein, L., *Philosophical Investigations* (Oxford, Blackwell, 1953), p. 32.

with my neighbour.' This usage is an exception to the obvious criterion that education is something that we consciously contrive for ourselves or for others. This does not mean, however, that there are *no* criteria of 'education' which are co-extensive with most of its central usages. It only means that terms in a natural language develop a life of their own and send out shoots which take them far away from the central trunk of the concept. But this does not imply the abandonment of the criteria; rather it leads us to distinguish between central and peripheral usages of the term. The important thing is that we should recognize the differences in the uses as well as the similarities. The formulation of criteria, which started with Socrates, is an attempt to make explicit what binds the uses together. It is like a guide to the customs of a people rather than a definitive statement of their law.

Another widespread error about meaning to which Wittgenstein also drew attention was the assumption that all words have meaning on the model of names which are associated with some typical referent. This had led to the postulation, as in Plato's theory of Forms, of abstract referents or essences for abstract terms such as 'justice', and of mysterious inner entities and processes to which words like 'mind' or 'intuition' might refer. Wittgenstein did not wish to deny that something is going on when people are thinking or having intuitions. He only wished to deny that there is any one special sort of thing which *must* be going on, and that reference to such a special process is essential for giving meaning to the concept in question. The term 'intuition' for instance calls attention not to a peculiar inner process but to a type of public claim that is made when people claim to know things 'by intuition' or to have intuitions about other people's motives. For they are intimating that they are sure of what they say or think but that they can produce no grounds to back their convictions.

Many might claim that Wittgenstein was in fact mistaken in the application of this thesis to the analysis of particular mentalistic terms; but few would deny that his general thesis was a salutary if unoriginal one. Not all terms have meaning on the model of names by being associated with some typical referent. And surely 'education' is a term of this sort. 'Education' is not a term like 'gardening' which picks out a particular type of activity. Something, of course, must be going on if education is taking place and something must have been gone through for a person to emerge as an educated man. For education is associated with learning, not with a mysterious maturation. But no specific type of activity is required. A man can do it himself in solitary confinement, or acquire it by constant activity in a small group. He can be trained on his own by a tutor or be inspired by lectures given to 500. In this respect 'education' is rather like 'reform'. It picks out no particular activity or process. Rather it lays down criteria to which activities or processes must conform.

2. THE NORMATIVE ASPECT OF 'EDUCATION'

There is another respect in which 'education' is like 'reform'. Both concepts have the criterion built into them that something worth while should be achieved. 'Education' does not imply, like 'reform', that a man should be brought back from a state of turpitude into which he has lapsed; but it does have normative implications, if along a slightly different dimension. It implies that something worth while is being or has been intentionally transmitted in a morally acceptable manner. It would be a logical contradiction to say that a man had been educated but that he had in no way changed for the better, or that in educating his son a man was attempting nothing that was worth while. This is a purely conceptual point. Such a connection between 'education' and what is valuable does not imply any particular commitment to content. It is a further question what the particular standards are in virtue of which activities are thought to be of value and what grounds there might be for claiming that these are the correct ones. All that is implied is a commitment to what is thought valuable.[1] This connection with commendation does not prevent us either from speaking of 'poor' education, when we think that a worth-while job is being botched, or of 'bad' education, when we think that much of what people are working at is not worth while, though it is a nice question to determine at what point we pass from saying that something is 'bad' education to saying that it is not education at all. There is, too, a more neutral way of using such a term. A sociologist or anthropologist might speak of the education system or moral code of a community without implying that he thought it desirable. But in such cases the implication is that those whose system or code it is consider that it involves what is desirable. The social scientist would be merely describing what others think worth while. But if he went on to say that he did not think that the educational system of a community had any educational value he would be passing a judgment himself which intimated what he thought worth while.

[1] For questions of justification see Part Two of this book.

(a) The task-achievement analysis of 'education'

It is this implication that something worth while is being passed on or promoted that makes 'education' a special case of what Ryle calls an 'achievement word'.[1] Ryle distinguishes what he calls 'task' words from 'achievement' words. 'Hunting' denotes a task, 'finding' an achievement. His main point is that words like 'finding' and 'winning' and hence epistemological words like 'concluding' and 'hearing' do not pick out activities or processes in addition to 'looking', 'running', 'reasoning' and 'listening'. Rather they are indicative of the successful outcome of the tasks in question. But there is no implication that the achievements in question are necessarily worth while or that the tasks are morally unobjectionable. There is nothing necessarily desirable about hearing or finding something. With 'education', however, there is such an implication. For to educate someone implies not only some sort of achievement, but also one that is worth while. It also implies that the manner of doing this should not be morally objectionable. Conditioning might be ruled out as a process of education on these, as well as on other grounds.[2]

There are other differences, too, between 'education' and Ryle's achievement words. 'Education' covers a range of tasks as well as achievements. It is used to cover both trying and succeeding. 'Teaching' has a similar double aspect, as Scheffler has already indicated.[3] Educational practices are those in which people try to pass on what is worth while as well as those in which they actually succeed in doing so. Success might be marked by general virtues such as a sense of relevance, precision, and the power to concentrate and by more specific virtues such as courage, sensitivity to others, and a sense of style.

This points to another difference between 'education' and other achievement words. It has already been shown that 'education' picks out no specific activities, though, as will be argued later, it does rule out some.[4] Similarly a multitude of different achievements or valuable states of mind are gathered together under the aegis of being worth while. Most of Ryle's achievement words pick out more specific states of mind and more specific activities which count as 'tasks' in relation to them. It is this multiplicity of worth-while states of mind

[1] See Ryle, G., *The Concept of Mind* (London, Hutchinson, 1949), pp. 149–53.
[2] See *infra*, Section 4.
[3] See Scheffler, I., *The Language of Education* (Springfield, Illinois, Thomas, 1960), pp. 38–44.
[4] See *infra*, Section 4.

which can be passed on in education which leads to so much dispute about its 'aims'.

(b) Aims of education

I have argued elsewhere[1] that much of the confusion about 'aims of education' comes about through extracting the normative feature built into the concept of 'education' as an extrinsic end. Given that 'education' suggests the intentional bringing about of a desirable state of mind in a morally unobjectionable manner, it is only too easy to conceive of education as a neutral process that is instrumental to something that is worthwhile which is extrinsic to it. Just as gardens may be cultivated in order to aid the economy of the household, so children must be educated in order to provide them with jobs and to increase the productivity of the community as a whole.

But there is something inappropriate about this way of speaking; for we would normally use the word 'train' when we had such a specifiable extrinsic objective in mind.[2] If, however, we do specify an appropriate 'aim' such as the development of individual potentialities or the development of intellect and character, then the aim would be intrinsic to what we would consider education to be. For we would not call a person 'educated' who had not developed along such lines. It would be like saying that the aim of reform is to develop an individual's sense of responsibility. This would give content to our understanding of making a man better, which is what it means to reform him, just as the development of intellect and character gives content to the notion of developing what is worth while, which is what it means to educate someone. If a dispute started about such 'aims'—e.g. whether a sense of responsibility was more important than respect for others or whether the development of intellect was more important than the development of character—this would not be a dispute about ends which were extrinsic to reform or education; rather it would be a dispute about what was the most important characteristic of a reformed or educated man. Such aims mark out specific achievements and states of mind that give content to the formal notion of 'the educated man'.

Another way of arriving at the same point is by an examination of the concept of 'aim'. The term 'aim' has its natural home in the context of limited and circumscribed activities like shooting and throwing. 'Aim-

[1] See Peters, R. S., *Education as Initiation* (London, Evans Bros., 1963).
[2] See *infra*, Section 3(c).

ing' is associated with the concentration of attention within such an activity on some object which must be hit, or pierced. Its internal accusative 'target' covers anything conforming to this specification. When the term 'aim' is used more figuratively it has the same suggestion of the concentration of attention on something which is the focus of an activity. It is odd to use it like the term 'purpose' or 'motive' to suggest some explanatory end for the activity in question. We can reasonably ask a person what his purpose is in building a new house or his motive in visiting a sick friend when we want to know what he sees these activities as leading up to; but it would be odd to ask for the *aim* of these activities, if we wanted to remove our puzzlement about their explanation. To ask for an aim is to ask for a more precise specification of what an action or activity is. We ask people what they are aiming at when they seem rather confused about their purposes or when they are drawing up a plan of campaign and have to formulate what they intend to do in a coherent way. Asking a person about his aims is a method of getting him to concentrate or clear his mind about what he is trying to do. 'Aim' also carries the suggestion that we are trying to achieve something that we might fall short of because of the difficulty involved in the task. Targets are things which we have to concentrate on if we want to hit them; so too, when we talk figuratively about what we are aiming at, we intimate the possibility of missing or falling short. If we say to someone 'What are you aiming at doing?' instead of 'What do you intend to do?' this is a quaint colloquialism which carries the suggestion both of concentration and of the possibility of falling short.

It is obvious enough, therefore, why the term 'aim' is used so frequently in the context of education. For this is a sphere where people engage with great seriousness in activities without always being very clear about what they are trying to achieve, and where genuine achievements are difficult to come by. To ask questions about the aims of education is therefore a way of getting people to get clear about and focus their attention on what is worth while achieving. It is not to ask for the production of ends extrinsic to education which might explain their activities as educators. Aims can be high level or low level. A teacher can write down in his lesson notes that his aim in the coming lesson is to reach the end of Exercise 6, or to get his pupils to speak some Latin, or grasp something about ancient Rome. Or he may say his aim is to train their character a bit by making them cope with a difficult unseen. But, whatever he says he is aiming at, the formulation of his aim is an aid to making his activity more structured and coherent by isolating an aspect under which he is acting. It is not something which he does in order to explain what he is doing; it is, rather, a more precise specification of it.

The natural way of asking for an extrinsic end is to ask what a man's purpose is in doing something or what his motive for it may be. These are strange questions to ask about education itself, for as 'education' implies the transmission of what is of ultimate value, it would be like asking about the purpose of the good life; but they are reasonable questions to ask about the activities that fall under education. For things like science and carpentry can be practised and passed on both for their own intrinsic value and because of the contribution which they make to extrinsic ends such as productivity, housing, and health. But in so far as they are regarded as part of someone's *education* they are regarded *ipso facto* as having value, and therefore as having reasons for doing them built into them, which he comes to accept. Confusion about aims of education often derives from saying things about education itself which are appropriate when said about activities which can be and usually are regarded as having educational value.

Of course a person who grasps these conceptual points about 'the aims of education' can quite reasonable reply: 'Well I am against education then. We have not time for such luxuries. We must equip people for suitable jobs and train enough scientists and technicians to maintain an expanding economy.' This is an arguable position[1]—provided that it does not masquerade as a view about the aims of *education*. To which the advocate of training might reply that the criteria for using the word 'education' have been unwarrantably tightened up; for the word is often used in contexts where some more limited exercise, such as vocational training, is envisaged. There are two points to make about such a reply. Firstly there is no reason why vocational training should not also be 'educational', as I shall show in more detail later in this chapter. But using the word 'education' suggests a rather different dimension for the exercise than that of simply equipping people with necessary skills for a job. A book called *Educating our Rulers* suggests more than purely vocational training. We do not naturally talk of educating men *as* rulers, soldiers, or economists; we talk of training them. But their training can

---

[1] Arguable, that is, in certain limited contexts, but difficult to defend to the last ditch; for presumably an expanding economy is a necessary base for a way of life that is thought desirable. And what is to be done about handing *that* on?

be conducted in such a manner that it may *also* have educational value. Secondly, even if the word were consistently used in such a limited way, we would need another word or circumlocution to distinguish between training people with a view to some limited extrinsic objective and educating them. The concept of educating people, as distinct from merely training them, has developed and is mirrored in the different words that people use who have developed this differentiated concept. The fact that there may be many people who do not have this concept, or who have it but use words loosely, does not effect the conceptual distinction to which I am drawing attention.

3. THE COGNITIVE ASPECTS OF 'EDUCATION'

So far attention has been focused on the moral requirements built into 'education' especially in relation to the achievement aspect of it. In Section 4 the moral as well as the conceptual requirements of the task aspect will be considered. But before examining what criteria processes have to satisfy in order to fall under the concept of 'education' as a family of tasks, more has to be said about the formal requirements built into the concept of 'being educated' as an achievement over and above the moral one. These have to do with knowledge and understanding.

(a) Knowledge and understanding

We do not call a person 'educated' who has simply mastered a skill even though the skill may be very highly prized such as pottery. For a man to be educated it is insufficient that he should possess a mere know-how or knack. He must have also some body of knowledge and some kind of a conceptual scheme to raise this above the level of a collection of disjointed facts. This implies some understanding of principles for the organization of facts. We would not call a man who was merely well informed an educated man. He must also have some understanding of the 'reason why' of things. The Spartans, for instance, were militarily and morally trained. They knew how to fight and they knew what was right and wrong; they were also possessed of a certain stock of folk-lore, which enabled them to manage provided that they stayed in Sparta. But we would not say that they had received a military or moral education; for they had never been encouraged to probe into the principles underlying their code.

This kind of knowledge which an educated man must have must also satisfy further requirements about which Whitehead has written much.[1]

[1] See Whitehead, A. N., *Aims of Education* (London, Macmillan, 1929), Ch. I.

It cannot be inert in two senses. Firstly it must characterize his way of looking at things rather than be hived off. It is possible for a man to know a lot of history in the sense that he can give correct answers to questions in class-rooms and examinations; yet this might never affect the way in which he looks at the buildings and institutions around him. We might describe such a man as 'knowledgeable' but we would not describe him as 'educated'; for 'education' implies that a man's outlook is transformed by what he knows. Such knowledge must not be inert in another sense, which was first stressed by Socrates and Plato in their doctrine that 'virtue is knowledge'. It must involve the kind of commitment that comes from being on the inside of a form of thought and awareness. A man cannot really understand what it is to think scientifically unless he not only knows that evidence must be found for assumptions, but knows also what counts as evidence and cares that it should be found. In forms of thought where proof is possible cogency, simplicity, and elegance must be felt to matter. And what would historical or philosophical thought amount to if there was no concern about relevance, consistency, or coherence? All forms of thought and awareness have their own internal standards of appraisal. To be on the inside of them is both to understand and to care. Without such commitment they lose their point. I do not think that we would call a person 'educated' whose knowledge was purely external and inert in this way.

(b) Cognitive perspective

The account of the cognitive requirements of 'being educated' is still, however, incomplete. For a man might be a very highly trained scientist; yet we might refuse to call him an educated man. This would not be because there is nothing worth while about science; for it is a supreme example of a worth-while activity. It would not be because such a man cares nothing about it and has no grasp of its principles; for the hypothesis is that he is dedicated to it and has got a good grounding of principles. What then is lacking which might make us withhold the description of being 'educated' from such a man? It is surely a lack of what might be called 'cognitive perspective'. The man could have a very limited conception of what he is doing. He could work away at science without seeing its connection with much else, its place in a coherent pattern of life. For him it is an activity which is cognitively adrift.

'Wholeness' is often emphasized in educational circles. At conferences things are said such as 'education is of the whole man', which sound wise and profound. Yet this saying surely belongs to a class of sayings such as 'the whole is more than the sum of its parts' and 'freedom does not consist purely in doing what one wants' whose truth depends upon the connections between the concepts involved. 'Education is of the whole man' bears witness not simply to a protest against too much specialized training, but also to the conceptual connection between 'education' and seeing what is being done in a perspective that is not too limited. On occasions there is point even in enunciating tautologies such as 'the function of a government is to govern'; so the fact that 'education is of the whole man' is a conceptual truth imprecisely expressed is not necessarily a reason for avoiding such a remark. But it is just as well to realize whence its obvious truth derives. We talk about a person being trained as a philosopher, scientist or cook, when we wish to draw attention to his acquired competence in some sphere; we do not use the phrase 'educated *as* a philosopher, cook, or scientist'. For 'education' cannot be tied down in this way to a specialized competence. We can, however, ask the further question whether such people are educated men. To ask this question is at least to probe the limitations of their professional vision.

(c) *Education and training*

Confirmation of this conceptual connection between 'education' and cognitive perspective is provided by exploring the different implications of talking about 'education' and 'training' in less specialized spheres. The hypothesis to be tested is that 'trained' suggests the development of competence in a limited skill or mode of thought whereas 'educated' suggests a linkage with a wider system of beliefs. A man with a 'trained mind' is one who can tackle particular problems that are put to him in a rigorous and competent manner. An 'educated mind' suggests much more awareness of the different facets and dimensions of such problems.

In the different manifestations of mind the link of 'education' with a wider system of beliefs is amply demonstrable. Why is it, for instance, that we talk more naturally of educating the emotions than we do of training them, whereas we talk more naturally of training the will than we do of educating it? This is surely because the different emotions are differentiated by their cognitive core, by the different beliefs that go with them. The fundamental difference, for instance, between what is meant by 'anger' as distinct from 'jealousy' can only be demonstrated by reference to the beliefs appropriate to them. A man who is jealous must think that someone else has something to which he considers himself entitled; but a man who is angry need only think that someone else is frustrating him. If, therefore, we are contemplating changing people's emotional attitudes or reactions, our main task consists in trying to get them to see the world differently in relation to themselves. The eye of the jealous man must be made less jaundiced by altering his concept of what he has a right to, or by getting him to put a different interpretation on the situation. We speak of 'education' because of the work that has to be done on his beliefs.

If, on the other hand, we speak, as we sometimes do, of training the emotions, the implications are different. What comes to mind is a situation where it is important that a person should not give way to emotion, or where he should express the appropriate emotion in the appropriate context. We think, for instance, of schooling a person not to give way to grief in a public place and to show courage in the face of danger and adversity. There is no suggestion of transforming a person's appraisal of a situation by working on his beliefs; rather of developing fairly standardized appraisals such as those connected with pity, anger, and fear in relation to appropriate objects and of not feeling such emotions so strongly that he is overcome by them. 'Training' suggests the acquisition of appropriate appraisals and habits of response in limited conventional situations; it lacks the wider cognitive implications of 'education'. Alternatively 'training the emotions' may be connected with the development of strength of will. A man with a weak will is a man who knows what he wants or ought to do but is sidetracked or deflected by emotions in the doing of it. That is why we speak of 'training the will' rather than of 'educating' it. For 'will' is associated with holding steadfast to some principle, purpose or plan in the face of temptation and distraction. Its sphere of operation is defined by the purpose in hand; it is a reinforcement of purpose, not a source of alternative purposes. Wants, of course, can be educated because of the diverse dimensions of belief built into the description of what may be wanted; but will is the executive that has to be trained for the more menial function of sticking fast to a plan, principle, or purpose. Will, as Plato put it, is the warrior of the soul; its function is to make sure that the purposes and principles decided on by reason are carried out. People can be educated in respect of their wants or purposes; for these depend upon how they see the world. But in respect of their will, which is parasitic on such purposes, they can only be trained.

C 33

In the moral sphere we talk naturally of 'the training of character'. This is because, in one sense of 'character', when we talk of people as 'having character',[1] what we have in mind is the development of persistence, incorruptibility, and integrity in relation to their practice of principles. This is more or less equivalent to strength of will. We might, on the other hand, be thinking of 'character' in a more non-committal sense, as when we speak of a person's character or character-traits. 'The training of character' would then suggest efforts to ensure reliability of response in accordance with a code. This would essentially be rather a limited sort of operation. It would not suggest any endeavour to get the trainees to understand the 'reason why' of things. When, on the other hand, we speak of 'moral education' we immediately envisage tackling people's beliefs; we think of questions of fact and questions of justification in relation to such beliefs. To make the same point even more sharply: 'sex education' consists in initiating adolescents into a complicated set of beliefs about the working of the body, personal relationships, and social institutions. 'Sex training' consists in passing on various skills to do with making love. 'Physical training' suggests merely disciplining the body in relation to a narrowly conceived end such as physical fitness; 'physical education' suggests the cultivation of physical fitness as a necessary foundation for a balanced way of life.

The general point that is illustrated by these examples is that the concept of 'training' has application when a skill or competence has to be acquired which is to be exercised in relation to a specific end or function or in accordance with the canons of some specific mode of thought, or practice. If it is said that a person is 'trained' the questions 'To do what?', 'For what?', 'As what?', 'In what?' are appropriate; for a person cannot be trained in a general sort of way. Training has its natural home in the realm of skills where something has to be done or manipulated. It is, of course, used in an extended sense, as when we speak of a 'trained philosopher', a 'trained observer' or a 'trained mind'. But even in these uses the notion is conveyed that the person in question can go through some sort of routine, make circumscribed moves, perform some kind of operation, or attack a problem in a specific and skilful way. With 'education', however, the matter is very different; for a person is never described as 'educated' in relation to any specific end, function, or mode of thought. Soldiers, historians and cooks may be educated men; but

[1] See Peters, R. S., 'Moral Education and the Psychology of Character' in *Philosophy*, January 1962.

men are not educated for fighting, as historians, or in cooking. To say that 'education is of the whole man' is at least to make the negative point that it is not something that pertains to a person in respect of his competence in any specialized skill, activity, or mode of thought.

4. CRITERIA OF EDUCATIONAL PROCESSES

'Education', it has been argued, involves the intentional transmission of what is worth while. To raise questions about its 'aims' is to invite clarification of and concentration on what is worth while in the enterprise. But there are many different ways of initiating others into what is worth while. Traditionally the assumption was that the teacher was the authority on these matters; his job was to imprint them on the mind and heart of the pupil. This he tended to do by formal instruction backed by a variety of coercive techniques which included plenty of corporal punishment. The models of moulding resistant material or of filling up the structure of the mind with valuable items was used to described educational transactions.

The 'child-centred' revolt against this conception of education was based on moral as well as on psychological grounds.[1] Morally speaking the movement represented an emphasis on what might be called procedural principles to the detriment of valuations about content. Attention was focused on the manner rather than on the matter of education. What was required of the teacher was respect for the child and a maximum of non-interference, together with psychological understanding of his interests, needs, and stages of development. This would provide the social environment in which the child could learn by experience, learn to choose for himself, 'grow' and develop his own natural bent.

Few democrats nowadays would dispute the moral desirability of the principles of liberty and respect for persons presupposed by this movement, though their justification is a difficult matter to which educational theorists have paid too little attention.[2] Adherence to them, however, cannot serve as a substitute for valuations about content, which determine the direction of growth and what interests are worth developing. The child-centred teacher who believes in the principle of liberty has

[1] For further discussion of this contrast between 'traditional' and 'child-centred' education see articles by Perry, L. R., and Peters, R. S., in Archambault, R. D. (Ed.), *Philosophical Analysis and Education* (London, Kegan Paul, 1965) and Cremin, L., *The Transformation of the School* (New York, Knopf, 1961).
[2] See Part Two of this book.

35

therefore, like the parent, the moral problem of choosing between letting children pursue their interests, which may be not at all in their interest, and getting them to pursue what is in their interest. For the teacher is institutionally concerned with fostering interests which it is in children's interest to develop. This is what education involves. Talk about 'growth', 'self-realization', and gearing the curriculum to the interests of children glosses over this fundamentally normative aspect of education.

No doubt some more formal educators were neglectful of and ignorant about facts of development and motivation; no doubt they sometimes treated children with lack of respect and with little regard for the principle of liberty. But they did at least have a clear idea that their function as educators was to hand on what is worth while in the way of content. They concentrated on the matter of education but were sometimes rather rigid, unreflective and unperceptive about its manner. The child-centred reaction, on the other hand, glossed over the matter of education with talk about growth, self-realization, and the development of individual potentialities; but it altered radically the manner of education by drawing attention both to facts about childhood and the conditions of learning and to principles regulating the treatment and development of children.

Adherents of the 'child-centred' ideology often make the conceptual point that 'education' is connected with 'educere' = 'to lead out' rather than with 'educare' = 'to bring up' or 'rear', thus moulding the concept towards the development of what is within rather than imposition from without. Thus what Stevenson[1] has called a 'persuasive definition' of 'education' can emerge, which is one in which there is a definite tightening up of the connotation of a term with a commending function (such as 'democracy') along lines which prescribe a preferred policy. In this case it is stipulated that nothing is to count as 'education' in which such procedural principles to do with 'leading out' are not implemented.

The point has already been made in Section 2 (b) that moral policies cannot be extracted from definitions or conceptual analyses even if they follow fairly closely the lines of ordinary usage. When, as in this case, they are based on dubious etymology and represent an obvious tightening up of ordinary usage, even less is to be said in favour of them as a method of backing a cause. But the question still remains whether there is any rationale underlying this conceptual shift. It can be argued, I

[1] See Stevenson, C. L., *Ethics and Language* (New Haven, Yale University Press, 1944), Ch. IX.

think, that there is a conceptual point about 'education' which, if clumsily handled, can be blown up into a moral principle to do with 'leading out'. The inner workings of such a conceptual shift will now, it is hoped, be made explicit.

It has been argued that 'education' picks out no particular process; it implies criteria which processes must satisfy. One of these is that something worth while should be immanent in them. Another is the built-in suggestion of understanding and of cognitive perspective. The question is whether there are additional criteria which must be satisfied, which characterize the tasks of education rather than the achievements. The suggestion of the growth theorist is that 'education' must involve processes of the 'leading out' type. There is some plausibility in this thesis; for we certainly would not call brainwashing or conditioning 'education', and, as has already been suggested in Section 3 (*a*), we certainly would not call a person 'educated' who was well informed about some cultural activity but never bothered much about conforming to the standards immanent in it. This does suggest that education involves getting people to grasp and possess for themselves those worth-while things which are essential to education and to care for them once they have mastered them. Notions to do with 'leading out', 'interest' and 'learning by experience' therefore seem peculiarly appropriate, together with the observance of principles such as those of non-interference and respect for persons on the part of teachers. On the other hand it would seem highly arbitrary to rule out as 'education' some of the very harsh things practised in institutions as a result of which very cultured and sensitive gentlemen eventually emerged.

To make more explicit these conceptual intimations we must revert to the distinction developed in Section 2 between 'education' as a task word and as an achievement word. As an achievement word it certainly implies that a person cares about and is interested in what is worth while as well as being knowledgeable about and in command of such things. We would not call a man 'educated' who knew about science and who could go through the motions of scientific thought and experiment but who cared nothing for finding out the truth or who regarded science purely as a means to material advancement. But, although to be 'educated' he must eventually come to care about something like science in this way and make it his own, it does not follow that he must have been brought to care about it by educational processes which always enlisted his interest and encouraged his autonomous activity. In other words the

37

implications of 'education' as an achievement word do not necessarily carry over to it as a task word. The scientist may have been forced, while he was a boy, to do experiments in which he had not the slightest interest. But by being trained to do them repeatedly under rigorous supervision he may eventually have come to develop an interest in doing scientific experiments and gone out of his way to do them, irrespective of whether he was made to do them or not. Whether or not making boys do things in which they have no initial interest, without trying to harness them to their existing interests, is an effective technique is an empirical question. The fact is that it has been practised in many educational institutions which have turned out educated and dedicated men. It might be argued that this has happened in spite of rather than because of the methods of instruction used. But this is an empirical question on which it would be rash to pronounce without a lot of evidence. Whatever the truth about it may be it is unwarranted to build in this condition of motivation into the meaning of 'education' as a task word.

There is another connected conceptual point which tends to strengthen this connection between 'education' and 'leading out'. So far the 'tasks' involved in education have been referred to rather jauntily without it being made clear whose tasks are being spoken of—those of the teacher or those of the learner. Obviously both are usually involved; but it is important to realize that the tasks of the teacher could not be characterized unless we had a notion of the tasks of the learner. For whereas 'learning' could be characterized without introducing the notion of 'teaching', 'teaching' could not be characterized without the notion of 'learning'. The tasks of the teacher consist in the employment of various methods to get learning processes going. These processes of learning in their turn cannot be characterized without reference to the achievements in which they culminate; for to learn something is to come up to some standard, to succeed in some respect. So the achievement must be that of the learner in the end. The teacher's success, in other words, can only be defined in terms of that of the learner. This presumably is the logical truth lurking in the saying that all education is self-education. It also explains the temptation to think that an educational process must be one of 'leading out'; for, in the end, education is something that only the individual can achieve himself. He must get going on some task, or series of tasks, in which he eventually achieves some degree of success. But this connection cannot be extended.to cover the additional demand that he must be initially drawn to the tasks in which he eventually succeeds.

Indeed gifted educators are precisely those who can get children going on activities which have no initial appeal to them.

If teachers confined themselves to teaching then the temptation to conflate the achievement and task aspects of education would be, perhaps, legitimate; for, to quote Scheffler: 'Every culture, we may say, normally gets newborn members to behave according to its norms, however these are specified, and many cultures have agencies devoted to this job. But not every way of getting someone to behave according to some norm is teaching. . . . Teaching may, to be sure, proceed by various methods, but some ways of getting people to do things are excluded from the standard range of the term "teaching". To teach, in the standard sense, is at some points at least to submit oneself to the understanding and independent judgment of the pupil, to his demand for reasons, to his sense of what consitutes an adequate explanation. To teach someone that such and such is the case is not merely to get him to believe it: deception, for example, is not a method or a mode of teaching. Teaching involves further that, if we try to get the student to believe that such and such is the case, we try also to get him to grasp it for reasons that, within the limits of his capacity to grasp, are *our* reasons. Teaching, in this way, requires us to reveal our reasons to the student and, by so doing, to submit them to his evaluation and criticism.

'To teach someone, not that such and such is the case, but rather how to do something, normally involves showing him how (by description or example) and not merely setting up conditions under which he will, in fact, be likely to learn how. To throw a child into the river is not, in itself, to teach him how to swim; to send one's daughter to dancing school is not, in itself, to teach her how to dance. Even to teach someone *to* do something (rather than how to do it) is not simply to try to get him to do it; it is also to make accessible to him, at some stage, our reasons and purposes in getting him to do it. To teach is thus, in the standard use of the term, to acknowledge the "reason" of the pupil, i.e. his demand for and judgment of reasons, even though such demands are not uniformly appropriate at every phase of the teaching interval.'[1]

This brings out well the connection between teaching and the giving of reasons on the part of the teacher together with the activity expected on the part of the learner. Teaching is a complex activity which unites together processes, such as instructing and training, by the overall inten-

[1] Scheffler, I., *The Language of Education* (Springfield, Illinois, Thomas, 1960), pp. 57–8.

tion of getting pupils not only to acquire knowledge, skills, and modes of conduct, but to acquire them in a manner which involves understanding and an evaluation of the rationale underlying them. It is pre-eminently concerned, therefore, with the adoption of methods appropriate to the development of knowledge and understanding of principles involved in the second type of criterion of 'education'. Teaching, however, is not synonymous with education as should be obvious from what has been argued earlier in this chapter. To start with, teaching is an activity, though a complex one; educating is not. 'Educating' intimates that other activities such as teaching, training, or instructing satisfy certain criteria; it does not pick out any distinctive activity. It is similar to 'teach' in that it can be used, and is used, predominantly in an achievement sense; but the achievements of a teacher may be morally neutral or pernicious whereas those of an educator cannot be. A teacher could teach astrology or the art of forgery; but he would not be regarded necessarily as educating people by so doing. Indeed there are few 'moral communities' nowadays where astrology or forgery would be regarded as part of any-one's education. He could also concentrate on teaching mathematics to the exclusion of all else. He might accordingly be denied the title of being an educator because of the lack of cognitive perspective which he and his pupils displayed. In other words teaching could be ruled out as education because it failed to satisfy aspects of the two types of criteria of 'education' which have already been made explicit. Nevertheless, if those who were meant to be teachers did nothing other than teach, the tendency to merge the achievement with the task aspect of education would be defensible in relation to the type of activity involved. For teaching involves discussion and explanation as methods for bringing about an ability to discuss and explain on the part of the learner. These methods cannot be operated without active co-operation on the part of the learner.

Teachers, however, do not always teach. They sometimes pursue the activities which are components of teaching without the overall intention of bringing about rational understanding and by methods which do not encourage or exhibit it. Sometimes they simply instruct, which is quite compatible with the authoritarian exposition of inert ideas; sometimes their activity approximates more to training which involves getting students to practise things for which no explanations need be given; sometimes they put students in situations where they expect them to 'learn by experience' without anything being explicitly imparted by the teacher. All these can be components in teaching if they are undertaken with the required intention and accompanied by the appropriate encouragement and explanation. But they *can* take place in isolation and might still be regarded as processes of education, even though they were not part of the specific activity of teaching. Indeed with young children they might be regarded sometimes as necessary preliminaries to teaching.

Is it the case, then, that 'education' as a task word rules out no transactions between teacher and learner provided that the result is an educated man? It has been already mentioned that conditioning and brainwashing would scarcely count as techniques of education. Why is it that they seem to be ruled out while techniques involving command and mere instruction are not? There is, of course, a moral objection to them because they involve lack of respect for persons; but this moral objection obviously depends upon the nature of the processes involved. The point is, surely, that even if boys are commanded to do things or treated as passive receptacles, there is an important sense in which they know what they are doing. They understand what is expected of them; they are initiated into the content of the activity in a meaningful way. They are not treated as a bundle of reaction tendencies without a mind of their own. A child might be conditioned, in a strict sense, to avoid dogs or induced to do something by hypnotic suggestion. But we would not describe this as 'education' if he was not conscious of something to be learnt or understood. The central cases of 'education' are tasks in which the individual who is being educated is being led or induced to come up to some standard, to achieve something. This must be presented to him as something which he has to grasp. The concept of 'education' is only derivatively applied to goings on in which this general condition, definitive of a task, is not satisfied.[1] Some forms of drill might also be ruled out on these grounds, if the individual was made to repeat mindlessly like a seal a series of narrowly conceived stereotyped acts.

An interesting implication of this point is that indoctrination cannot be ruled out as a process of education on the same sort of grounds as conditioning can. The reason is that whatever else 'indoctrination' may mean[2] it obviously has something to do with doctrines, which are a species of beliefs. These have to be understood and assented to in some

---

[1] It is true that all sorts of things to which the learner may not be explicitly attending can be 'picked up' in an educational situation—e.g. mannerisms, nuances of style, attitudes. But such things are usually, as it were, on the fringe of things to which the learner *is* attending. They are *imparted*. (See *infra* p. 60.)

[2] See articles by Wilson, John, and Hare, R. M., in Hollins, T. H. B., *Aims in Education: The Philosophic Approach* (Manchester University Press, 1964).

embryonic way, for indoctrination to take place. Conditioning, on the other hand, in a strict sense, has no connection with beliefs. It is of reactions, such as salivation and eye-blinks, and of simple movements which are not seen as bringing about anything by the subject. Movements of a random sort are made which are positively or negatively reinforced. If the movements form part of an action, in the sense of being seen by the subject as bringing something about which may be pleasant or unpleasant, it is only by analogy that the concept of conditioning is applied. Indoctrination, of course, may be ruled out on other grounds as a process of education. As a process it involves, it might be argued, lack of respect for the learner. Or it might be argued that it is intended to produce a state of mind, which constitutes the relevant achievement, in which an individual has either no grasp of the rationale underlying his beliefs or a type of foundation which encourages no criticism or evaluation of his beliefs (e.g. an appeal to authority). Such objections to indoctrination would fall, however, under the first two types of criteria of education, rather than under the minimal criteria of wittingness and voluntariness which rule out conditioning.

For something to count as an educational process, then, a minimum of comprehension must be involved. This is quite compatible with formal instruction and commands, and in this respect with indoctrination; for in methods such as these children do understand, in an embryonic way, what is being passed on; they know what they are learning or doing and grasp the standards which they are expected to attain. Furthermore, there is a minimal sense in which they act as voluntary agents; for they can rebel and refuse to do what is required of them. Indeed they very often do. This dual implication of the meaningfulness of the material transmitted and of voluntariness on the part of learners can very easily, if not handled with care, be inflated into the ideal of autonomous activity enlivened by interest, which is essential to the 'leading out' concept of 'education'. The temptation to puff up such minimal intimations of the concept of 'education' into a procedural principle to do with self-direction would be encouraged if the implications of 'education' as an achievement term were carried over into 'education' as a task term.

The suggestion is not that, as a matter of historical fact, growth theorists pondered on the concept of 'education' and mistakenly puffed up some minimal conceptual intimations into a procedural principle. More probably their concept of education was moulded by their consciences; for they were morally indignant at the lack of respect shown for children as individuals and appalled by the lack of psychological understanding evident in the ways in which they were treated. Their moral indignation and increasing psychological insight were combined in procedural principles demanding that children should be treated with respect, not indoctrinated, coerced and ordered around, and that they should be allowed to learn by experience and choose for themselves. But their conception of education derived additional plausibility from certain minimal criteria built into the concept of 'education' itself.

5. 'EDUCATION' AND 'LIBERAL EDUCATION'

The concept of 'education' here developed, it might be said, is almost indistinguishable from that of 'liberal education'. There is, actually, a good reason why this should be so which is connected with the function of the word 'free', 'liberal' presumably still retaining its connection with its root meaning. If the demand is made that a man should be free to do what he wants or allowed to do what he wants freely, this does not imply that he should do anything else; rather it implies that restrictions on or impediments in the way of doing what he wants should be removed. Thus the demand for liberal education might not be for a special kind of education, but for the removal of certain restrictions or impediments that might hinder education as ordinarily understood. The function of 'liberal' would then be the negative one of emphasizing one or other of the three types of criteria of 'education' in a context where these were being made difficult to realize. A brief examination of what lies behind the demand for 'liberal education' should bear this out.

Traditionally the demand for 'liberal education' has been put forward as a protest against confining what has been taught to the service of some extrinsic end such as the production of material goods, obtaining a job, or manning a profession. In other words it has been a plea for education rather than vocational training or training of hand and brain for utilitarian purposes. For, as was argued in Section 2, in so far as science or carpentry are to be regarded as part of someone's 'education', then they are to be thought of as having intrinsic worth, whatever they may as a matter of fact contribute to extrinsic ends. The function of 'liberal' in this context would be therefore to emphasize this aspect of education, to oppose the restriction of the curriculum to what is deemed to be relevant to extrinsic ends. This affects very much the manner in which something is taught as well as the details of the syllabus. Suppose, for

43

instance, that in teacher-training psychology were taught purely for vocational purposes. The various experimental findings would be assembled, which would be obviously relevant to the teacher's task, e.g. about learning, remembering, motivation, intelligence, class-room climates, etc. The trainee would be encouraged to assimilate as much of this material as he could, which would be skilfully related to his teaching practice. If, on the other hand, psychology were regarded as part of his education or 'liberal education' as a teacher, then he might be introduced to it by starting with investigations which were relevant to his task as a teacher, but he would be encouraged to go deeper into the discipline, to begin to grasp from the inside what this form of scientific thought entails, and to be attracted and absorbed by the values immanent in this form of inquiry.

There is, however, another interpretation of 'liberal' which is more in line with the point that has been developed in Section 3 about cognitive perspective. This is the plea that education should not be confined to specialist training however liberally conceived, in the first sense of 'liberal'. The notion here is of the mind being confined by or restricted to one mode of thought. No scientist should emerge, for instance, without a good understanding of other ways of looking at the world, historically, for instance, or aesthetically. Whether or not this is equivalent to the concept of an 'educated' man here advanced depends on the rigour with which these other modes of thought are pursued. On the view here put forward an 'educated' man could be trained in one sphere, e.g. science, and yet be sufficiently cognizant of other ways of looking at the world, so that he can grasp the historical perspective, social significance, or aesthetic merit of his work and of much besides. Some modern advocates of 'liberal education',[1] however, envisage that people should be trained, to some degree at least, in such other ways of thinking. This is a much stronger requirement. Nevertheless it is obviously derivative from what is intimated by the criterion of cognitive perspective; it involves emphasizing this essential aspect of all education.

Thirdly those who agitate about education being 'liberal' are often protesting against the illiberal tendency to constrain people's beliefs along narrowly conceived or doctrinaire lines, thus emphasizing procedural principles to do with liberty picked out in the extension of my third type of criterion.

[1] See, for instance, Hirst, P. H., 'Liberal Education and the Nature of Knowledge' in Archambault, R. D. (Ed.), op. cit.

In discussions about 'liberal education' it is important to be clear which sense of 'liberal education' is being used, although obviously a lot is to be said for all types of emphasis. For instance it is often said that vocational training should be 'liberalized'. This could mean firstly that people were taught cooking, carpentry, and 'home economics' in such a way that the intrinsic standards involved in the activities were constantly stressed and not merely the consumer value of the end-product; or it could mean secondly that these practical interests should be used as centres of interest from which people could be encouraged to develop an interest in wider areas of knowledge that were relevant to the practice of them. Cooking, for instance, can lead to an interest in where the various materials come from and hence in geography; mending fuses to a general interest in and knowledge about electricity. Or it could mean thirdly that the knowledge required for vocational purposes should be transmitted in a less dogmatic way, that trainees should be encouraged to be more critical about what they are taught. All such approaches to vocational training could be attempts to increase its educational value. But they would involve a rather different approach and emphasis.

This analysis of the different ways of conceiving of 'liberal education' has revealed, perhaps, some of the ambiguities in the concept of 'liberal'. It has also helped to confirm that the criteria implicit in central cases of 'education' are those which have been made explicit in this chapter. These are:

(i) that 'education' implies the transmission of what is worth-while to those who become committed to it;

(ii) that 'education' must involve knowledge and understanding and some kind of cognitive perspective, which are not inert;

(iii) that 'education' at least rules out some procedures of transmission, on the grounds that they lack wittingness and voluntariness on the part of the learner.

Indeed the analysis of 'liberal education' has served as an effective and concentrated summary of these basic criteria. It has revealed, also, both the necessity for and the limitations of conceptual analysis. For a much clearer grasp of the fundamental issues underlying current controversies is made possible by mapping the area of the concepts and revealing the contours of the criteria built into them. But a detached and clear-sighted view of the shape of issues and institutions is all that conceptual analysis provides. It cannot of itself determine the lines of practical policy.

CHAPTER II

EDUCATION AS INITIATION

INTRODUCTION

So far three main criteria of 'education' have been considered, the first concerning its matter, the second its manner, and the third its cognitive perspective. No attempt has been made either to produce a definition of 'education' or to attempt any account of a synthetic nature which pays due attention to all three criteria. It could be said, however, that some of the models of the educational situation so far considered have proved inadequate because they tend to emphasize one criterion to the exclusion of the others. The traditional view of 'education', for instance, emphasized the matter and cognitive perspective of 'education' rather than its manner; the child-centred view drew attention to questions concerned with its manner and rather evaded the question of its matter; views which build up an account of 'education' by extrapolating what is involved in acquiring skills ignore its cognitive perspective. All such views are inadequate in the way in which caricatures are; they distort the features of the concept in a particular direction. But they are valuable, like caricatures, in emphasizing salient features. It should, however, be possible to say some general things about 'education' which takes due account of all the criteria instead of emphasizing one to the exclusion of the others. This would be a synthetic sketch rather than a definition; for in such a field as Bacon put it long ago 'subtleties of definitions are but curiosities'. Such a synthetic sketch is necessary both to draw together the implications of the analysis in the preceding chapter and to prepare the way for the problems of justification that lie ahead.

I. THE DEVELOPMENT OF MIND

The distinction has previously been made between 'education' conceived of as an achievement and 'education' as covering a number of tasks. An educated man is one who has achieved a state of mind which is characterized by a mastery of and care for the worth-while things that have been transmitted, which are viewed in some kind of cognitive perspective. The requirement built into 'education' that it should be of the 'whole man' implies the possibility of a man being trained in some more limited respect. In other words the concept of 'education' pre-supposes not only the development of beliefs but also the differentiation of mind in respects which can be developed to the exclusion of others. How, then, is the development of such a differentiated mind to be conceived?

There is a view about the development of mind, which has been very influential in England since the time of the British Empiricists (Locke, Berkeley, Hume), in which the development of the individual mind is regarded as a slow process by means of which generalized beliefs are acquired as a precipitate of individual experience. Atomic sense data, it was argued, are admitted through the inlets of sense. Gradually the individual mind, consisting of complex ideas and expectations established on the basis of the co-existence and constant conjunction of sense qualities, begins to emerge. The function of the educator is either to provide a suitable environment in which this individual development can proceed or to intervene more actively and implant the appropriate ideas in the mind of the child in accordance with some carefully articulated programme.

This rather botanical picture of the development of mind is correct in one important respect. It singles out 'consciousness' as the hall-mark of mind. The Greeks did not really have an explicit and articulated concept of 'consciousness'. Not that they thought of men as machines or failed to note that men lost consciousness from time to time; for conscious activity—especially that of reasoning—was regarded by them as a matter of great significance. Indeed Plato and Aristotle were so struck by the wonder of reasoning that they regarded it as a divine characteristic. But they did not stress the common core of consciousness in varied phenomena such as mathematical reasoning, purpose, pain, dreaming, and emotional states. Aristotle, for instance, singled out goal-directedness as the hall-mark of soul. This was exhibited at the plant, animal, and human level. The hall-mark of 'mind' was the imposition of plans and rules, associated with 'reason', on this goal-directedness.

Historically the emphasis on private individual experience, in which consciousness was stressed as the hall-mark of mind, presupposed the development of individualism as a social movement; for the Greeks of the city-states lived in a public world of public feats and public concerns in which the term ἰδιώτης (idiot) disdainfully picked out the man who concerned himself only with private matters. Socrates, with his stress on individual self-knowledge and the care of the individual soul, was a moral innovator. With the conquests of Philip and Alexander of Macedon and the break-up of the small autonomous Greek states such moral innovation became systematized in the codes of the Stoics and Epicureans. The ideal of the self-sufficiency of the individual as a citizen of the world developed as a substitute for the much lauded self-sufficiency of the city-states. He must either discipline himself and purify his individual soul (Stoics), or slip through life unobtrusively by cutting down the possible sources of suffering (Epicureans). This led to an increase of interest in the will and emotions, and to an emphasis on the importance of individual consciousness.

This turning inwards was institutionalized by Christianity with its stress on personal salvation and purity of soul. Introspection vied with revelation as a source of knowledge. St Augustine paved the way for Descartes' first certainty—Cogito; *ergo* sum. With Descartes the Platonic view of the soul and of knowledge was reinterpreted in the light of the rise of the mathematical sciences, but with a difference—the stress on the certainty of the individual's knowledge of his own mental states. 'Mind' was no longer simply associated with Reason; it was that inner world of consciousness to which each individual has private access and whose rational activity it is self-contradictory to doubt. The British Empiricists explicitly rejected Descartes' account of knowledge with its more precise rendering of Plato's innate ideas. Knowledge, they argued, was not spun out of the recesses of mind by the activity of reason; it was a precipitate left by sensory experience in the mind of the individual. But they implicitly accepted Descartes' emphasis on consciousness as the hall-mark of mind.

On this fundamental point surely both Descartes and the British Empiricists were right; for even if the importance of the Aristotelian criterion of goal-directedness is stressed, a distinction has to be made between behaviour in which there is consciousness of an end and in which means to it are seen or devised, and that in which, as in the case of plants, there is persistence towards an end without consciousness of it. If this distinction is not made minds could be attributed to machines; and one thing we know about machines is that mentality is not one of their attributes. The ideas and expectations of an individual centre of consciousness, however, do not develop as deposits out of an atomic individual experience. This is one of the misleading features of the empiricist account. On the contrary they are the product of the initiation of an individual into public traditions enshrined in the language, concepts, beliefs, and rules of a society.

A child is born with a consciousness not as yet differentiated into beliefs, purposes, and feelings. Indeed it is many months before consciousness of his mother as an entity distinct from himself develops. His 'mind' is ruled perhaps by bizarre and formless wishes in which there is no picking out of objects, still less of 'sense-data', in a framework of space and time, no notion of permanence or of continuity, no embryonic grasp of causal connection or means-ends relationships. The sequence of children's questions—'What is it?', 'Where is it?', 'When did it happen?', 'Why did it happen?' mark the development of this categorial apparatus. The differentiation of modes of consciousness proceeds *pari passu* with the development of this mental structure. For they are all related to types of objects and relations in a public world. The child comes to want things that there are means of obtaining instead of threshing around beset by unruly and unrealistic wishes; he comes to fear things that may hurt him, and to believe that things are the case which experience has confirmed for him. Later he comes to create predictability in his social world by stating his intentions and making promises, as well as to guide his behaviour through his grasp of the rules which he finds there.

In the history of philosophy Kant rightly achieved fame for outlining this structure of concepts and categories by means of which order is imposed on the flux of experience; this he attributed to an active reason at work in the experience of all individuals. Later on, in the early part of the twentieth century, the psychologist Piaget, much influenced by Kant, laboriously mapped the stages at which these concepts and categories develop. But neither of these thinkers speculated about the extent to which the development of mind is the product of initiation into public traditions enshrined in a public language. Hegel, perhaps, with his notion of 'objective mind' articulated in institutions, and Marx, with his stress on the social determinants of individual consciousness, were vividly aware of this social dimension of the development of mind. But for different reasons their accounts of mind failed to take root in the empirical tradition of Western thought and to correct the undue emphasis on individual experience. Indeed their collectivist, holistic approach to social phenomena tended to go to the other extreme of ignoring the importance of individual centres of experience.

The point is that consciousness, which is the hall-mark of mind, is related in its different modes to objects. The individual wants *something*, is afraid of or angry with *somebody* or *something*, believes or knows that *certain things are the case*. The objects of consciousness are first and foremost objects in a public world that are marked out and differentiated by a public language into which the individual is initiated. The learning of language and the discovery of a public world of objects in space and time proceed together. But the individual, as owner of experiences welded to each other in a unique life-history, represents a particular and unrepeatable viewpoint on this public world. As Leibniz put it, each one mirrors the world from a particular point of view. Furthermore, as he develops, he adds his contribution to the public world. His consciousness, as well as his individuality, is neither intelligible nor genetically explicable without the public world of which he is conscious, in relation to which he develops, and on which he imprints his own individual style and pattern of being. But that does not make individual consciousness any the less important both as the hall-mark of mind and as a centre of ethical concern.

The development of a structure of categories and concepts for picking out objects in a space-time framework and for noting causal connections and means-ends relations is only a stage in the development of mind. Further differentiation develops as the mastery of the basic skills opens the gates to a vast inheritance accumulated by those versed in more specific modes of thought and awareness such as science, history, mathematics, religious and aesthetic awareness, together with moral, prudential and technical forms of thought and action. Such differentiations are alien to the mind of a child or preliterate man—indeed perhaps to that of a pre-seventeenth-century man.

Each of these differentiated modes of thought and awareness is characterized both by a content or 'body of knowledge' and by public procedures by means of which this content has been accumulated, criticized, and revised. Each has its own family of concepts peculiar to it and its own distinctive methods of validation. In learning science, for instance, concepts such as 'mass', 'force', 'velocity', and 'gravity' have to be understood, together with the procedures of experiment and observation by means of which hypotheses making use of such concepts are tested. All these are public. Many do little more than develop a familiarity with such a mode of thought together with a mastery of some portion of its body of knowledge. A few, however, develop this form of thought themselves to a pre-eminent degree and contribute themselves to the criticism and development of its content. But for all who get on the inside of such a form of thought and who make it, to a certain extent their own, the contours of the public world are to that extent transformed. The process of initiation into such modes of thought and awareness is the process of education.

2. THE INTERSUBJECTIVE CONTENT OF EDUCATION

The foregoing sketch of 'mind' and of its development has been necessarily brief and selective. Its point should be obvious enough—to correct the conceptions of education that were derivative from the empiricist picture of mind and its development as well as to give an account of education that is consistent with the criteria that were made explicit in the first three chapters. The same sort of corrective is necessary also for the Kantian concept and its derivative in Piaget. For although a view which stresses the activity of mind in selecting from and imposing order on the flux of experience by means of a developing categorial and conceptual structure is a great improvement on the *tabula rasa* or 'empty cabinet' view of the classical empiricists, it is still deficient if mental structure is regarded as innate or simply as the product of maturation. What is lacking is the notion that such a structure develops out of and as a response to public traditions enshrined in language.

Plato once described philosophy as the soul's dialogue with itself. It is a pity that this clue was not followed up. For the notion would not then have developed that reason is a sort of mental gadget that can be used by the individual or, as Hume described it, a 'wonderful and unintelligible instinct in our souls'. The ability to reason, in the philosophical sense of thinking critically about one's beliefs, develops only if a man keeps critical company so that a critic is incorporated in his own consciousness. The dialogue within is inseparable from the dialogue without. In a similar way the individual's sense of guilt is inexplicable unless he is brought up amongst others who blame or shame him for things that they call 'wrong'.

The moral and psychological defects of what were dubbed the 'moulding' and 'growth' models of education were touched upon in the first chapter. But the point was not made that they both share a common defect: that of regarding the educator as a detached operator who is working for some kind of result in another person which is external to him. On the moulding model some kind of content is judiciously imprinted on or implanted in the child's mind; in the parlance of modern associationism, represented by Skinner, the individual is 'shaped' to conform to some approved pattern. On the child-centred model the child is encouraged to 'grow' according to the laws of his own development. What both these models lack is a sense of what D. H. Lawrence called 'the holy ground' that stands between teacher and taught. To conceive of 'education' as imposing a pattern on another person or as fixing the environment so that an individual 'grows' fails to do justice to the shared impersonality both of the content that is handed on and of the criteria by reference to which it is criticized and developed. It ignores the cardinal fact that education consists essentially in the initiation of others into a public world picked out by the language and concepts of a people and in encouraging others to join in exploring realms marked out by more differentiated forms of awareness.

In the early stages, of course, language counts for little. The exploration of the public world begins with taste and touch. In this amorphous world there may well be a few natural objects, such as the mother's breast, that all children pick out as primordial patterns. But most of the objects explored are put there for a purpose and have the imprint of the public mind upon them. The human world, even at this level of concrete objects, is largely a selective world of social artifice. This is especially the case in civilized communities. It may well be, of course, that the manipulation and exploration of natural materials such as faeces, water, earth, and sand are necessary to the unstunted development of the child. But there are few universal objects of this sort, and communities vary both in the social significance with which they invest them and in the access which they permit to them. Most objects with which the child has contact are concretizations of social purpose and belief.

Very soon, the child has to adapt himself to the multitude of rules and customs that are going to mark for ever the channels of his individual life. For the social world, as Durkheim put it, confronts the child *comme les choses*. To live at ease he has to get on the inside of it, to incorporate it in his own mental structure. This he does mainly by learning a language; for a people's language is the key to the form of life which they enjoy. By means of it they pick out and create the public world peculiar to them. The working class man, for instance, who has access only to a limited vocabulary and to a limited set of symbolic structures, literally lives in a different world from the professional man who has a much wider and more varied vocabulary and whose education in the various differentiated forms of thought has continued for nearly a decade longer. It is a grave error to regard the learning of a language as a purely instrumental matter, as a tool in the service of purposes, standards, feelings, and beliefs. For in a language is distilled a view of the world which is constituted by them. In learning a language the individual is initiated into a public inheritance which his parents and teachers are inviting him to share.

If anything in education is purely instrumental the basic skills of reading and writing are. They give access to and make participation possible; but they have no content built into them. Everything depends on what is read or written. With arithmetic, however, the case is different. For to manipulate numbers and to see relationships between them is to begin the exploration of a special world, to learn a new sort of language. With the development of more differentiated modes of thought, made possible by the mastery of basic skills, the paramount importance of public traditions becomes more palpable. For there are books and journals in which bodies of knowledge are arranged and accumulated; there are intersubjective methods of inquiry and argument, rules of evidence and criteria of criticism. The cardinal function of the teacher, in the early stages, is to get the pupil on the inside of the form of thought or awareness with which he is concerned. At a later stage, when the pupil has built into his mind both the concepts and mode of exploration involved, the difference between teacher and taught is obviously only one of degree. For both are participating in the shared experience of exploring a common world. The teacher is simply more familiar with its contours and more skilled in finding and cutting pathways. The good teacher is a guide who helps others to dispense with his services.

In recent times it has been fashionable to attack the old view, associated with the moulding model, that education is concerned with the transmission of a body of knowledge. Stress is placed instead on critical thinking, individual exploration and experimentation. This emphasis was salutary enough at a time when bodies of knowledge were often handed on as 'inert ideas' and without any attempt being made to hand on also the public procedures by means of which they had been accumulated and could be criticized and revised. But it is equally absurd to think that procedures can be handed on without content. Critical thought is vacuous without anything concrete to be critical about and there are as many brands of 'critical thinking' as there are disciplines. In the various modes of thought such as science, history, and philosophy there is a great deal to be known before the peculiar nature of the problem can be grasped. The procedures of a discipline can only be mastered by an exploration of its established content under the guidance of one who has already been initiated.

In these differentiated modes of thought and awareness both the content and the procedures are intersubjective. A body of knowledge is an accumulated heritage that has stood up to public scrutiny and discussion and which has structured the outlook of countless men and women with its built-in conceptual scheme. The critical procedures by means of which established content is assessed, revised, and adapted to new discoveries, presuppose public principles that stand as impersonal standards to which both teacher and learner must give their allegiance. In science or philosophy it is truth that matters; in morals it is justice as well; in religion it is reverence for the contingency of the natural order. These fundamental principles mark out 'the holy ground' of which D. H. Lawrence spoke.

Once this social dimension of the development of mind has been grasped together with the intersubjective character of its more differentiated modes of awareness, the likening of education to a process of initiation is obvious enough. For it is a peculiarly apt description of the essential feature of education which consists in experienced persons turning the eye of others outwards to what is essentially independent of persons. 'Initiation', too, even when connected with various ceremonies or rites, suggests an avenue of access to a body of belief, perhaps to mysteries that are not revealed to the young. One is not initiated into something that involves a mere know-how or knack. To liken education to initiation is therefore consistent with the second group of criteria of 'education' which connect 'education' with some depth of understanding. Furthermore 'initiation' picks out types of processes leading up to a successful outcome which are consistent with the third criterion. For just as 'education' requires that those who are educated should be brought to this state by various processes which only have in common the minimum requirements of wittingness and voluntariness, so too does 'initiation' convey the same suggestion of being placed on the inside of a form of thought or awareness by a wide variety of processes which at least involve some kind of consciousness and consent on the part of the initiate. There are no processes which are specifically required for something to count as either initiation or education. In other words both are highly general terms. 'Education', however, is more specific in that it requires, according to the first criterion, that something worth while should be or have been transmitted. Initiation, on the other hand, can be into things that are not worth while such as gambling or devil-worship. 'Education', therefore, has to be described as initiation into activities or modes of thought and conduct that are worth while in order to do justice to all three criteria that are built into it.

3. EDUCATION AND THE EMPHASIS ON THE INDIVIDUAL

It might be said that this account of 'education' which has stressed the intersubjective content of education, does too little justice to the personal element in it. This could mean that it ignores matters to do with the individual differences of the pupil or that it ignores the personal bond which must exist between teacher and taught for education to proceed in a satisfactory way. These two aspects of the personal element in education must be considered separately.

It is almost a platitude of democratic thinking that the aim of education is to develop the potentialities of each individual or to enable the individual to realize himself. It might seem as if the account of education here given was inconsistent with such an aim. But deeper reflection would surely reveal not inconsistency but a proper perspective for it. It is salutary to stress the aim of individual self-realization when an educational system is either geared to the demands of the state, such as for more scientists or technicians, or when individuals are being relentlessly moulded in accordance with some doctrinaire pattern. There is point, under such conditions, in stressing the differences between people and the ethical principle of respect for each individual's unique viewpoint on the world, together with the aspirations, abilities, and inclinations that are peculiar to him. But no educator, when confronted with abilities and inclinations such as those of a lotus-eater or a Marquis de Sade, would say that these ought to be developed to the full. His plea for self-realization is a plea for the principle of options within a range of activities and modes of conduct that are thought to be desirable. For not all desirable things are within the scope of every individual; not all of them fan in some minds even the faintest spark of inclination. The plea is both for cutting the coat of what is desirable according to the cloth of the individual and for the procedural principle that individuals should be allowed to experiment and choose their own manner of life over and above those modes of conduct that are essential for them as members of society.

The self-realization, then, of the individual is limited to the development of the self in activities and modes of conduct that are regarded as desirable, or at least as not undesirable. Furthermore, these activities and forms of conduct are almost always social in character. They are engaged in with others; there is usually a body of knowledge or at least some kind of 'lore' attached to them even if they take the form of games or pastimes; there are good and bad ways of proceeding which the individual has to pick up from others more experienced in them. The 'potentialities' of the individual can only be developed within the framework of some socially structured pursuit into which he has to be initiated.

In the matter of avenues of initiation as well as in the matter of aims of education the foregoing account of education is perfectly consistent with an emphasis on individual differences. Indeed a very shrewd criticism of traditional theories of learning is that they emphasize too much the general conditions of learning and neglect the matter of individual style.[1] Though the banal slogan 'We teach children, not subjects' ignores the fact that the verb 'to teach' takes a double accusative, it does at least draw attention to the importance of individual differences. In the early stages of education, especially, while the minds of young children are comparatively unformed by public traditions, the importance of individual differences is paramount. Hence the relevance of activity methods which cater well for individual idiosyncrasies and divergent rates of growth. Such a 'child-centred' approach is as appropriate in dealing with the backward or difficult adolescent as it is at the infant stage. For the crucial difference is not one of age, but of the development of cognitive structure, and of degrees of initiation into public and differentiated modes of thought. At the other end of the enterprise of education, however, in universities, adult education classes, and the later stages of secondary education, the emphasis is more on the canons implicit in the forms of thought and awareness than on individual avenues of initiation. Of course points have to be made in different ways to different people; some poems or problems appeal to some, others to others. But the presumption, at the later stages of education, is that the argument is followed or the opinion considered; its source is ignored unless the

[1] See Riessman, Frank, 'The Strategy of Style' in *Teachers College Record*, March 1964, pp. 484–9.

idiosyncrasy is so striking that the common enterprise is held up. This is one of the respects in which education differs from group therapy.

Others who emphasize individuality may have in mind the importance of individual inventiveness and creativity. This is another desirable aspect of education which must be put into perspective. For talk of inventiveness is empty unless the individual is brought up in a tradition which enables him to see and find a way round a problem when it arises. Some situations are called problematic because they cannot be dealt with by an established tradition. Unless an individual has mastered the tradition in respect of which such situations are regarded as problematic, no problem exists for him. Similarly talk of creativeness is cant unless a child is equipped with competence; for he can have no skills with which he can exhibit his creativeness. Whitehead[1] very wisely put the matter in perspective when he argued that individuals have to pass from the stage of romance, when their interest is awakened, to a stage of precision when their interest is disciplined. They are then ready to pass to the stage of generalization when they can proceed under their own steam. In other words they are on the inside of the activity and have mastered both its established content and the procedures by means of which it has been developed. They are now in a position to revise and develop it for themselves, to invent and cut new pathways in their exploration. But such individual inventiveness can only emerge against a background of a public tradition which has provided both the milieu for problems and the procedures for tackling them.

Similarly an individual's character, which many consider it the business of education to develop, represents his own distinctive style of rule-following. But it represents an emphasis, an individualized pattern, which is drawn from a public pool. Character-traits are internalized social rules such as honesty, punctuality, truthfulness, and selfishness. A person's character represents his own achievement, his own manner of imposing regulation on his inclinations. But the rules which he imposes are those into which he has been initiated since the dawn of his life as a social being.

4. EDUCATION AND PERSONAL RELATIONSHIPS

There are many who emphasize the importance of personal relationships in teaching and it might be thought that the foregoing account is

[1] Whitehead, A. N., *The Aims of Education* (London, Macmillan, 1929), Ch. 2.

oblivious of them in its stress on impersonal standards to which both teacher and taught owe allegiance. Again it is a matter of placing the emphasis in perspective.

It must be said, first of all, that the ability to form and maintain satisfactory personal relationships is almost a necessary condition of doing anything else in a manner that is not warped or stunted. If the need to love and to be loved is not satisfied the individual will be prone to distortions of belief, ineffectiveness or lack of control in action, and unreliability in his allegiances.[1] His attempts to learn things will also be hampered by his lack of trust and confidence. A firm basis of love and trust, together with a continuing education in personal relationships, is therefore a crucial underpinning to any other more specific educational enterprise. The teacher himself must obviously be an exemplar in this respect if he is to do his job effectively. But so must a nurse, a psychiatrist, or a social worker. More needs to be said about what is specific to a *teacher's* relationship with his pupils.

Too many accounts of an educational situation are haunted by the notion that it approximates to a confrontation between one teacher and one pupil. This is a very rare situation for a school teacher to find himself in for any length of time. Usually an educational situation is a form of group experience. At its developed stages, when all are to varying degrees on the inside of a form of thought or awareness, it is a shared exploration conducted in accordance with rigorous canons, in which all are united by a common zeal. A feeling of fraternity unites those who share a common pursuit. The teacher himself, who conducts the enterprise, will be affected by this contagious feeling. But he will also have a special regard for the members of his class which derives from his special responsibility for guiding them in a region which he has explored before.

A teacher will inevitably like some pupils more than others, just as some will be attracted by him whereas others will not. Such mutual attractions are part of the situation in which he is placed; that they should exist or not exist is not part of his intentional concern as an educator. Indeed they are very little under his control. This is just as well, for what is required of him is not an intense liking for his pupils but a respect for them as persons. This respect is perhaps peculiar to the special relationship in which he is placed in regard to them; for there is no one form of

---

[1] See Peters, R. S., 'Mental Health as an Educational Aim' in Hollins, T. H. B. (Ed.), *The Aims of Education, A Philosophic View* (Manchester University Press 1964).

love or respect. Such feelings are inseparable from the view one has of people as sons or brothers, as colleagues or competitors. In general respect for persons is the feeling awakened when another is regarded as a distinctive centre of consciousness, with peculiar feelings and purposes that criss-cross his institutional roles. It is connected with the awareness one has that each man has his own aspirations, his own viewpoint on the world; that each man takes pride in his achievements, however idiosyncratic they may be. To respect a person is to realize all this and to care.

In the teaching situation this general respect for persons is overlaid with the awareness that one is confronted with *developing* centres of consciousness. The teacher must be unswerving in his allegiance to the principles which mark out his 'holy ground'. But, especially in the early stages of initiation, he must not be brutal in applying them to the halting or misdirected ventures of his pupils. For that would be to disregard how such a contribution looks to its author, to trample on another's inchoate formulation of what he thinks or feels. People learn by committing themselves and finding out where they are mistaken. Much can be done to anticipate criticism by rehearsals in the imagination. But there is a sense in which no one quite knows what he thinks or feels until he has made a view his own by identifying himself with it and defending it in public. To take a hatchet to a pupil's contribution, before he has much equipment to defend it, is not only likely to arrest or warp his growth in this form of thought; it is also to be insensitive to him as a person. When Socrates described himself as a midwife in the service of truth he used a brilliant image to illustrate this dual aspect of a teacher's concern. He must care both about the principles of his discipline and about his pupil's viewpoint on the world which he is being led to explore. *Both* forms of concern are obligatory. Respect for persons must not be pursued with a cavalier disregard for standards. The art teacher who is content simply to let his pupils express themselves without comment on their form of the expression is as deficient as the seminar leader who ruthlessly ridicules all contributions that are not obviously apposite.

Another important dimension of the personal element in teaching is much more elusive and applies especially to the final stages of the educational enterprise when the teacher's role is that of *primus inter pares*. This is to do with the development of skill and judgment. It is one thing to understand the canons of any discipline or mode of conduct and to be able to proceed in a more or less autonomous fashion; it is quite another

59

to apply these canons with skill and judgment in particular circumstances. Judgment, said Longinus, is the final flower of much experience. But such experience has usually to be acquired in the company of a man who already has judgment. Aristotle's teaching about the development of practical wisdom and, in more recent times, Oakeshott's[1] strictures on formalistic attempts to contrive political education, confirm the widespread conviction that such subtleties in an educational situation are caught rather than taught. Presumably they depend on imitation and on the mechanism known as 'identification' about which psycho-analysts have written so much. Presumably those who acquire them are drawn by some sort of attraction towards a particular practitioner of an art or of a mode of thought, who functions as an exemplar for them. And so skill and judgment are handed on from generation to generation, each master contributing his individual increment to the common stock.

It might be said that it is strange that the final fruits of the enterprise of education should be so chancy. For, it was argued that the central cases of 'education' are task-like; yet it looks as if the final reward of a teacher, the emergence of a pupil who has developed enough skill and judgment to correct him, is not something that can be consciously contrived. The answer to this is surely that the imparting of such skill or judgment may be a chancy business; but it is not quite like falling in love or other such irrational possessions to which a man is subject. For the teacher has actively to engage in exhibiting some art, attitude, or form of thought for the contagion to spread. There is a Polish proverb to the effect that the marksman takes aim but that, in the end, it is God who determines whether the target is hit. It is the same with teaching. The final flower will only bloom if the teacher is devoted to exploring his 'holy ground' with all the skill, perseverance, and enthusiasm which he can muster. He may acquire genuine disciples if he is single minded enough to care little whether he has them or not.

5. EDUCATION AND MOTIVATION

This waywardness of the final flower of education introduced another crucial aspect of it, that of motivation; for it is often claimed that admiration felt for the teacher is one of the most potent incentives to learning.

[1] See Oakeshott, M., 'Political Education' in *Rationalism in Politics* (London, Methuen, 1962).

If this is so there is a chanciness that infects the whole educational enterprise. For, as has already been pointed out, such attractions and repulsions cannot be planned or summoned at will. Maybe they depend on whether the teacher reminds the child of an adored parent; maybe his face, tone of voice, or smell is in some way reassuring. What is the perspective in which to see this elusive bond?

Little service is done to education if the cardinal point is evaded that the activities and modes of conduct which define a civilized form of life are difficult to master. That is why the educator has such an uphill task when he is competing with modern mass-media which lead children so gleefully along less exacting paths. The teacher may initially win the interest of children; but it is when what Whitehead called the stage of precision arrives that they may find the going hard. That is why the factor of motivation is so crucial.

Motivational factors in learning can be divided into those that are intrinsic and those that are extrinsic. Intrinsic factors are of two main sorts—general and specific. The general ones have long been familiar to common sense before more precise investigation by psychologists confirmed them. They include the desire just to find out things and to explore the environment, the desire to manipulate things, the sense of competence and of mastery, and the achievement motive.[1] These can be harnessed to things that are both futile and wicked; they can degenerate into compulsiveness and obsessiveness. But if they are harnessed to worth-while activities and modes of conduct they are a very powerful source of motivation.

The specific motivations depend upon being on the inside of the activity or the form of thought in question and having mastered the appropriate procedures. Scientists, mathematicians, and philosophers do not just desire to discover the truth; they desire also to devise ingenious experiments, to construct elegant proofs, and to develop clear and cogent arguments. Writers desire to construct neat plots, to make witty remarks, and to fix their feelings in just the right form of words. These joys are intrinsic to the activities and modes of thought in question; they reinforce the more general motivations which urge men on above the level of their 'necessary appetites'.

[1] See Berlyne, D. E., *Conflict, Arousal and Curiosity* (New York, McGraw Hill, 1960), White, R., 'Competence and the Psycho-sexual Stages of Development' in *Nebraska Symposium on Motivation*, 1960, McClelland, D., *The Achievement Motive* (New York, Appleton-Century-Crofts, 1953).

The aim of the educator is to get others on the inside of such worthwhile activities and forms of awareness so that they will explore them for the ends which are intrinsic to them. But in the early stages he may have to use extrinsic motivations both to get children started on them and to sustain their interest when the stage of precision begins to exert its irksome discipline. The 'moulding' school of educators used rewards and punishments with, perhaps, an over-emphasis on punishments. The 'child-centred' school attempted to harness basic skills and worth-while activities to the existing interests of children. They tried to erect skill and discrimination on a foundation of existing wants. Others have used all sorts of techniques to appeal to the imagination and thus to create new wants and interests. Amongst such extrinsic motivations perhaps the most powerful is the admiration which a child may have for a teacher and his infectious enthusiasm for his subject. If a teacher attracts such admiration he is then in a position of danger. For it is only too easy and too human for him to wish to keep his disciples dependent upon him instead of using their admiration for him to turn their interest outwards towards the objects of the educational enterprise, to the ends which are intrinsic to the activities. In this respect the teacher is like the analyst who finds himself in the transference situation. The test of his integrity as a teacher is how he deals with this felicitous situation.

When all has been said about intrinsic and extrinsic motivation the sobering truth remains that education is a very chancy business. The teacher can only work away with enthusiasm, insisting on the standards immanent in his subject, but adapting it and presenting it in accordance with the idiosyncrasies of those whom he is trying to initiate into it. Some catch on, others do not. In education, as in other meetings between human beings, the wind of the spirit bloweth where it listeth. In the end all education is self-education. Somehow or other the individual must come to care sufficiently about what is intrinsic to these worth-while activities so that he no longer has any need of extrinsic motivation. (There are some rules for aiding this process but none for ensuring it.) Perhaps the greatest educators are those who can convey insensibly the sense of quality in these activities so that a glimmering of what is intrinsic is constantly intimated. The result is that others are drawn along with them to join in the shared experience of exploring a different level of life. But how many of us are much more than just quiet men working at our job?

THE CONCEPT OF 'EDUCATION' AS APPLIED TO CONTEMPORARY ENGLISH INSTITUTIONS

INTRODUCTION

Much has been said to date about education, but very little about the institutions in which it should take place. It is very difficult, as a matter of fact, to pronounce in general terms about institutions such as schools or universities. Objectively speaking a sociologist could examine what the functions of such institutions are in the community in the sense of the actual jobs that they do. He might note, for instance, that universities provide positions of prestige in a community and that schools act as agencies of selection and socialization But few would argue that such generalizations would reveal much of what was distinctive about such institutions. To get at this an attempt would have to be made to find out what those manning such institutions conceived of themselves as doing in so far as they are members of them. Extrinsic purposes such as earning a salary would not be relevant; neither would idiosyncratic motives such as satisfying a desire to dominate. For a man might also have these as a member of the police force; they would reveal nothing specific either about schools and universities or about the institution of the police force. Some reference to the enforcement of the law or the preservation of public order would surely have to be brought in to characterize the police force as an institution. The behaviour of its members would be inexplicable unless they conceived of themselves as attempting to do something like this. A simpler case still would be an institution like the Society for the Propagation of Christian Knowledge, for which a clear-cut aim provides the essence of the institution.

Universities and schools, however, are not such clear-cut institutions

[1] This appendix was added after the book had been written in order to meet the objection that it was not clear how the concept of 'education' here developed applies to institutions as different from each other as universities and primary schools. It therefore has the very limited purpose of spelling this out. In so far as it contains comments about contemporary policies and practices, these are approached from the limited point of view of their relevance to the concern of differect types of institutions with education, having regard to the different criteria of 'education' explicated in Ch. 1. The appendix, therefore, adds little to the main argument of the book and contains very little philosophy in a strict sense. Those who have grasped the conceptual points about 'education' already made, and who are not interested in contemporary English institutions, are therefore advised to miss it out.

as these; for their members have different ways of conceiving of what they are meant to be doing. These may constitute divergent views about the aims of education or aims which compete with strictly educational ones. These possibilities must now be briefly explored.

I. UNIVERSITIES

It might be thought, for instance, that if the preceding analysis of 'education' is more or less along the right lines the place *par excellence* where it should take place is in a university. But this would exhibit a certain *naïveté* about the conception which many university teachers have of a university. They might argue that what is essential to a university is the pursuit of truth in its various forms. To educate, on the view put forward in this book, involves at least the intentional transmission of such a worth-while pursuit, and many scholars and research workers might regard the instruction of others as extraneous to their concept of a 'university'. Of course if others like to be around while the pursuit of truth is proceeding there is no harm in their listening in and, perhaps, joining in. There are plenty of opportunities for this as the pursuit of truth is essentially a public matter involving discussion with colleagues and the publication of findings. All this could go on with little explicit attempt being made to teach anyone.[1]

This is certainly a possible concept of a university but it is neither the British nor the American concept. 'University' suggests to us not only the disinterested pursuit of truth in its various forms but education as well—at least in the minimal sense of the initiation of others into this pursuit. But once concede that a university is concerned with education and vast vistas open up. For to what extent is a university concerned with the development of that cognitive perspective which, it has been argued, is one of the hall-marks of an educated man?[2] To admit that education is the concern of a university is to insert a wedge that can easily open the door to the demand for the exploration of many forms of thought and awareness. Particular stress might even be placed, as at Balliol in the old days, on moral awareness and a social conscience. It might be claimed (more or less *a priori*) that such moral awareness is encouraged by some form of studies rather than others. Snow and Leavis at least agree on one thing—that moral sensitivity can and should

[1] For defence of this concept of a university see Griffiths, A. P., 'A Deduction of Universities' in Archambault, R. D. (Ed.), *Philosophical Analysis and Education* (London, Kegan Paul, 1965).
[2] See Ch. 1. Sec. 3(b)

be encouraged by distinct forms of disinterested pursuit; they disagree about the respective merits of science and literary studies when viewed under this aspect.

Clearly, then, if 'education' is to be included in the concept of 'a university' there must be some decisions about priorities. In the USA, for instance, different emphases have been given to different types of institutions. Liberal Arts Colleges have concentrated on 'the whole man'; Graduate Schools and Institutes of Technology have been left the task of expanding the frontiers of knowledge. In England, however, all universities have viewed themselves in recent times as concerned primarily with research and with education in the limited sense of initiating others deeply into the different disciplines in the context of the advancement of knowledge; but they have differed very much in the extent to which they have thought that education in a wider sense is their explicit concern. Perhaps they have made concessions to this view by insisting on subsidiary subjects or by instituting joint and general degrees; perhaps they have assumed that the all-round understanding of an educated man is picked up informally in common-room conversation and in discussions going on into the small hours. They have also instituted schools of professional training and technology and have attempted to educate people in some sense or other while they are undergoing a training. But they have always held fast to their primary concern with the pursuit of truth and with the initiation of others who may continue it. This provides a distinctive context for technology and teaching.

Given, however, that 'education' is already part of our concept of 'a university', it would be understandable if the concept were stretched more in the direction of 'education' than heretofore; for concepts are usually stretched by the development of something that is already intimated by them. This does not usually happen because clear-headed men sit down and think out the business afresh, but because economic and social change and the accompanying social pressures exert a steady and insensible influence. Such pressures have been exerted on the universities in the past ten years to an unprecedented degree by the phenomena labelled the 'bulge' and the 'trend'. British universities have almost trebled their numbers since 1939; eight quite new universities are now being developed; and in so far as this expansion is linked with demands for specific types of education, the claims of science, technology and professional training have been pressed together with a more diffuse demand for education in a wider sense as distinct from specialist training in one discipline, i.e. for the development of 'whole men'. The Robbins Report represents a well-documented expression of these various pressures. The section on 'the aims of higher education'[1] resonates with those confused and sonorous hosannas which one has come to associate with such statements; but it is clear enough at least to exhibit the pressures. It brings to the forefront 'instruction in skills suitable to play a part in the division of labour'. It secondly draws attention to the need to conduct vocational training in such a way that it will promote 'the general powers of the mind', and then proceeds to conflate giving 'practical techniques' a good theoretical basis with producing 'cultivated men and women' instead of 'mere specialists'[2] It is only when the authors come to their third aim, the advancement of learning and the disinterested pursuit of truth, that they mention the more central aim of universities.

It might be expected, therefore, that the demands implicit in the report might lead to the moulding of the concept of 'a university' along the lines of these pressures—especially in the case of the new universities. But an examination of their explicit statements does not confirm this expectation. It suggests rather that they are attending to their academic arrangements in ways which take account of the pressures, while keeping to the forefront the emphasis on the advancement of knowledge to provide the appropriate context.

A common expedient is to eschew the traditional organization in faculties and departments which is thought to ossify the apartness of different disciplines. It is hoped that staff and students from different disciplines will thus be thrown more into daily contact with each other and will thus have more chance to develop that 'wholeness' which, as has been argued, is a characteristic of an educated person. Another move in the direction of education is to have some broadly-based course or courses in the first year (like the controversial 'Foundation Year' of the University of Keele) to bridge the gulf between school and university. Interestingly enough no university has put forward a plan for starting with specialized training and broadening out in the third year into more general courses, though in fact this might be more desirable on *educational* grounds.

---

[1] *Higher Education* (London, HMSO, 1963).

[2] In other words it conflates criteria of 'education' which are distinguished from other each in Ch. I. Secs. 3(a) and 3(b). Needless to say these 'needs' are very different.

Over and above these general expedients there are, roughly speaking, two ways in which the curriculum is contrived so as to guard against the alleged danger of premature specialization. The first is to encourage or force students to pursue more than one subject to an advanced stage, as is being done at Keele, York, Lancaster and Warwick. The second and more radical attempt to extend the concept of 'a university' in the direction of 'education' is to start from some 'field' to the exploration of which many disciplines naturally contribute, and to develop specialization gradually out of a many-sided approach to such a field. This development is occasioned partly by the fact that many of the most promising areas of research now cut across boundaries which have traditionally separated the different disciplines—e.g. the common area between chemistry and biology or between history and sociology—and partly because a common criticism of the Joint degrees of the past (e.g. PPE and PPP at Oxford; BA General, Philosophy and Economics, Philosophy and Psychology at London) has been that such disciplines either are not linked or, if they are, they are in fact pursued in a very compartmentalized way. Sussex, East Anglia, and Essex are adopting this approach. Kent is adopting this approach for Part I of the degree and the first type of approach for Part II.

'Education' also intimates something about the *manner* of initiating others into a quality of life; and the new universities are mindful of the 'leading out' aspect of it. Emphasis is given to the provision of tutorials in most of them; some—in particular, York—are developing on a collegiate basis in which the college is thought of as the centre of social and intellectual life; enlightened thought is being given to problems of accommodation and to staff and student participation in university government. In brief there is no confidence that either a civilized outlook or the more intangible qualities of a university education will be rubbed in by casual contact with eager contemporaries or with dedicated dons in buildings hallowed by tradition and sometimes by architectural grace. All this has to be contrived by institutional arrangements and physical planning.

There is as yet, then, in Britain at any rate, no new concept of 'a university'; rather the established one is being extended more in the direction of 'education' in ways which, it is hoped, will not damage the advancement of knowledge. But institutions have a logic of their own; they often develop, in response to internal strains and external pressures, in ways which run counter to the explicit intentions of their founders.

Many major institutional and conceptual shifts have been set in motion by those who never intended them, e.g. those connected with the Reformation. It remains to be seen whether the lines of institutional provision will in fact so determine the emphasis that in some cases it will be said either that the concept of 'a university' has changed or that the institution in question has become something else, e.g. a Liberal Arts College. And which of these is said may prove to be very important for the future quality of our university provision.

2. INSTITUTES OF TECHNOLOGY AND TECHNICAL COLLEGES

It has been argued that, in so far as universities have an essence, it is the disinterested pursuit of truth in its many forms together with the initiation of others into this pursuit. It has been shown that, in spite of modern pressures to extend this concept in the direction of education, British universities have attempted to do this in ways which do not seriously damage their essence. The question is largely one of the relative emphasis given to research and to teaching.

Another influential modern demand is that universities should be less rather than more concerned with education. But this, in the eyes of enthusiasts like Lord Bowden,[1] does not mean that they should concentrate more on their essential function of being centres of learning and of the disinterested pursuit of truth. Rather they should model themselves on the American 'Cow-Colleges' and become centres of the 'knowledge industry'. They should devote themselves, like MIT and Caltec, to providing the theory necessary for solving the practical problems of the community.

Few would question the desirability of having such institutions; but it would be odd to regard them as paradigms of universities, especially when the established title of 'Institute of Technology' conveys much more appropriately their predominant preoccupation. In Britain many universities already have incorporated large technological schools; the new Universities of Essex and Lancaster are explicitly making large-scale provision for them; and the Colleges of Advanced Technology are being granted university status, which involves the right to grant degrees amongst other things. Whether or not such institutions are properly called 'Universities' or 'Institutes of Technology' depends on the extent to which the pursuit of the practical predominates.

[1] In the Foundation Oration given at Birkbeck College, University of London, in December 1964.

A distinct issue is the extent to which such institutions are educational institutions; for their predominant concern with the practical need not, as advocated by Lord Bowden, entail that they are not concerned with education as well. MIT, for instance, prides itself on its School of Humanities, on its philosophy as well as its physics, and students have to devote one-fifth of their time to studies in the humanities. This could mean the attempt to encourage the grasp of fundamental principles as distinct from technical know-how. The Robbins Report is emphatic on the desirability of this: 'And it is the distinguishing characteristic of a healthy higher education that, even when it is concerned with practical techniques, it imparts them on a plane of generality that makes possible their application to many problems—to find the one in the many, the general characteristics in the collection of particulars.'[1] Alternatively it could mean the development of 'the whole man' which involves the cognitive perspective conveyed by 'education'. How this is to be achieved within a technological context is a much debated question. There are three main views about it which correspond roughly to the views in the new universities about how students are to be more broadly educated. One view is that students shall be made or encouraged to develop in a more or less disconnected way a different perspective on life from that associated with technological concerns. Courses on literature, history, philosophy, and similar subjects should be mounted, as it were, in their own right. Another view is that an attempt should be made to develop such a perspective by linking these studies with the main course, e.g. history and philosophy of science as arising from the particular sciences studied. The third view is that such a liberal attitude develops more as the result of conversation than of courses. Those who argue in this way deprecate the setting up of separate technological institutions; for they claim that, if these institutions are incorporated within a university, contact with other students pursuing other disciplines, and pursuing them for their own sake—especially under residential conditions—provides an environment which is mutually beneficial to both types of student.

The third type of view raises issues vital to the future of regional Technical Colleges as educational institutions. These, at the moment, are not so exclusively concerned with technology as the Colleges of

[1] *Higher Education*, Report of the Robbins Committee (London, HMSO, 1963), p. 6. Presumably this relates to the criterion of 'education' picked out in Ch. I, Sec. 3(a).

Advanced Technology. Their advanced students tend to take the London External Degree as well as the Diploma in Technology. It had been assumed that they too would either gradually be granted university status or be incorporated within new or existing universities. Recently, however, the Government has announced its intention of developing a 'binary system' of higher education, which has called a halt to such evolution. An alternative route to a degree, awarded by the Council for National Academic Awards, is to be provided for students in regional colleges and other institutions such as Area Colleges and Colleges of Commerce, which are all to remain under local education authorities. The link will thus be preserved between such colleges and their local communities—especially their industries who use them extensively for 'sandwich courses', day release and part-time study. These colleges will, of course, be, for the most part, non-residential. Their students, it is hoped, will eventually have 'parity of esteem' with those who take the alternative university route. They will simply have a different type of education, geared more closely to the realities of commerce and industry. The universities will benefit from competition from this other form of higher education and far more students will have a chance of attaining a degree than they would have had if they had to obtain a place in a slowly expanding system of university education.

This decision is obviously dictated in large part by economic necessity. A place at a university costs the country far more than a place at a Technical College and the country's economic viability depends upon training a vast number of technicians. But it is a pity that it should have been dressed up in such shabby clothes. The suggestion that a technically or vocationally based education is the proper concern of the local education authority may have some logic to it; but it is a strange argument to use at a time when CATs are being converted into universities and in the light of the amount of technology and professional training that is already the concern of universities. The claim of 'equal but different', too, sounds suspiciously like the pious hope that heralded the advent of the ill-fated secondary modern school. Whatever the realities of the matter may be, no one will accord the same status to a degree awarded by the CNAA to a student at a Regional College as is accorded to a proper university degree. Second-class citizens will be created at the level of higher education just as they were created at the level of secondary education by the 1944 Act.

As a matter of fact there is a lot to be said for refusing to extend the concept of a 'university' further to include institutions which will be minimally concerned with research and for preserving a distinctive concept of a 'university' as one form of institution of higher education amongst others. But the crucial issues are obscured by the undiscriminating advocacy of the extension of university education as an alternative to the development of a binary system. For what advocates of the extension of universities are concerned about, in addition to questions of 'parity of esteem', is the facilities afforded by universities for educating students as distinct from merely training them.[1] They argue that universities provide communities which are humanely in touch with each other, the paradigm of which was the community of scholars of the medieval universities. They provide also a grounding in subjects which are of lasting human concern, which represent man's fundamental ways of understanding his environment. They contrast this sort of atmosphere with that of a college in which there is little opportunity for meeting other students, no contact with leaders of thought, and where the main subjects studied are concerned with ephemeral applications rather than with fundamental principles—accountancy rather than the theory of numbers, cosmetology rather than chemistry. In brief they argue for the extension of universities on educational grounds, without inquiring whether education is the essence of a university.

This is surely to weaken the case; for it cannot be maintained that this type of educational environment is the peculiar property of residential universities. For, on the one hand, there are universities which are soulless and dead. Lectures are given to vast assemblies without any follow-up in tutorials or small seminars. Physical conditions and intellectual traditions are absent which might encourage the lively meeting of minds. They approximate to supermarkets where knowledge is available for those who wish to pick it up. On the other hand some of the non-residential Educational Settlements such as Morley College, and the Walthamstow Educational Settlement, which cater for part-time students, are most lively centres of intellectual stimulation and cross-fertilization. Residence does not of itself impart magical properties to an institution. If proper facilities for communal life are provided there is no reason why this sort of informal education should not take place in non-residential colleges. Similarly the tutorial or seminar system and the insistence on written work related to the students' interests, which is so

[1] See, for instance, Niblett, W. R., 'Expansion and Traditional Values' in Reeves, M. (Ed.), *Eighteen Plus* (London, Faber, 1965).

closely connected with the 'leading out' aspects of education, is not practised solely within universities. I would hazard the guess that by such purely educational criteria the Workers' Educational Association and Tutorial Classes movement has proved itself one of the most successful educational ventures in Britain. Yet this has been conducted on a part-time, non-residential basis, often without any proper physical centre for its classes. Such educational criteria, which are insisted on by the WEA and Tutorial Classes, could equally well be insisted on in Regional Colleges with the right sort of staff and with imaginative direction.

What would be lacking in such institutions need not therefore be conditions which make *education* possible. It is not this that distinguishes non-residential centres of education from universities. The crucial difference is the absence of many people who are themselves advancing the frontiers of knowledge, who are acknowledged authorities in their field. A university, it has been argued, is a community of scholars and research workers who also regard it as their business to initiate others into the pursuit of truth. Their educational activities are set in a context of the advancement of knowledge. In a Regional College, on the other hand, the emphasis is much more on teaching than on the advancement of knowledge.

The logical course of evolution should surely be that adopted in the past. Colleges should develop firm links with established universities in the way in which they developed them in the past with the University of London by means of the external degree. But this should be done on a more regional basis, not centred on the overworked External Department of the University of London. When such colleges reach the stage of themselves having a reasonable proportion of staff concerned with the advancement of knowledge as well as with teaching, then they should themselves become autonomous universities granting their own degrees, or be incorporated within existing universities. This type of evolution would avoid many of the glaring anomalies implicit in the proposed 'binary system'. Obvious objections, perhaps, are the time it would take and the conservative attitude of the universities. But one of the great dangers of the present 'escalation' of education is that educational developments will be determined mainly by economic considerations. More need not mean worse; but it will do if educational decisions are left to economists. The question is not simply one of increasing the quantity of education and training in a community; it is also that of contriving it in a manner which is also likely to improve its quality.

3. COLLEGES OF EDUCATION

A paradigm for this type of evolution could be that of Colleges of Education, if those who work in them have their way. Such colleges are either voluntary colleges with a direct grant from the Department of Education and Science or the responsibility of the local education authorities. In the past they were called Training Colleges; but, with the lengthening of the course from two to three years, and with the increasing emphasis on education as distinct from mere training,[1] their name was changed, as a result of the recommendations of the Robbins Committee.[2] They are mainly residential and stress the importance of tutorials, seminars, and individual supervision which have often been thought to be the prerogative of universities. They are thus educational as well as training institutions, but the absence of research has made it reasonable for them to be outside the universities.

After the Second World War it was increasingly realized that education, like politics, involves practical activities which require a well-established theoretical basis. Without research in psychology, sociology, philosophy, and history, decisions and practices are likely to be very much a matter of hunches, hit or miss, and prejudice. The need for a closer link with the universities, where such subjects are studied in a more concentrated and disciplined way, became apparent. The McNair Report of 1944 advocated a closer link between Training Colleges and universities, as a result of which University Institutes of Education were established to act as examining bodies for the colleges situated near the relevant universities, to co-ordinate academic arrangements, and to act as centres for research and advanced courses. The Robbins Committee in 1963 proposed the renaming referred to above, the possibility of selected students taking a BEd degree of the relevant university, after a fourth year at college, and the handing over of administrative and financial control of the colleges by the local education authorities to the University Institutes which were to be called Schools of Education. The Labour Government, elected in 1964, decided to implement the first two proposals but ruled, under strong pressures from the local education authorities, that *for the present* the colleges must remain administratively and financially outside the university orbit. The strains created by this decision to keep academic arrangements separated from financial and administrative control are not difficult to imagine.

[1] See *supra*, Ch. I, Sec. 3(c) and p. 44.
[2] For rationale behind this see Ch. IX, Sec. 4.

Such strains, however, are endurable for a brief period, provided that the blessed phrase 'for the present' intimates the eventual inclusion of the colleges within the universities. Such a slow evolution would be logical in that the Institutes have been very uneven in their development of research. The BEd degree, together with the increased emphasis placed on educational research, should do much to raise academic standards in the colleges and should in time bring about a situation where colleges do in fact have lecturers who can properly be said to be advancing knowlege as well as just educating teachers. This, it has been argued, is the crucial criterion for determining whether an institution should be incorporated within a university. It would be outrageous, however, if the colleges, staffed by lecturers of good academic standing, became welded into the universities by solid academic links, but remained administratively and financially under the control of the local education authorities. One could only conclude, in such an eventuality, that it was power and prestige rather than logic and educational considerations that had determined the outcome.

4. SCHOOLS

Not all schools are concerned with education and most schools are not concerned only with education. There are schools of motoring and golf-schools, for instance, where education plays a minimal part; and most schools which are concerned with education have also to act as agencies for selection and training for careers. Such schools, under modern conditions, have taken over many functions of the home. They have doctors and dentists attached to them; they worry about matters of diet and dress. They have almost become orphanages for children with parents. In other words the school has to take careful account of what is in the interest both of the State and of individual children. It cannot be concerned purely with the general pursuit of what is worth while.[1] This means partly concerning itself with things that are of only instrumental value and partly adapting what is worth while to children who vary a great deal in interest and ability. These subsidiary tasks of the school should not be lost sight of, though few would dispute that its essence should be education.

It is often said by child-centred educators from Rousseau onwards that each stage of education has its own values and that adults should not

[1] See *infra*, Chs. V and VI, for elaboration of this distinction.

74

try to impose their values on children. It is difficult to make much sense of this; for education necessarily involves the initiation of children into what is thought to be valuable. Without education children would be incapable of valuation and choice. Also if something is valuable, it is valuable. It does not become so because children rather than adults are concerned with it.[1] It is true, however, that only a limited range of what is valuable is accessible to children in the early stages of education, and that simpler rather than complex forms of what is valuable must be enjoyed. A child may delight in a well-made boat who is unmoved by a cogent argument. Presumably the point of the child-centred doctrine is to warn adults who may be interested in cogent arguments against neglecting the values inherent in well-made boats.

This is salutary advice, if this is how it is to be interpreted; but it is unfortunate advice if it encourages teachers to work away at one stage of education without considering how what they are doing relates to a more general concept of education. It has been argued that the aims of education are intrinsic to it in the sense that they are ways of emphasizing different aspects of what it means to be educated. If teachers in primary schools lose sight of what they consider an educated man to be, they are bound to have a truncated concept of their task. An educated person, it was maintained, is a person who pursues some worth-while things for their own sake, who has knowledge and understanding that is not inert, and whose understanding is not narrowly specialized. The school is concerned with different aspects of the achievements involved at different stages of development.

(a) The primary school
The first stage of education, which lasts roughly to about the age of 6+,[2] is basically concerned with the child's exploration of and attitude to the world and other people as distinct from himself. Objects with their qualities have to be picked out and named in a framework of space and time. Causal and means-to-ends connections have to be distinguished from the products of wishes, fears and imaginings. The modes of consciousness—cognizing, wanting, and feeling—have to be differentiated in relation to objects in a public world. In the sphere of intellectual

---

[1] See Chs. III and V.

[2] The ages singled out in this section are only rough approximations and allow for great individual differences. Obviously, too many debatable psychological assumptions underlie this section. It represents a commentary in general theory of education, not just an attempt to apply the concept of 'education'.

development this is the crucial stage for concept formation and the development of the categorial apparatus referred to in Chapter II, Sec. 1. Without this both social and emotional development will be stunted. Appropriate objects for wants have also to be learnt together with appropriate means of satisfying them, and, in the emotional sphere, realistic appraisals of the environment together with appropriate feelings towards it and the control and canalization of such feelings have also to be acquired. Standards have to be internalized for the regulation both of wants and of emotional reactions to natural objects and people. The child, at this stage, is not closely bound by social ties to his peers. His own sense of identity gradually emerges out of his dependence on his mother. He has to learn, by waiting his turn and sharing, that he is a member of a peer group.

Crucial for the child's education at this stage are his own activity, particularly his play, his imitation of and identification with his parents, and, above all, talk. It is often thought that his own manipulative and exploratory activity in relation to his environment will of itself equip him with the concepts which teachers think it desirable that he should acquire at this stage. This overlooks the social dimension of initiation.[1] The concepts will probably only come if such self-originated activity is constantly accompanied by talk and explanation on the part of adults. Obviously such activity assists his motor development and provides satisfaction. Indeed it used to be defended as crucial to the emotional development of the child—especially by Freudians. But with the increasing emphasis in modern times on intellectual development and the importance of 'concrete operations' as an aid to this, it is often assumed that concepts can be learnt by the child on his own. The proper view, surely, is that concepts must be learnt both by talk and explanation and by being confronted with concrete examples to which concepts apply. Ideas are inert if they are not concretely related to the relevant experiences; but experiences themselves are structureless without the differentiations picked out by language. It is basically through learning a language that a conceptual apparatus is developed. This requires constant and canalized talk.

It might be very reasonably maintained that if this is all that is happening in education up the age of 6+ there is little point in children going to school. All this can be picked up in the home. It is only when the child is ready for reading and writing, that the child should go to

[1] See *supra*, Ch. II, Sec. 2.

school. For the teaching of such skills requires an expertise which few parents possess. There is a lot to be said for such an argument, especially at a time of a great shortage of teachers. The fact, too, that Britain is one of the few countries where children go to school at 5 adds to its cogency. A strong case can only be made for children going to school at this early age if it can be shown either that most homes are ill-equipped to carry out this early education or that there are aspects of it *in relation to what is to come afterwards* that only specially trained people are competent to handle. These are, of course, educational arguments for children going to school at this age; they are quite distinct from arguments based on economic and social needs which stress the importance of mothers being released from domestic duties a year earlier.

There is much to be said for both types of educational argument. The cultural impoverishment of countless British homes can be cited. The homes of a large percentage of the population are so drab and cramped that the child is not provided with a rich and varied enough environment for the required early development. Above all the language of their inmates, as Bernstein[1] has shown, is so restricted that the necessary conceptual apparatus simply cannot be acquired. Also the method of social control tends to be so hit and miss and authoritarian, rather than intelligently adapted to the idiosyncrasies of the individual child, that moral and emotional development is likely to be stunted. Finally there are few opportunities for constant mixing with other children which is a prerequisite for any adequate social development. If early learning is as decisive as psychologists maintain, then a strong case can be made for removing children as early as possible for part of the day from such an impoverished environment. The corollary of this argument, however, is that the school must provide facilities for intelligent and articulate adults to supervise the exploratory and linguistic activities of children in groups which are small enough for plenty of talk as well as for plenty of enriched experience. The size of classes in most of our infant schools makes such a requirement a Utopian dream.

Suppose, then, that children come to school at this age. Into what can the teachers initiate children which is vital for later development and which might be missed in the average home? There should be much more explicit emphasis on a range of concepts which are crucial for the

[1] See Bernstein, B., 'Social Class and Linguistic Development' in Halsey, A. H., Floud, J., and Anderson, C., *Education, Economy and Society* (New York, Free Press, 1961).

modes of thought which children are later to learn. In other words the environment should not be enriched in a haphazard way but in ways that lead naturally on to the more disciplined and articulate explorations that are to follow. But equally important at this stage is the development of attitudes and habits without which children will never later get on the inside of worth-while activities. These are developments of the universal tendency of children to explore their environment, and to shape, master, or manipulate it. Out of these generalized drives there has to develop, on the one hand, the determination to get things right, to find out the truth, to get to the bottom of things and, on the other hand, the pride in finishing things, in shaping things with accuracy and precision. Without these attitudes no one will ever emerge as an educated man;[1] but they are learnt from teachers and parents who insist on standards at every stage. They are not the product of unguided exploration.

There is much emphasis nowadays on appealing to the child's spontaneous curiosity and allowing him to discover things for himself. This is a welcome reaction against the old system of sitting children down and telling them things which were of little interest to them. But a certain scepticism is appropriate about the reliance on such an approach as being sufficient in itself. This is not due simply to the virtual impossibility of employing such methods with large classes in cramped conditions. There is also the fact that the curiosity of children is sporadic and wayward; it is often directed towards things that lead on to little else; it is subject to great individual differences. Children have to develop a disciplined curiosity. The approval and example of adults is crucial in this. An educated man, it has been argued, has to be intrinsically motivated. He must be drawn to worth-while pursuits by what is intrinsic to them. But he may have, in the early stages, to catch this attitude from others who have it. In relation to the development of such disciplined curiosity many now advocate 'discovery' methods, both in the infant and in the junior school. But children so often forget what they 'discover' and even keep on 'discovering' the same thing. They also frequently 'discover' what is false.[2] It would be folly to neglect the importance of practice and precision in extolling the virtues of self-origination.

This reaction against 'formalism' can also go too far in the context of 'creativity' and the moulding of materials. Self-expression may be

[1] See *supra*, pp. 37 and 60–62.
[2] See Friedlander, B. Z., 'A Psychologist's Second Thoughts on Concepts, Curiosity, and Discovery in Teaching and Learning' in *Harvard Educational Review*, Vol. 35, 1963, No. 1.

therapeutically important; but a teacher is not just a therapist. His task is to get children to delight in creating things that conform to the appropriate standards. The precision required cannot come without practice. In the old days children were sat down in rows and had to learn laboriously how to cut out things, make envelopes, use a paint-brush and almost create things by numbers. The healthy reaction against this in favour of self-origination has often involved the neglect of standards and of the practice and learning of basic skills which are necessary to achieve them. Often it is possible, necessary, and indeed desirable for children to learn such skills together by instruction and practice in small-scale 'lessons' which can alternate with more individual forms of exploration and creation.

These points about the 'progressive' approach to education are meant as correctives to it rather than criticisms of it. There is surely a case for a rational, experimental approach to such matters which are too much associated with causes and with emotional and ideological attachments. No good teacher, with 'formal' tendencies, ever just treats children like intelligent seals or rows of pint pots to be topped up with learning. Perhaps she emphasizes instruction; but this is a polymorphous concept including all sorts of things like asking leading questions, dropping hints, making suggestions, converting interests into tasks and practices, and so on. Most 'progressive' teachers employ such methods also;[1] but they sometimes tend to caricature 'formal' teaching, e.g. by assuming that this involves a devotion to 'rote learning'.

The harsh reality in the primary school is that classes are well over forty and premises are cramped. Our concept of infant education has been much influenced by the ideals of the Froebel Kindergarten which was never intended for groups of over twenty children. Usually the children in them, like those in the schools of other pioneers such as Susan Isaacs and Dora Russell, came from well-to-do homes with its consequent effect on the intelligence and attitudes of children. The application of such methods to the large classes of the infant school, which contain countless culturally deprived children (and increasingly the children of immigrants) raises all sorts of problems. It is very difficult, under such conditions, to 'follow the interests' of each child and to keep track of the stage of cognitive and emotional development that he has reached, and to let him acquire desirable habits because he sees their necessity. The constant learning of new words, which is also necessary

[1] See Gardner, D. E. M., and Cass, J., *The Role of the Teacher in the Infant and Nursery School* (Oxford, Pergamon Press, 1965).

for cognitive development, is very difficult to contrive on an individual basis under such conditions. *Of course* no full-scale return to the old regimentation and dead learning is being advocated—only an empirical eclectic attitude by teachers which takes account of existing conditions. The problem of the primary teacher under such conditions is very much that of relating educational ideals to institutional realities. This requires flexibility, empiricism, and a grasp of underlying principles. Neither recipes nor ideological clichés can serve as a substitute for dedicated intelligence.

It would be a rash person nowadays who would pronounce on the stage at which reading and writing should be taught or on the extent to which they should be taught. But certainly once the child has had time to explore his immediate environment and has learnt to complete tasks, he must somehow acquire these basic instrumental skills so that he can extend the range and articulateness of his experience and learn how to control and communicate his expression of it. The way is then open soon after about 8 + for the beginnings of a more detailed, differentiated approach to the world. Mathematics, elementary science, history, music, art, geography, religious knowledge and so on begin to feature as definite 'subjects' on a curriculum. At this stage children are inveterate Aristotelians. What is required is plenty of experience, both first-hand and through books and visual aids, and classificatory schemes to structure it. Children of this age can cope with much more formal instruction; they are avid for facts and are good at retaining them. The 'peer group' has taken definite shape by now which makes co-operation and group projects much more a feature of the educational situation. The classroom can become a Lyceum in miniature and the development of a more autonomous type of morality marks the beginning of the possibility of Kant's 'kingdom of ends'.[1]

At this late primary stage there must, of course, be the same emphasis on self-origination and intrinsic motivation, which is such an important characteristic of an educated person.[2] But this must not be at the expense of values such as precision on the one hand and of 'facts to be stored' and 'knowledge to be acquired' on the other. The 1931 Hadow Report was salutary in emphasizing the importance of 'activity' and 'experience' as procedures for encouraging lively interest and for avoiding inert ideas. But there is a grave danger nowadays of overlooking the value of knowledge. Apart from its value in itself an individual simply is

[1] See p. 226 *infra*.   [2] See Ch. II, Sec. 5.

not viable in a highly industrialized society without a great deal of sheer knowledge. There are some, too, who have the strange idea that children can pick up 'scientific method' without knowing any science. They also confuse a 'do it yourself' attitude with the discipline involved in systematic experimentation. This is equivalent to encouraging children to be critical without giving them anything concrete to be critical about, or to suggesting that they 'decide' on their own moral principles without giving them a firm basis of moral rules, so that they can know from the inside what morality is and be vividly aware of conflicting rules between which they have to discriminate in concrete circumstances. The acquiring of knowledge is just as important as the inquiring attitude. Both, it has been argued, are features of an educated person.

Education at this late primary stage should be very much concerned with acquiring a solid body of knowledge in a differentiated way without which all talk of 'understanding principles' and of developing a critical and inquiring mind is sheer cant. But this body of knowledge must be acquired in a way that does not discourage curiosity, interest, and the desire to strike out on one's own. The overall aim of education is to get children *on the inside* of the activities and forms of awareness characterizing what we would call a civilized form of life.

In relation to the primary school there are four further considerations which are important when it is considered as an institution.[1] The first is that its function is much more diffuse than that of a secondary school because of the difference in degree of the child's capacity to take responsibility for the wider aspects of his life. At one end of the continuum, though nursery schools, as distinct from day nurseries, pride themselves on their educational emphasis, a nursery school teacher has also to spend a great deal of time on matters to do with the toilet, clothing, eating, and so on, which the secondary teacher, at the other end, can leave in the main to the children. The primary school stands in between the two and its teachers vary enormously in the amount of attention which they give to these wider processes of 'socialization'.

Any teacher must secondly attend to matters to do with the health and general welfare of the child without which education cannot proceed. But she has to attend much more to this at early stages when children can assume less responsibility for their own welfare. It is a nice question

[1] See Blyth, W. A. L., *English Primary Education* (London, Routledge & Kegan Paul, 1965), Vol. 1, Ch. VII, Sec. C. This book was unfortunately published too late to be carefully consulted.

to determine the extent of the teacher's responsibilities in this sphere, at any stage of teaching. Obviously a knowledge of the home, contact with parents, and so on, are vital for teaching a child and not merely a 'subject'. But if the teacher knows that there is a danger of a home being 'broken', is it her business to exert influence in the interest of the child? This raises not only the general question of the rationale of social work in relation to parental responsibility, but also the more particular question of the extent to which teachers must also assume the role of social workers. Obviously they must do so much more in the primary than in the secondary school. The fact that infant teachers have sole responsibility for one class marks this difference in emphasis.

Thirdly in the primary school the teacher has, to a certain extent, to act as an agent of selection on behalf of the community. The 11+ examination made this function a very pressing one in the junior school and led to all kinds of anomalies connected with streaming and cramming, which are being systematically investigated by the National Foundation for Educational Research. But in any educational system a teacher has to act, to a certain extent, in this capacity.

The fourth and final consideration is much more a problem connected with the rather *ad hoc* way in which primary education has developed in Britain. The exposition given above was predominantly in terms of developmental stages rather than in terms of administrative breaks. It raised no obvious questions about individual differences in these stages or about the possibility and desirability of speeding them up. Neither did it relate them carefully to the function of the junior as distinct from the infant school. This is because there seems little rhyme or reason in the way in which the breaks occur in Britain. Children attend an infant school from five to seven, a junior school from seven to eleven and then qualify for whatever form of secondary education is thought appropriate on the basis of some version of the 11+. These breaks do not coincide with anything which is of great general developmental significance. They were partly a product of the 1918 Act which made attendance up to fourteen compulsory. It was thought that about three years was necessary for the provision of any adequate form of secondary education. So 11+ seemed the most suitable stage at which to divide primary from secondary education.[1] The senior school would

---

[1] See *Report of the Consultative Committee on Education of the Adolescent* (HMSO, 1926) and *Report of the Consultative Committee on the Primary School* (HMSO, 1931) which are usually referred to as the Hadow Reports.

ensure, it was hoped, a reasonable standard of secondary education. The division at seven between the junior and the infant school seems retrospectively equally arbitrary. The junior school emerged gradually in the '30s after the second Hadow Report in 1931, because the Consultative Committee thought that this age range has particular needs and problems which justified provision for it in a separate school. But no clear concept of junior as distinct from secondary or infant education emerged. Its function became related much more to what happened afterwards in the secondary school than to what happened before in the infant school, which had a long tradition to draw on. The continuous progression was never properly thought out in the light of a clear concept of education or of adequate knowledge about the stages of child development.

The issues raised in this area are extremely complex, and as the Plowden Committee is soon to pronounce on them, it would be out of place to pursue discussion of them any further at this juncture.

(b) The secondary school

It was argued in Ch. I, Sec. 3(a), that a man is not educated if he is merely well informed, even though he may have a passion for accuracy and an avid curiosity. He must also have some grasp of underlying principles. At about 12 + the child passes from what Piaget calls the stage of concrete operational thought to that of hypothetico-deductive thinking. He is not so tied in his thought to the immediate environment. A postulate like that of the conservation of motion becomes possible for him as well as the inversion of propositional forms. He can begin to think like a scientist in systematically eliminating possibilities. Such an understanding of principles does not depend upon the accumulation of extra items of knowledge. Rather it requires reflection on what is already known so that a principle can be found to illuminate the facts. This often requires the postulation of what is unobservable to explain what is observed. The 'experience' and 'activity' so much lauded in the primary school can be deepened by reflection about the form in the facts and by experiments in the imagination. Critical discussion about alternative interpretations becomes possible, together with a grasp of the procedures by means of which a decision can be made between them. The few who manage to master these procedures are those who will eventually help to develop the frontiers of knowledge. But from the point of view of education what is essential is the grasp of the more abstract conceptual schemes rather than skill in research. At the secondary school level, too, the turning inwards of the adolescent and his increased interest in personal relationships makes a range of social and historical studies possible which are of little interest to younger children. It also adds depth and vitality to the study of literature and to creative achievements in a variety of media.

It is often said that the specialization of the secondary school is what prevents that all-round development and cognitive perspective which is a criterion of being educated.[1] But integration presupposes differentiation; 'wholeness' in the sphere of a man's outlook presupposes parts which are in some way related. The structuring of knowledge into differtiated forms of thought and awareness is not an accidental or arbitrary matter; for there is no other way in which knowledge in depth can be developed. Mathematical concepts are different from moral, scientific or religious ones; the criteria of truth and the methods of testing are different.[2] There is, however, a certain arbitrariness about what constitutes school-subjects, and many think that novel ways of organizing the curriculum in terms of fields of study to the illumination of which different forms of thought are necessary, may serve as a method of preventing a too fragmented outlook. This way of developing 'the whole man' is being attempted, as has already been explained, by some universities such as Sussex and East Anglia. The topic and project methods at the level of the secondary and juniors schools exemplify it on a smaller scale. This may prevent too one-sided a view of problems; but as soon as any student really wants to understand anything, as distinct from having a kind of panoramic view of it, he must go deeper into one of the forms of thought by means of which the different facets of experience are explored.

It would not be in place here to discuss the rival merits of teaching the different forms of thought independently from each other or as related to or arising from some central field of interest. The important thing to emphasize is that one form of knowledge, e.g. science or literary studies, should not be pursued at school to the exclusion of others. It is the tendency towards such one-sided diet in the sixth form of the secondary school that justifies the attacks on specialization as being the enemy of education. This is in the main due to traditional pressures in the universities which determined the form of entrance qualifications and to the role which the school has had perforce to play in the machinery of

[1] See Ch. I, Sec. 3 (b).

[2] For full treatment of this see Hirst, P. H., 'Liberal Education and the Nature of Knowledge' in Archambault, R. D. (Ed.), *Philosophical Analysis and Education* (London, Kegan Paul, 1965).

84

selection. The history of this problem, the half-hearted attempt of the Crowther Report to tackle it, and more radical attempts in recent times to remedy matters form too complicated and too familiar a saga to recount.

Another extraneous factor, which might side-track the efforts of the school as an educational institution, is the necessity of concerning itself with training. For it cannot be impervious to the interest of the child in entering a career and to the needs of the community for technicians, typists, and so on. But this instrumental function of the school can be used equally well as a powerful incentive in the cause of education. Indeed for many boys and girls it may prove to be the only effective one in adolescence when the realities of the adult world begin to crowd in. It depends on how this extrinsic incentive is used. It can be used as an urgent centre of interest around which knowledge, understanding, and cognitive perspective can be developed or it can be treated as a goal to which everything has to be instrumentally geared. Similarly, children may be initially induced to study something seriously because they see its utilitarian value; but once they get started they may come to appreciate the values which are intrinsic to it. In these ways both the first and the second type of criteria of 'education' can be satisfied.

The current controversy about whether secondary education should be organized on the tripartite system, which was a consequence of the 1944 Act, or in accordance with various interpretations of the 'comprehensive' principle, is difficult to relate to any straightforward issues about the educational essence of the school. In so far as arguments fall under this heading they are not concerned with whether the school should educate people but with which institutional arrangement best promotes education. They are far too complicated to discuss here.[1] The more urgent issues, however, are to do with fairness and with the community's best use of its resources. They will be dealt with in more detail in Chapter IV.

An obvious consequence of the 1944 Act was that the school system, especially the junior and secondary schools, came to be used increasingly as agencies of selection in the community. The educational activities of the school suffered consequently because of the system which was exacerbated by a shortage of places in universities. The 11 + examination is on the way out, but 'O' level stands still as a watershed in the secondary school. Examinations, of course, serve useful functions other than that of selection. They act as tests of attainment and as incentives. But if their

[1] For brief summary of different possibilities see Elvin, H. L., *Education and Contemporary Society* (London, Watts, 1965). Ch. VII, and Ch. IV, Section 4 *infra*.

main function is a selective one, then the teacher may find himself caught in the logic of a situation where he has to use his expertise in order to get children through them rather than in the cause of education. A constant complaint of secondary school teachers is that the examination system prevents them from doing what they regard as educationally desirable. They have become agents of a bureaucracy. Their task has become an instrumental one. Many would not mind their task becoming more frankly instrumental. For they would argue that more direct vocational training is suitable for certain types of children and that it does provide a concrete incentive around which education can be developed. But an examination-geared curriculum is neither educational in itself nor does it provide an appropriate core for educational activities. It is to be hoped that the new Certificate of Secondary Education, which will be more directly related to what it is thought desirable to teach in schools, and for which teachers themselves will have more direct responsibility, will alleviate matters by providing a less harsh selective instrument which is also educationally desirable.

Another factor which militates against education at the secondary level is the deplorable state of many of our secondary modern schools and the attitude towards education of many of their inmates.[1] To what extent this is a product of the 1944 Act and to what extent it is a product of more general social conditions—especially family background and previous 'education' of an inferior quality—is debatable; but the fact is that the task of many secondary school teachers at present must of necessity be one of 're-socialization' rather than of education. There must be a concentration on the development of basic skills and attitudes that children should have acquired years before. Problems of discipline and of incentives to learning proliferate. It is small wonder that many nowadays confuse the role of the teacher with that of the social worker. In schools such as these the roles tend to merge. The existence of such schools calls for immediate action of a drastic sort. But it should not lead us to lose sight of the ultimate objectives of education.

Because of the unsatisfactory state of many of our primary and secondary schools, and because of the deplorable family conditions from which so many children suffer in the critical early years of their lives, there are many children in England who are permanently stunted and denied avenues of exploration in later life which might otherwise have been

[1] See *Half our Future*. A report of the Central Advisory Council for Education (England) (HMSO, 1963).

86

open to them. But even under ideal conditions some children, because of their heredity and brain structure, will have less potentiality for such explorations than others. There are also great individual differences in motivation and interest as well as in cognitive capacity. It can, therefore, never be the function of the secondary school simply to lay on worth-while activities in an undiscriminating way, but to tailor them very much to individual differences. Some children, for instance, may have a very practical and vocationally-oriented approach to any sort of learning. Others may be fascinated by animals, machines, or cooking. If the curriculum is not too closely geared to examinations and if the teachers are interested in children as well as in 'subjects', it should not be impossible to arrange courses in such a way that the coat of worth-while activities is cut according to individual aptitude.

In this way a concrete approach can be made towards implementing the educational cliché that the aim of education should be the self-realization of the individual. This, as has been argued before, cannot mean that any individual must be encouraged to develop in any way that he thinks fit; it must mean that within the sphere of what is desirable every individual should be encouraged to engage on those things which are within his capacity and with which he can identify himself. No child should be a stranger to the feeling of mastery and of satisfaction which comes from doing something well which is worth doing. Education involves both the absorption in disinterested activities and the development of a differentiated and disciplined view of the world. Some children may be severely limited in their potentiality for development in regard to the cognitive aspects of education; but this does not mean that they are necessarily incapable of developing a pride in doing more simple things for their own sake. Objectively speaking such things may be of less value. But a school is concerned with individual children as well as with what is worth while. The problem created by mass education, which has not been satisfactorily solved either by the American or the English educational systems, is that of providing adequate avenues for self-realization in a way which does not involve a depreciation in the quality of education available for those who are gifted enough to benefit from it.

5. INFORMAL EDUCATION

It should never be forgotten, finally, that education is not confined to the class-room and study. There are institutions such as youth clubs where education goes on in a much more informal way. A boy may join in the first place because a friend is a member or because he wants to meet a girl. But he may find himself gradually drawn into activities which absorb him and which give him a sense of standards and of achievement which gradually transform his outlook. In the sphere of moral education especially both schools and clubs accomplish informally much more than can ever be laid on in more formal situations. The necessity for co-operation on common tasks and for mutual adjustment, the example of older boys and adults, and the general tone of the community exert a far more pervasive influence than any lesson, even if it is given by a Leavisite who thinks that literature lessons are the key to moral education. The school is, of course, pre-eminently concerned with moral education. Boarding schools, which approximate to what sociologists call 'total institutions', are most effective in this sphere precisely because of the scope which they provide for such informal education.

And so we return to the universities, with which we started, whose residential basis gives great potentialities for moral education, which many university teachers think to be their concern. In the more general sphere, too, of the development of 'the whole man' such informal influences probably accomplish as much as formal courses. No doubt formalized correctives to specialization are necessary, though it is arguable that the proper place for them is at school rather than at university. But the classical way of ensuring an integrated outlook has surely been not courses but conversation. Conversation is not structured like a discussion group in terms of one form of thought. In a conversation, lecturing to others is bad form; so is using the remarks of others as spring-boards for self-display. The point is to create a common world to which all bring their distinctive contributions. By participating in such a shared experience much is learnt, though no one sets out to teach anyone anything. And one of the things that is learnt is to see the world from the perspective of another. To be able to take an active part in a real conversation is, of course, an achievement. It is not possible without knowledge, understanding, objectivity and sensitivity to others. But it is also a learning situation of an informal sort. One of the greatest achievements perhaps is really to be able to listen to what another says irrespective of the use which can be made of it or him. This is perhaps one of the main hall-marks of an educated man. Are we beginning to lose faith in the likelihood of anything valuable emerging if it is not carefully contrived? Or are we just the victims of shortage of space, pressure of numbers, and the bureaucratization of our educational system?

PART TWO

ETHICAL FOUNDATIONS OF EDUCATION

CHAPTER III

CLASSICAL THEORIES OF JUSTIFICATION

INTRODUCTION

That educational issues should give rise to ethical questions is not a contingent matter; for the analysis of the concept of 'education' in the first section of this book has shown why this must necessarily be the case. 'Education' has notions such as 'improvement', 'betterment', and 'the passing on of what is worth while' built into it. That education must involve something of ethical value is, therefore, a matter of logical necessity. There is, however, no logical necessity about the particular values ascribed in particular societies to the variable of 'being worth while'. The justification of such values, too, must go beyond the realm of conceptual analysis into that of ethical theory.

Most writers dealing with 'the aims of education' persuasively parade the particular values which they commend such as 'the self-realization of of the individual'; but they have little to offer by way of justification. Attitudes are articulated without arguments derived from a solid foundation in ethical theory. To deploy such arguments adequately would require a major treatise. All that can be done in an introductory book is to present a brief critique of classical theories followed by an outline of a positive position. This is bound to be most inadequate and open to all sorts of objections as it stands. This does not much matter—provided that it has the prime philosophical virtue of being clear enough to be obviously mistaken. The important thing is that it should be there for others to criticize. The philosophy of education is in too undeveloped a state to wait for a lifetime before committing perfected arguments to paper. It will only develop as a rigorous field of study if a few philosophers are prepared to plough premature furrows which run more or less in the right direction.

There are two main aspects of education which stand badly in need of ethical foundations. These are its matter and its manner, to revert to the distinction made in the first two chapters of this book. On the one hand, arguments must be given for initiating children into activities and forms of awareness such as science and poetry rather than into Bingo and horror films; on the other hand, arguments must be given to justify some procedures of initiation rather than others. It has been argued that the concept of 'education' intimates no special processes, though it may rule out some. Nevertheless it may be possible to justify on ethical grounds principles such as fairness and freedom in dealing with children. But arguments for such principles have to be produced. No philosopher can rest content simply with the articulation of attitudes towards the treatment of children.

Obviously enough these questions about matter and manner are interrelated. Indeed many would argue that the manner is to be justified if it can be shown to promote a form of life characterized by the required matter. Liberty, for instance, might be justified by claiming that it was the only effective procedure for promoting various forms of worth-while activity. Others might argue that the end does not always justify the means or that the means-end distinction has no proper application in this sphere. These are both positions within ethical theory and will have to be considered in due course. In the opening critique of classical theories only incidental reference will be made to this distinction between worth-while activities and principles of procedure. In sketching a positive theory, however, there will be separate chapters dealing with the justification of these different facets of the moral life.

I. ETHICS AND THE TEACHER

When a teacher asks whether art is a more worth-while activity than cooking or whether or not a boy ought to be punished for bullying, his questions arise from a highly structured matrix of presumptions and expectations. His role as a teacher will demand certain modes of conduct of him as well as certain attitudes to children; from his own experience as a pupil and training as a teacher he will have certain attitudes to school-subjects. He will have built into him the general customs of the community and its attitudes to learning; he will be aware of the law, of the ideals of the headmaster and of the examination system. Furthermore, although he may not be aware of it, the very questions he asks presuppose a highly differentiated form of consciousness in which different forms of question presuppose quite different forms of answer. He will know, for instance, that no laboratory experiment or dissection of a child's body will provide an answer to the questions about whether he ought to be punished. For terms like 'good', 'worth while', and 'ought' are not used to describe what is found out by such methods.

The fact, however, that the teacher can ask these different forms of question and sometimes know how to answer them and that he can feel quite at home in different forms of discourse, does not imply that he is explicitly aware of the rationale underlying them. In more settled times when social change was negligible there was little need for awareness of such a rationale. Tradition prescribed what ought to be done in stock situations and society was not highly differentiated so as to make conflicts of standards a frequent occurrence. Teachers were initiated on an apprenticeship system into established traditions which prescribed standard methods of teaching and attitudes to children. There was little controversy about what was to be included in the curriculum and little disagreement about the aims of education. If the teacher was worried about what ought to be done the appeal to tradition or to an authoritative mouthpiece of it was usually sufficient to provide guidance.

Nowadays all this is changed. There are no set systems of teaching and no agreed aims of education; there is constant controversy about the curriculum and a welter of disagreement about how children ought to be treated. In more settled times only the very reflective teacher was led to probe behind tradition for a rationale of what he ought to do; nowadays it is only the lazy or the dogmatic teacher who can avoid such probing. Neither can the modern teacher find in the appeal to authority much more than a temporary resting place; for authorities disagree, and on what grounds is the advice of one rather than another to be heeded? The unpalatable truth is that the modern teacher has no alternative to thinking out these matters for himself. Teachers can no longer be merely trained; they have also to be educated.

If the teacher begins to ponder about the rationale underlying the various recommendations which confront him about the matter and manner of education he enters a realm which is not so well structured and marked out as the one which his more theoretical interests presuppose. He may not know why iron expands when it is heated or why canals run from Tring to Wales. But he knows pretty well how to find out such things. He knows how experiments are conducted and how to consult books and records. He knows that, in the end, answers to such questions depend upon comparing what is stated in some hypothesis with what can be observed. But he also knows, if he reflects, that questions about

93

what is good or bad or about what ought to be done cannot be settled in this perspicuous manner. He cannot see wrongness written over the face of a bully or cup his ear and listen for the goodness of poetic composition. Nevertheless people discuss such matters with great seriousness on the assumption that they are dealing with answerable questions. Slavery and murder, he reflects, are palpably wrong whereas gambling and extra-marital sex relations may be wrong but are not palpably so. There must be some rationale in virtue of which such obvious gradations of moral knowledge obtain. To make explicit this rationale is the task of moral philosophy.

2. NATURALISM

An obvious suggestion, when confronted with questions about what ought to be done, is to assimilate them to the more straightforward questions about what is, was, or always will be the case. It has often been argued, for instance, that if man's nature could be clearly deter-mined, then it would be clear how man ought to live. A whole succession of eminent philosophers have argued that man is essentially rational by nature. He differs from other animals in the development of reason as exhibited in his ability to impose plans and rules on his desires and in his capacity for abstract thought and the development of highly compli-cated symbolic systems; his behaviour can only be understood if account is taken of his rationality so defined. Therefore, it is argued, those activities are best which exhibit rationality in the highest degree. Mathematics is obviously preferable to bingo in that it satisfies more fully man's nature as a rational being.

An argument of a similar form is often advanced for the importance of personal relationships. It is argued that only men are capable of treating other members of their species in this way. Other animals may have innate or acquired social tendencies but they are incapable of appreciating their fellows, as distinct centres of consciousness and of encountering them as persons. Therefore, it is argued, man should live his life as much as possible on the plane of the personal rather than merely as an organism or as an individual occupying a purely functional position.

Few civilized people—especially teachers—would wish to dispute the moral desirability of such policies for living. There may well be, too, some sort of connection between their desirability and man's rationality. But there are all sorts of difficulties about the form of argument in which such policies feature as a conclusion. There are difficulties, first of all about what is meant by 'nature' when any premiss is formulated about 'the nature of man'. In the arguments here cited 'nature' is interpreted as indicating some important respect in which man differs from other animals. An initial objection might be made on the score of the arbitrariness involved in the selection of man's capacity for reason or for forming personal relationships. No other living thing laughs like man or spends so long rearing its young; the possession of a prehensile thumb which enables man to use tools might be mentioned as being of more importance than his capacity for abstract thought. Genetically speaking this might well have developed from the ability to perform concrete operations made possible by the possession of such a thumb. Indeed Julian Huxley has indicated about twenty important ways in which man is different from other animals.[1] But *whatever* capacity is suggested as being crucial in determining man's difference from other animals the form of the argument remains the same. And it is difficult to see how the fact that man is different from animals in a certain respect constitutes, of itself, a reason for claiming that it is this respect that ought to be developed. Indeed Rousseau was willing to agree that man differs from animals in that he thinks, but went on to maintain that a thinking man is a depraved animal. The use of reason leads to an alienation of man from the rest of nature, which is undesirable. If contradictory conclusions can be 'inferred' from the same set of premisses there must be something wrong with the form of argument.

Others have argued that, because man is the same as other animals in respect of his aggression or need for a horde, it is these tendencies that ought to be developed. Philosophers have seldom advanced this as an argument. But this is surely because *for other reasons* they have been committed to a policy of rationality rather than brutishness. It cannot have been because a premiss which contains 'different from' rather than 'same as' as part of an empirical generalization is logically preferable.

This point can be generalized into an attack on simple naturalistic theories in ethics which try to base ethical recommendations on empirical generalizations. Naturalism is sometimes represented as the view that tries to infer moral judgments from statements of fact. But this way of characterizing naturalism is too loose; for the notion of what constitutes a fact is loose. Etymologically the word 'fact' intimates something that is palpably done. Facts can be contrasted with theories, with fiction, and

[1] Huxley, J., *The Uniqueness of Man* (London, Chatto and Windus, 1941).

with opinion.[1] So presumably the contrast arises between 'facts' and 'values' because what is valuable is thought to be a matter of opinion. But it is perfectly good English to say 'let us start from the fact that pain is evil' or 'it is a palpable fact that men ought to keep their promises'. Empirical observations, on the other hand, provide the most obvious hard core of what is *not* a matter of conjecture, fiction, or opinion. So it is easy to see how the notion of what is a matter of fact can be sucked up into the notion of what can be observed.

Goodness or desirability, however, are not things, relations, or qualities that can be observed to be present in man's activities, neither can statements about what is good or desirable be straightforwardly inferred from what can be observed. Empirical generalizations about man's nature, in so far as these involve judgments of comparison with animals, provide no basis for inference either. If it is argued that men *ought* to develop their reason because in this respect they are different from animals, this is only valid if the implicit principle is made explicit, that men ought to develop that capacity in which they differ from animals. Once this principle is made explicit, which makes man's reason or his possession of a prehensile thumb a relevant consideration, it is obvious that there is a problem about the justification of such a basic principle.

The invalidity of this form of argument does not derive simply from the interpretation of what is natural to man in terms of the comparison with animals. Any empirical generalization is subject to the same objection if it is put forward as a premiss unsupported by an ethical principle. Hobbes, for instance, argued that man ought to accept simple rules necessary for the preservation of peace because he was by nature afraid of death as well as zealous for power and advantage over other men. Mill tried to base an argument for the desirability of happiness on man's universal tendency to desire it. The logical difficulty about all such arguments is that answers to practical questions about what ought to be done are inferred from answers to theoretical questions about what is the case. As Hume put the matter at a time when men were beginning to get clearer about such forms of argument:

In every system of morality which I have hitherto met with, I have always remarked that the author proceeds for some time in the

[1] For a most illuminating discussion of the category of 'fact' see Hamlyn, D., 'The Correspondence Theory of Truth' in *Philosophical Quarterly*, July 1962.

ordinary way of reasoning, and establishes the being of God, or makes observations concerning human affairs; when, of a sudden I am surprised to find, that instead of the usual copulation of propositions, *is*, and *is not*, I meet with no proposition that is not connected with an *ought* or *ought not*. This change is imperceptible; but is however of the last consequence. For as this *ought* or *ought not* expresses some new relation or affirmation, it is necessary that it should be observed and explained; and at the same time that a reason should be given for what seems altogether inconceivable, how this new relation can be a deduction from others, which are entirely different from it.[1]

Hume is here asserting what is nowadays called the autonomy of ethics which is the claim that no moral judgment can be deduced from any set of premises which does not itself contain a moral judgment or principle. Naturalism as an ethical theory ignores the requirement of a strict deductive argument that nothing should be drawn out by way of a conclusion that is not contained implicitly or explicitly in the premises. If there is no practical principle, which enjoins some form of actions or expresses some preference, in the premises, how can a judgment of this form ever emerge as a conclusion?

Consequentialist theories which attempt to base the desirability of courses of action on their consequences are open to the same objection unless an ethical principle is stated which makes some forms of consequences relevant. Supposing, for instance, it were argued that it was wrong to stick sharp instruments into other people because of the pain that was caused by so doing. This would only be a valid argument against this form of conduct on the assumption that pain is undesirable. Another person might argue that this was a most desirable form of conduct because it tended to make people bleed. Blood being red, this form of conduct tended to increase the amount of redness in a drab world. Hence its desirability. To most of us this would seem to be an argument which only a lunatic would advance. This is because the principle that pain ought to be minimized seems more perspicuous than the principle that redness ought to be maximized. But the argument, though bordering on lunacy, does at least bring out the point that an ethical principle is needed to pick out the relevance of consequences as well as the point that some principles for doing this seem more acceptable than others.

[1] Hume, D., *Treatise on Human Nature*, Book III, Part I, Section 2.

The naturalist might reply that the example brings out the point which he wishes to stress—that some consequences rather than others are relevant because of human nature. The fact is that human beings universally avoid pain whereas they do not universally seek redness. Hence the tendency to pick out consequences which involve pain rather than redness. There is something in this argument but not all that the naturalist might claim. For in general the existence of a human want is not a sufficient ground for maintaining the desirability of what is wanted. If Freud is right there might well be a universal desire amongst men to seduce their mothers and to kill their fathers. But the desirability of such forms of conduct would not depend on demonstrating the universality of the desires which might prompt it. Indeed, as Freud himself argued, one of the main functions of moral rules is to regulate such 'natural' desires. Nevertheless it would be very odd if there were *no* sort of connection between moral rules and human wants; for one of the distinguishing features of moral rules is that they guide conduct. If there were no connection between what they enjoined and some things which human beings tend to want the actual guiding function of practical discourse would be inexplicable.

The defect of naturalism is that it makes the connection between human nature and this guiding function of moral discourse too tight. It suggests that generalizations about human nature function as premises from which rules of conduct can be inferred. Alternatively it is suggested (e.g. by Hobbes) that 'good' means 'that which a man desires'. This is a most implausible suggestion. For there is no logical contradiction in asserting that peace is good but that no one desires it. We can also, with perfect logical propriety, remark that people want things that are not worth wanting or that they want all the wrong things. Furthermore, when we bring up children we tell them that they ought to do things or that certain things are good when we know perfectly well that these are not things that they want to do or have.

If in reply it is asserted that 'good' means what a man wants on the whole and in the long run, when he carefully considers what is in his interest, there is then the problem of explicating these qualifications without smuggling in some norm by reference to which the variety of human wants can be assessed.[1]

It would be inconceivable, however, that words like 'good' and 'ought'

[1] See Griffiths, A. P., and Peters, R. S., 'The Autonomy of Prudence', *Mind*, April 1962.

could function as they do in a public language to guide people's behaviour if there were *no* connection between what was prescribed and what might be wanted. It would be odd, for instance, to say that something was good, such as making the world much redder, if it were inconceivable that anyone should want such a state of affairs.

The truth is surely that words such as 'good' and 'bad' are taught as words in a public language in connection with objects and states of affairs such as eating food and experiencing pain which are universal objects of desire or aversion. They could only have the guiding function which they do have if they were typically associated with such paradigm objects of desire and aversion. But once they have, as it were, got off the ground as words in a public language, they can be used to guide people towards things which they do not actually want but which are possible objects of desire. Indeed 'good' and 'ought' are used very frequently for educating people in respect of their wants, once they have grasped the commending function of such words.

Perhaps one of the strongest points of naturalism as an ethical theory is that it does do justice to what is usually called the 'objectivity' of moral judgments. By 'objectivity' is meant the assumptions that error is possible in moral matters and that whether or not a person is in error depends on facts independent of the opinions or attitudes of any particular person or group of persons. To claim objectivity is to deny that the adoption of moral values is merely a matter of personal taste or group allegiance. Words like 'ought', 'wrong', 'good', and 'bad' typically feature in a form of discourse which has not only the practical function of determining action but also the function of doing this by the production of reasons. To give reasons, if it is done seriously and with a determination to decide in terms of reasons, is to put a matter up for public discussion. It is tantamount to the admission that the decision must depend not on the authority or private whims of any individual but on the force and relevance of the reasons advanced. It is to assume, too, that truth and error are possible about the matter under discussion. For how could *discussion* have any point without such an assumption?

Naturalists are united in assuming that moral matters admit of such discussion and that the reasons adduced as backing to moral judgments must consist of empirical generalizations—usually to do with human nature or human wants. This is salutary in its insistence on the connection between moral discourse and the giving of reasons. But it falls short by ignoring the ethical principle or principles which are necessary

99

to make such reasons relevant, and to bridge the gap which Hume detected between 'is' and 'ought'. In brief naturalism does justice to the
objectivity of moral discourse; most forms of it do justice to its guiding
function by connecting it with human nature or human wants; but it
does not do justice to its autonomy.

3. INTUITIONISM

The strongest point of the second classical theory that has to be considered, which is usually called 'intuitionism', is that it does preserve
the autonomy of ethics. In all its forms it is clear about two points,
namely that terms like 'good' and 'ought' do not stand for observable
qualities or relations and that moral judgments are not inferences from
any form of empirical generalization. In this respect intuitionism is a
great improvement on naturalism. Unfortunately, however, its critique
of naturalism and the theory which is developed as an alternative, preserve the main feature of the theory which it criticizes. For it assimilates
moral judgment to the providing of answers to a very special form of
purely theoretical question. It supposes that in the end the goodness of
an activity like artistic creation or the rightness of a principle such as
that of justice or liberty is a matter of 'seeing' or grasping a quality or
relation.

This process of 'seeing' has been interpreted in terms of two distinct
sorts of models, both of which attempt to ground moral knowledge on
some kind of indubitable and self-evident propositions. One type of
theory assumes that terms like 'good' designate some sort of property
that is grasped by a reflective mind. G. E. Moore,[1] for instance, a
modern Platonist, held that 'good' refers to a simple non-natural un-
analysable property. It is non-natural in the sense that it is not to be discovered by use of the senses or by the ordinary processes of introspection by which anyone might, for instance, become aware of thirst
or pain. Nevertheless it depends for its existence on such observable
qualities in that it is only to be discerned when some such observable
qualities are also present. The goodness of artistic creation, for instance,
is not something that can be observed by means of the senses; neither is
it an inference that can be tested by observation. Nevertheless it is only
discernible by the inner eye of intuition, when other observable qualities
are present, in virtue of which it can be said, for instance, that a man is

[1] Moore, G. E., *Principia Ethica* (Cambridge University Press, 1903).

painting a picture. This theory uses the model of looking at a simple quality like yellow, which many have taken to be the sort of experience which is the ground of our certainty about the world and to issue in incorrigible statements like 'This is yellow.' It then postulates a special non-natural type of object or quality, a Platonic form, as the object of a special inward type of 'seeing'. Moral knowledge is thought to be based, in the end, on this intellectual type of grasping in the same sort of way as empirical knowledge is thought to be based on our sensory experience of simple qualities and relations. 'Intuition', being derived from the Latin 'intueor' which meant 'I gaze on', is the name given to this intellectual process of 'seeing' which is crucial for this type of theory.

When confronted with moral principles rather than with good activities, intuitionism often has employed another model of 'seeing' which is much more closely linked with the grasp of the self-evident which many once thought to lie at the root of mathematics. Mathematics was taken by Plato, and by later thinkers such as Descartes, as the paradigm of knowledge; so it was concluded that moral knowledge, if it is to be knowledge at all, must resemble mathematical knowledge in its structure. Mathematical knowledge, especially geometry, was thought to be based on a clear and distinct apprehension of basic Forms or simple natures between which relations could be grasped intuitively. From this self-evident foundation of axioms demonstrations could be made which issued in theorems. Descartes held that certain knowledge was possible in science and morals as well as in mathematics provided that this type of logical structure of propositions could be articulated.

This view of moral knowledge was later held by the post-Renaissance theorists of natural law. In the hands of John Locke it formed the epistemological basis for the conviction that there are certain inviolable rights of man—to life, liberty, and estate—a conviction which later provided a rationale for revolutionary doctrines as well as for the American Declaration of Independence. In more recent times moral philosophers such as Sir David Ross[1] have held that all moral duties are founded upon a limited number of basic prima facie obligations, such as that promises ought to be kept, which are known intuitively.

This form of intuitionism, then, which had its source in the importance ascribed by Plato to mathematics as a form of knowledge, has had a long and influential history in the development of ethics. There

---

[1] Ross, Sir David, *The Right and the Good* (Oxford, The Clarendon Press, 1930).

are, nevertheless, many basic objections both to this type of intuition-ism and to the type stated so precisely by G. E. Moore, which employed the model of inspecting qualities rather than that of grasping relation-ships, to characterize the foundations of moral knowledge.

To start with, the view that mathematics itself must be based on in-tuitively grasped axioms is not now widely accepted. Furthermore, since the attacks by Hume and Kant on Cartesian rationalism, the fact that mathematical systems sometimes fit the world presents itself as a problem, the rationalistic assumption having been abandoned that mathematical thinking must somehow mirror the world, or at least the real structure of the world beneath the appearances, which was what Plato assumed in his theory of Forms and Descartes in his theory of simple natures. Whether or not a postulate about the world is true depends, in the end, on whether consequences deduced from it can be confirmed by observation, not on the self-evidence of the postulate itself.

The intuitionist view usually goes hand in hand with some notion of self-evidence which is alleged to characterize the grasp of both mathe-matical and moral axioms. 'Self-evidence' is a term which combines both logical and psychological attributes. Psychologically speaking some sort of inner flash is alleged to occur when such axioms are grasped; logically speaking the 'evidence' is thought of as being internal to what is affirmed. The logical requirement is most easily exhibited in statements when the truth of what is affirmed derives from the rules governing the terms which are combined. Examples would be 'a square contains some right angles' or 'every effect has a cause'. The truth of statements about the world, however, does not depend in the end upon such conventions for the use of terms. The definition of the term 'father' does not reveal the truth of the Freudian assumption that fathers are hated by their sons in the way which it reveals the truth of the statement that if a man is a father he must have either a son or a daughter. Of course statements about the world can be so well confirmed that an internal relation of this sort can grow up. For instance 'gold is yellow' has been found so often to be true that we would not be inclined to call anything a piece of gold which did not reveal this colour under standard conditions. But this connection had to be established by observation; it was not created by convention like some of the truths of mathematics. People may also come to experience a feeling of conviction about such statements. But this feeling depends upon the truth of the statement being established in some other way; it is an accompaniment of a statement being true, not a criterion of its truth. It may be useful to have such feelings of conviction; for they curtail the area of doubt and leave the mind free to speculate about a limited realm of problems. But an aid to practical living should not be exalted into a criterion of truth.

Some moral judgments such as 'murder is wrong' may come to have such a feeling attached to them. Many such judgments, too, are almost true by convention in the sense that 'murder' is almost equated with 'wrongful killing' in the public consciousness, whatever its legal definition may be. But this only puts the problem back as to what makes the sort of killing, picked out by the term 'murder', wrong. Definitions cannot of themselves determine what is right or wrong. Still less can the strength of people's feelings of certainty or 'self-evidence'. Many people feel just as strongly about abortion or about homosexuality between consenting males. Their feelings are regarded as highly arbitrary by others who make different judgments about these matters.

The basic objection, therefore, to intuitionism as an ethical theory is that the probing for fundamental principles is encouraged to stop too soon and at too *arbitrary* a point. If it is put forward, as by Sir David Ross, that certain basic obligations are self-evident, there are many who may doubt this. A good example is the case of punishment where many have hotly challenged the intuitive conviction that pain ought to be inflicted on those who commit breaches of rules. And even if they agree, for instance, that promises ought in general to be kept they may deny that this is 'self-evident'; for, they will argue, there are very good reasons for keeping promises. Can it be seriously maintained that there are no further reasons for this important social practice? If obligations like this are held to be self-evident, what is to be said to people who insist that black men ought be to treated differently just because they are black, that one ought never to permit more redness in the world than is necessary, or that gambling is self-evidently wrong? They can say that they just know these things intuitively in the same sort of way as intuitionist philosophers claim that they know intuitively that they ought not to tell lies, break their promises, and be unfair. The attempt to justify principles stops at an arbitrary point. Where arbitrariness reigns, *de gustibus non est disputandum*. This is a very unsatisfactory basis for morality which intuitionists have always insisted is an impersonal and objective matter.

The other type of intuitionism, which likens being aware of goodness to 'seeing' in a more literal sense, is no better off in respect of the accusation of arbitrariness either. In ordinary cases of 'seeing' there are criteria for making the distinction between something being 'really' there or as it is described and something only 'appearing' to be so. Reference to standard conditions, perspective, etc., can be made. But what are standard conditions for 'seeing' the non-natural quality of goodness, which permit a similar escape from arbitrariness? Furthermore in ordinary cases of seeing there are established tests for determining whether there is something wrong with the observer if he fails to see what is there or sees things askew or is subject to hallucinations. What similar tests are there in the moral case? Can a man be assessed as morally blind in the same sort of way as he can be assessed as colour-blind?[1]

Both types of intuitionism suffer from a further fundamental defect which has been already hinted at and which was first stressed by David Hume. The stress on 'seeing', whether modelled on seeing qualities or grasping relations, makes morals a theoretical matter. If a man sees that a table is square or grasps a mathematical truth, there is no implication of any sort about anything being done. He may remark 'How interesting!' after noting what there is to note or grasping what there is to grasp. But whether or not anything is to be done is a further question. Now the palpable thing about the use of moral concepts such as 'good', 'wrong', and 'ought', is that there is some kind of close connection with something being done; they are used to guide people's choices. The precise form of this connection is difficult to determine; but that there is such a connection is one of the basic features of moral language. The intuitionists make the connection between seeing that something is good or grasping that something ought to be and doing something about it a purely contingent one.

Plato was one of the first to suggest an intuitive basis for moral knowledge. But he did not think of the connection with action as a contingent one. For he inherited from Socrates the conviction that virtue is knowledge and that no man wittingly does what he knows to be evil. He therefore believed that knowledge of what is good is accompanied by a passionate desire that it should be realized. This Socratic doctrine seems to err in the other direction; for it makes the connection between moral knowledge and action too close. It does not seem to be a logical contradiction for a man to say that he knows what is good but that he

[1] For further developments of this type of objection see Nowell-Smith, P. H., *Ethics* (Harmondsworth, Penguin Books, 1954), Ch. 1.

does not want or intend to do it. Yet Socrates maintained that such a man could not really know what is good.

The Socratic view, however, seems more defensible than that of the later intuitionists who assimilated moral knowledge to perception or to intellectual assent. For it does make the connection between moral knowledge and action, albeit in too tight a manner. The true view is surely that the *general function* of moral language is to guide action or to get people to do things. To say that something is good is to intimate that there are reasons for doing or promoting it. These must be reasons which could induce human beings of some sort to act. Otherwise moral language could never have the function which it does have in getting people to do things. But the reasons intimated in a particular case may not, psychologically speaking, be strong enough to get the person who is using or addressed in the public language to act in the way prescribed. He may say or agree that peace is good—meaning that there are very good reasons for having peace. But he may know well enough that he personally does not want it strongly enough to pursue it himself. Nevertheless it could not sensibly be said that it was good if there was nothing about it which would count, for some human being or other, as a reason for trying to promote it.

Though intuitionism, like naturalism, is inadequate as an ethical theory it nevertheless, like naturalism, intimates in a distorted way some of the important features of moral knowledge and discourse. It will be useful, therefore, at this point to make explicit what these features are. The point was made, in the foregoing criticism of intuitionism, that words like 'good' and 'ought' occur in a form of discourse that has the practical function of guiding people's action. This is not the only way in which people's behaviour is regulated by language. Another common form of practical discourse is the use of commands. What distinguishes moral language, in which terms like 'good' and 'ought' occur, is the suggestion that there are reasons for doing what is prescribed. 'Shut the door' and 'You ought to shut the door' both have a practical function. But 'ought' implies reasons for shutting the door in a way in which the use of imperatives does not. Nothing, of course, depends on the use of the particular words 'good' or 'ought' to perform this function. Once language has become sufficiently differentiated so that getting people to do things by giving them orders has become distinguished from getting them to do things by giving them reasons, any words could have done. So this is not a verbal argument in the sense that anything of substance is inferred from the use of particular words. Rather it is an argument which goes behind words and attempts to formulate in a general way what is presupposed by the differentiation of forms of discourse. What is presupposed, it is claimed, is the development of the concept of getting people to do things by giving them reasons, which is a very specific form of regulation associated with a specific family of words. 'Good', 'bad', 'ought', 'ought not', 'right', 'wrong' are the most general words in our vocabulary for performing this function. 'Intuitionism' as an ethical theory marks the point very strongly that reasoning in morals, or practical reason, is very different in respect of its justification from reasoning about what is, was or will be the case, for which the descriptive and explanatory discourse of science and history has been developed. But it does this in a very misleading way; for it preserves the model appropriate for answering theoretical questions by basing moral knowledge on 'seeing' in one of the two forms outlined.

This model caricatures another of the main features of practical discourse which is often referred to as its autonomy—the fact that statements about what is good or what ought to be done cannot be reduced to or inferred from empirical observations or generalizations. The postulation of 'non-natural' qualities and relations and of an inner eye for inspecting or grasping them make this point in a dramatic but misleading way. For by suggesting that the grounds of moral knowledge are grasped by a kind of gazing it ignores the practical function of moral discourse, its very close connection with action. In this respect, therefore, intuitionism employs a misleading model to make an important point about the analysis of moral terms and the justification of moral convictions.

In another respect, too, intuitionism makes an important point about moral discourse, though again in a misleading way. To claim that moral discourse is that form of practical discourse whose function is to regulate behaviour by the giving of reasons is, *ipso facto*, to claim some sort of *objectivity* for it. The claim that there are reasons for what is prescribed distinguishes moral language from that in which private likes and whims are canvassed. 'I like bull-fighting' conveys something very different from 'I approve of bull-fighting' just as saying that gardening is good is very different from saying that it is nice. Intuitionism attempts to convey this claim of objectivity, of interpersonal standards, by postulating the paradigm case of objectivity where some quality or relation is out there for all to behold. As has been shown it cannot sustain the claim to objectivity in this particular form. For 'non-natural' qualities and relations seen by an inner eye present problems of standard conditions and normal observers. But at any rate intuitionism does hang grimly on to this claim of objectivity. Rightly so; for this is implicit in the very notion of there being a reason for doing something.

Again, when this notion of the backing of reasons is pressed, both the strength and weakness of intuitionism are again revealed. Intuitionists, especially Plato, have always stressed that the ultimate experience of 'seeing' is only granted to reflective people who think detachedly and clearly about situations and activities. The 'intuition' provides, as it were, the basis beyond which further reasoning is impossible. Indeed the general function of saying that something is known 'intuitively' is to suggest that what is claimed is true, that one is sure that it is true, but to withdraw the usual claim that goes with 'know', that the grounds for saying it is true are patent. In this way intuitionism preserves the link with reason, but gives up too soon in the search for a foundation to morals in principles of a non-arbitrary sort. What these principles are in the sphere of practical reason and how they can be shown to be non-arbitrary must be left for later consideration.[1]

4. EMOTIVISM

Intuitionism as an ethical theory, it has been argued, is open to the criticism that it makes moral judgments arbitrary. This, however, was not the intention of those who advanced it; for without exception they thought of moral judgments as being objective like judgments in mathematics. Those who advanced some sort of 'emotive' or voluntaristic theory, on the other hand, accepted the arbitrariness of such judgments at least in the sense that they thought that no rational justification of them was possible. They compared them to expressions of tastes or to commands.

The strong point of such theories has always been that they have rejected the view that moral judgments are answers to special sorts of theoretical questions. In recent times the limited view of meaning, which went with the old theoretical model, has been the item most frequently singled out for attack. The assumption of naturalism and of intuitionism was that words must have meaning in the manner of names that 'stand for' things, properties, or relations. Hence the tendency to

[1] See *infra*, Chs. IV–VIII.

think that 'good' and 'ought' must really stand for observable properties or relations or for special kinds of 'non-natural' properties or relations. Once it was realized that not all words have meaning in the manner of names, possibilities were opened up for giving meaning to moral terms in ways which brought out what was distinctive of them. One such attempt has been to try out the notion of 'emotive' meaning popularized by Ogden and Richards.[1] Sophisticated versions of this approach to ethical terms have been developed by Ayer and Stevenson.[2] Terms like 'good' it is argued, have meaning by expressing how people feel and by getting others to feel in the same way. Stevenson's analysis of 'This is good' as 'I approve of this; do so as well' was perhaps the most notorious example of this approach.

Awareness of this guiding function of moral discourse is not new. In his *Principles of Human Knowledge* (Introduction, Section XX) Berkeley remarked that the communicating of ideas marked by words is not the chief and only end of language. There are, he says, other ends such as the 'raising of some passion, the exciting to, or debarring from an action, the putting the mind in some particular disposition'. He then went on to make the point, which is nowadays laboured by talk of the commending function of moral words, when he said 'May we not, for example, be affected with the promise of a *good thing*, though we have not an idea of what it is?' What is new is the realization that this guiding function is one of the distinguishing features of moral discourse.

Hume, of course, was well aware of this aspect of moral discourse. Indeed the most damaging criticism which he made of rationalistic theories in ethics was that they failed to account for this influence of moral discourse on the will. 'Morals excite passions and produce or prevent actions. Reason of itself is utterly impotent in this particular.'[3] Hume himself, however, was much more interested in the expressive aspect of moral discourse. It has been therefore the 'emotive' element in his theory which has exerted most influence historically in, for instance, the theories of Adam Smith and Westermarck. The importance of the voluntaristic element has not been stressed till recent times when

[1] See Ogden, C., and Richards, I. A., *The Meaning of Meaning* (New York, Harcourt Brace, 1923).

[2] See Ayer, A. J., *Language, Truth and Logic* (London, Gollancz, 1936) and Stevenson, C. L., *Ethics and Language* (Newhaven, Yale University Press, 1944).

[3] Hume, D., *A Treatise of Human Nature*. Book III, Part I, Section 1.

it has featured in the theories of Hare[1] and Popper[2] who have likened moral judgments to commands and decisions.

Hume relied on the emotive element in the analysis of moral discourse to bridge the gap which he detected between 'is' and 'ought'. He argued that ' . . . when you pronounce any action or character to be vicious, you mean nothing, but that from the constitution of your nature you have a feeling or sentiment of blame from the contemplation of it'.[3] On his view, and on that of all subsequent emotivists, moral distinctions marked by words such as 'good', 'ought', and 'wrong' must be explicated in terms of the emotions or feelings which they express. The autonomy of morals is thus preserved; for moral discourse is admitted to be *sui generis*. Because of its expressive and commending character it is irreducible to theoretical discourse; moral judgments cannot be inferences either from any combination of premisses which does not itself include a moral principle. But the autonomy of moral discourse is saved at the expense of its objectivity. For Hume was at pains to point out that the only sense in which moral judgments could be unreasonable would be if they presupposed faulty inferences about empirical matters concerning the causes, characteristics or consequences of situations which awaken our feelings. Similarly Stevenson stressed that moral disagreement often presupposes disagreement in beliefs about the world which are reconcilable by reason. In so far, however, as disagreement is based upon disagreement in attitude there is nothing, rationally speaking, that can be done; for attitudes are not the sorts of things that can be rationally justified. In the final analysis a moral judgment is a sophisticated sort of grunt.

This theory is often crudely stated and therefore exposes itself to the obvious objection that people frequently make moral judgments in a calm state. Hume himself admitted this when he said that the sentiment of approbation or disapprobation is often mistaken for reasoning because of its calmness. He noted too the tendency of people to approve and disapprove of actions as a result of their upbringing rather than out of a first-hand conviction of their wickedness or meritoriousness. He could also have argued, like Stevenson, that provided that on some occasions

[1] See Hare, R. M., *The Language of Morals* (London, Oxford University Press, 1952), *passim*.

[2] See Popper, K. R., *The Open Society and Its Enemies* (London, Routledge, 1945), Vol. I, Ch. 7.

[3] Hume, D., op. cit. Book III, Part I, Section 1.

a man's feelings have been aroused so that he has the first-hand experience necessary for making moral distinctions, he need not be emotionally excited on every subsequent occasion that he makes a moral judgment. For he could develop a relatively permanent attitude to situations of this sort. By refinements such as these this objection can be easily accommodated within a sophisticated statement of the theory.

A much more serious objection to the theory is one that attacks the unanalysed concept of 'emotion' or 'feeling' in terms of which it is alleged that moral judgments can be explicated. The first step in the analysis of concepts such as 'emotion' and 'feeling' is to show that any state of mind that can be called an 'emotion', such as fear, anger, jealousy or remorse, is characterized by an appraisal of an object or situation which is internally related to it. By this is meant that how a man sees a situation is basic to characterizing the state of mind as one of 'emotion' in general and as one of 'fear' or 'anger' or 'resentment' or 'jealousy' in particular. For to be so characterized a man has to see it as in general agreeable or disagreeable and, in the different emotions, as agreeable or disagreeable in a certain respect. A man who is afraid, for instance, sees a situation as disagreeable in respect of being dangerous. Jealousy can only be differentiated from plain anger by reference to what a man picks out in a situation. A jealous man sees a situation as involving the loss of something to which he considers he has a right, whereas an angry man sees a person or situation as frustrating him in a less determinate way. The 'feeling' involved in emotion is inseparable from the aspect under which he views the situation.

Now the emotive theory of ethics attempts to explicate moral judgments in terms of emotions, attitudes, or feelings of approval and disapproval. But how are 'approval' and 'disapproval' to be characterized except in terms of the appraisal of an action as being right or wrong? The theory tries to give an analysis of 'That is wrong' in terms of an emotion, attitude, or feeling of disapproval; but the concept of 'disapproval' presupposes the prior notion of 'wrong'. Typically this appraisal has a 'feeling' side to it; that is why it is properly called an appraisal. But the feeling gets its characteristic quality from the cognitive core of the appraisal. And the appraisal is of an action as 'wrong'. In brief the main weakness of the 'emotive' theory of ethics is that it lacks an adequate concept of 'emotion'.

As a matter of fact Hume's account of approval was much more sophisticated and tenable than modern versions. He associated this emotional reaction with the 'general view' of the disinterested spectator who is moved by the contemplation of actions which have the character of being useful or agreeable to the agent or to society. So he built a very specific sort of appraisal into the emotions of approval and disapproval. In classifying moral emotions as 'disinterested passions' which arise when the general view of the impartial spectator is adopted he wrote into the cognitive core of the moral emotions the stance which is indispensable to the use of reason.

It has been argued that objectivity is one of the distinguishing features of moral judgments, in the sense that terms like 'ought', 'right', 'wrong', 'good', and 'bad' suggest the backing of reasons. Giving reasons presupposes something like 'disinterestedness' or taking 'the general view'.

Thus in Hume's account the objectivity of moral judgments was unwittingly preserved by the analysis which he gave of the cognitive characteristics of approval. His denial that moral distinctions were based on reason derived from his narrow interpretation of reasoning as being either a matter of demonstrative proof or of scientific inference and from his failure to see that his sophisticated account of moral emotions incorporated much of what is essential to the use of reason in a general sense. It was left to Kant to extract from Hume's account of the 'disinterested passions' the norm of impartiality which is one of the basic presuppositions of rationality.

Perhaps the most important contribution of the emotive theory of ethics has been its insistence on the guiding function of moral discourse by linking it with feeling. The attempt to explicate forms of judgment in terms of feeling has to be abandoned for the same sort of reason as the attempt to explicate them in terms of the narrower concept of 'emotion'; for how can 'feelings' be characterized when cut adrift from their cognitive core? One can feel sure, happy, and pleased as well as angry, jealous, and afraid. But how are such feelings to be identified if separated from the aspect under which a situation is viewed? There are, of course, queer indeterminate feelings as well as more lasting moods which are not closely linked with specific ways of looking at situations. Examples are vague feelings of uneasiness and free-floating anxiety. But it is precisely their indeterminacy and free-floating characteristic that makes them queer and in need of special explanation.

The fact, however, that feelings are closely linked with appraisals of situations rather than self-subsistent entities does not affect the vital point that not all cognition is of this character. To think of a man as being six feet tall is quite different, in this respect, from thinking of him as dangerous or wicked. 'Dangerous' and 'wicked' are members of the class of cognitions which can be dubbed 'appraisals'. They have a 'feeling' side to them because the qualities picked out have a positive or negative valence for us. There is, as it were, a movement of the mind towards or away from the object or situation in respect of the way in which it is characterized. Such appraisals function either as motives for doing things or, in the case of emotions, as the explanation of things that come over us, which are intimately connected with the functioning of the autonomic nervous system.[1] We can act out of fear or shame or our teeth can chatter and our cheeks go red. Such 'feelings' can be identified by reference to the cognitive claims of the appraisals of which they form a part. But they cannot be characterized in any more fundamental way.

It does not follow from this analysis that when people appraise situations they must always be in a highly excited state. There are, after all, great variations in vehemence, intensity, and urgency. But it must be the case that on some occasions they must have appraised a situation for themselves in a first-hand way. For how else could they ever be induced to act or caused to suffer? There are, as a matter of fact, some appraisals such as those connected with fear and anger which are universal in the species and which provide paradigms for the learning of others. But once the relevant appraisals have been learnt they can be made with varying degrees of feeling. More permanent attitudes develop. But the cognitive core differentiating the various attitudes is always present.

There are two levels of moral appraisal depending upon the specificity given to the notion of 'moral'. In its most general sense, when it is linked with highly general terms like 'good', 'ought', 'bad', and 'wrong' a situation or action is appraised in a positive or negative way with the implication that there are reasons for it to be or be done or for it not to be or not to be done. These terms, in other words, intimate grounds for the positive or negative character of the appraisal without indicating precisely what they are. In its more specific sense it is connected with terms

[1] See Peters, R. S., 'Emotions and the Category of Passivity', *Proc. Aristotelian Soc.*, 1961-2, Section 2.

such as 'satisfying', 'benevolent', 'dangerous' and 'cruel' which are appraisals with grounds built into them.

The main problem of moral philosophy is to see why some such grounds are justifiable and not others. Hume's theory was that as a matter of fact all moral appraisals derive in the end from estimates of what is useful or agreeable to society or to the individual himself whose actions are being considered impartially. As, however, he claimed to be a Newton of the social sciences who was simply noting what men did and attempting as simple an explanation of it as possible, and as he held anyway that no rational arguments could be produced for such basic preferences, he never proceeded to a positive attempt to justify what he held to be the universal attitudes of man. Like all who have advanced an emotive theory he held that in the end no justification is possible for the basic moral principles built into such attitudes. The question is whether this somewhat depressing conclusion is warranted.

For educationists this is not an academic issue, and it should not be one for teachers; for at the moment in England education is a topic which arouses moral fervour both inside and outside the profession. The inequalities involved in its distribution are denounced with as much censoriousness as was once loaded on inequalities of income. The subject of how children should be treated in school is still one that can arouse public indignation, both when children are allowed to do what they like and when they are treated in an authoritarian manner. Punishment within the schools, especially corporal punishment, is still a focus of acrimonious debate. Education has become as moralized as marriage and politics.

The assumption behind all this discussion is that there are moral principles such as fairness, liberty, and the consideration of people's interests as well as valuations about what people's interests are. The controversies are largely about the application of these principles and valuations to a concrete situation. Questions are seldom raised about the justification of the principles themselves. Furthermore no basis has emerged, in the brief examination of classical theories in the present chapter, for claiming that any of these principles can be justified. Could it be that these debates, like some of the old debates over creeds, are meaningful to those who indulge in them but rationally undecidable for lack of procedures for arriving at the truth? Instead of having recourse to clubs, as did the monks in bygone disputes over creeds, we have recourse to elections. This would be a depressing parallel.

5. TOWARDS A POSITIVE THEORY OF JUSTIFICATION

The possibility of a rational basis for such moral principles, however, should not be abandoned too soon; for there is another form of argument, notably employed by Kant, which has not yet been examined. If this form of argument is valid it would not be surprising that people can be convinced about moral principles without being able to state explicitly how they can be justified; for basically this form of justification of principles consists in probing behind them in order to make explicit what they implicitly presuppose. Kant was impressed by two major phenomena—the rise of Newtonian physics and the challenge on grounds of justice and liberty to the existing order on the part of the French Revolutionaries. He asked of both phenomena: 'What have we to presuppose about the human mind for such phenomena to be possible? How can it be that formulae fit the world? How can ordinary men appeal to abstract standards of right and wrong in order to condemn the *status quo*?' The particular answers that he gave to these questions may be unconvincing, but the form of argument may be valid. Indeed, it may be the only form of argument by means of which general moral principles can be shown to be well grounded.

A revised form of this type of argument would be as follows. It has been assumed that a differentiated form of discourse has emerged which has the practical function of guiding people's behaviour by the giving of reasons. Men make use of it when they ask what they ought or ought not to do and when they judge things good and bad. The problem to which the classical ethical theories provided no satisfactory answer is that of justifying the principles which make such reasons relevant. If the account of the development of mind sketched in Chapter II is taken seriously one of the obvious comments to be made about the classical theories is that they treat the individual too much as an isolated entity exercising his 'reason', 'feeling', or 'intuition' as if he were switching on some private gadget. What they ignore is the public character of the situations in which such exercises occur together with their public presuppositions in the form of abstract principles.

It is always possible to produce *ad hominem* arguments pointing out what any individual must actually presuppose in saying what he actually says. But these are bound to be very contingent, depending upon private idiosyncrasies, and would obviously be of little use in developing a general ethical theory. Of far more importance are arguments pointing to what any individual must presuppose in so far as he uses a public form of discourse in seriously discussing with others or with himself what he ought to do. In a similar way one might inquire into the presuppositions of using scientific discourse. These arguments would be concerned not with prying into individual idiosyncrasies but with probing public presuppositions. They might draw attention to considerations of *meaning* in the sense of the established relationship between concepts within the form of discourse. If, for instance, a person refused to observe the principle of non-contradiction, it would be difficult to conceive how he could ever string together terms in an intelligible way. Arguments might be drawn from considerations about what conditions must obtain for anything said within a form of discourse to be established as true. It might not matter whether such conditions obtain if it were a system which might be true in some possible world. But if it is meant to have *application* in this world some truth conditions must be presupposed. There is no doubt, for instance, that theological statements are intelligible and often internally consistent. But there is a grave problem about the conditions which must be satisfied for them to apply to the world. Most important, finally, in the case of moral judgments are presuppositions to do with the *point* of a form of discourse, or its function as conceived by anyone who uses it. People do not use language in any one way. They may use it to communicate information or emotion. On the other hand they may use it as a systematic way of guiding people's conduct.

If it could be shown that certain principles are necessary for a form of discourse to have meaning, to be applied or to have point, then this would be a very strong argument for the justification of the principles in question. They would show what anyone must be committed to who uses it seriously. Of course, it would be open for anyone to say that he is not so committed because he does not use this form of discourse or because he will give it up now that he realizes its presuppositions. This would be quite a feasible position to adopt in relation, for instance, to the discourse of witchcraft or astrology; for individuals are not necessarily initiated into it in our society, and they can exercise their discretion about whether they think and talk in this way or not. Many have, perhaps mistakenly, given up using religious language, for instance, because they have been brought to see what its use commits them to, e.g. saying things which purport to be true for which the truth conditions can never be produced. But it would be a very difficult position to adopt in relation to moral discourse. For it would entail a resolute refusal to talk or think about what ought to be done, which would constitute an abdication from a form of thought into which all in our society are initiated in varying degrees. No adducing of reasons for the guidance of conduct would be permissible thereafter. It is difficult to conceive of the sort of life to which such a moral sceptic would condemn himself. He certainly would not read a book like this in the attempt to find a rational basis for his judgments. For this book is only written for those who take seriously the question 'What ought I to do?' It is the presuppositions of asking and trying to answer this question that are to be investigated.

CHAPTER IV

EQUALITY

INTRODUCTION

It may seem somewhat illogical to discuss the distribution of education before proceeding to the justification of its content and procedures; but there are reasons of a psychological rather than a logical type for this order of exposition. In the first place this order may not seem surprising to many readers who are embroiled in contemporary controversies about education, which centre largely on its distribution. Agitations about the plight of the educationally underprivileged abound, but few bother to reflect much about the nature of what they are missing. Tackling issues to do with 'fairness' and 'equality' may therefore provide an approach to the ethical foundations of education which is in accordance with the time-honoured educational practice of following the interests of the student.

In the second place the ethical foundations of 'equality' and 'fairness' may well seem more solid than those of the content of education. As was explained in the last chapter it is hoped to develop a particular form of argument to justify the manner and matter of education. This form of argument is not easy to grasp and many will question its validity. But it is much clearer in its support of the principle of fairness than in its bearing on the worthwhileness of activities which form the main substance of the curriculum. Indeed this form of argument has its natural home in support of the principle of fairness where Kant first developed a particular form of it. From an expository point of view, therefore, there is much to be said for starting with the principles of equality and fairness.

Ever since the Utilitarians raised the question of how we know that poetry is preferable to push-pin, philosophers have been trying unsuccessfully to produce arguments in support of their conviction that it must be preferable. But they have met with little success. It would be rash, therefore, from an expository point of view, to introduce this form of argument in an area where it has not previously been tried, and where people are more inclined to say that we are confronted with matters of taste rather than with matters of principle. Only the out-and-out sub-jectivist would maintain that belief in fairness is a matter of taste. If anything is a principle, this is. So from an expository point of view there is a lot to be said for starting with the justification of fairness or justice which is as near as we can get to rock-bottom in the attempt to establish ethical foundations.

I. EQUALITY OF CONSIDERATION

Those who adhere to the principle of equality are often accused of being committed to some empirical generalization about the nature of man. If they were they would be in a highly vulnerable position. For, taken as an empirical generalization, the statement that all men are equal is either vacuous or patently false. It is vacuous because the term 'equal' like the term 'same' is a term used for comparing people or things, and people or things can only be compared in some respects. Unless, there-fore, the respect in which people are being compared is made explicit, the statement is vacuous. It says too little because it says too much. If, however, it is made to do a descriptive job of work by making explicit the respects in which men are being compared, then it looks as if it is always false. For in respect of height, weight, intelligence, sensitivity, or any other property, men are manifestly not equal.

'All men are equal', however, seldom functions as an empirical generalization. In spite of its grammatical form as a statement its logical function is usually to lay down a rule rather than to state a generaliza-tion. It usually amounts to saying that men ought to be treated equally. But how is this rather bald and stark injunction to be taken? It surely cannot mean that all men ought always to be treated literally the same. Should all men, for instance, pay the same amount of tax irrespective of their income? Should manual workers be given the same amount of food in a ration scheme as office workers? Should very intelligent children be treated the same as mentally defectives? It might be possible to pro-ceed in this way in some areas of life, but it would surely be both un-wise and unjust. Equity or justice rather than flat equality demands that men should be treated differently if there are relevant grounds for so treating them. Injustice results just as much, as Aristotle pointed out, from treating unequals equally as it does from treating equals unequally.

The principle of distributive justice can thus be formulated which lays it down that equals should be treated equally and unequals un-equally. This sounds rather cryptic, not to say cynical, until it is explained that the first injunction refers to treatment within a category, the second to treatment between categories. To take an example: all children who are within the category of 'mentally defective' ought to be treated the same as each other and they all *as a class* should be treated differently from all children within the category of 'supra-normal'. The first injunction amounts to saying that a rule is a rule or that there must be no exceptions unless, of course, a category of exceptions is created. The second injunction lays it down that there should be rules placing people in different categories if there are relevant grounds for so doing. The problem of course, is that of determining what are the relevant grounds for making categories in the context of the second injunction or for making exceptions in that of the first. In relation to what problem of distribution, for instance, is the difference in intelligence between mentally defective children and supra-normal ones a relevant difference? Probably not in matters to do with distributing food. But what about the distribution of education? The 1944 Act laid it down that children should have different education in accordance with their differences in age, aptitude, and ability. Are such distinctions relevant in the case of educational provision? The principle of distributive justice does not dictate whether these criteria are relevant or not.

A believer in equality may get restive at this point; for he may well feel that it may always be possible, with sufficient ingenuity, to discover differences between people which might be thought to provide relevant grounds for treating people differently. It is this tendency towards difference in treatment which he finds obnoxious. He may, therefore, resist this tendency by proclaiming that there must be some respect in which all men are alike which justifies them in being treated alike. He may even be haunted by the thought that unless there are such grounds then there is no rational basis for equality of consideration. He may therefore look for some property of men *qua* men, e.g. their reason, capacity for suffering, or basic needs which puts men *qua* men all in the same category.[1]

If he attempts to justify equality of consideration along these lines he is, I think, doomed to disappointment. For if generic properties such as reason, capacity for suffering, or the possession of basic needs are singled out, it is palpably obvious that men differ in the degree to which they exhibit or possess these properties or capacities. All men

[1] See, for instance, Hobhouse, L. T., *Elements of Social Justice* (London, Allen & Unwin, 1922), p. 95.

may reason or be prone to suffering; but some men reason much better than others and some men are obviously more sensitive than others. All men need some food but different categories of men need different amounts and types of food. Obviously, therefore, such similarities cannot always be cited to justify equality of treatment if the issue is a distributive one between individual men or classes of men; for whether these differences are relevant will depend on what is being distributed and on the point of the distribution.

What might be meant, however, is that there are certain generic properties which men possess *qua* men which justify them all being treated *in this respect* differently from animals or angels. This argument, however, will not do for another reason; for it is a particular form of naturalism whose weaknesses as an ethical theory have been exposed in the previous chapter. Supposing, for instance, man's capacity for thought is singled out, and it is argued that man, as a thinking being, should be treated differently from animals who are not prone to reflection. This might provide grounds for treating all men the same, but, of course, it provides no basis for how they should be treated. It does not show why their capacity for thought or suffering should be respected, developed, or ignored. Indeed, as was mentioned in the last chapter, Rousseau accepted the fact that men differ from animals because of their capacity for thought; but in his *Discourse on Inequality* he argued that this is one of the unfortunate things about men which leads to alienation from the natural world. A thinking man, he argued, is a depraved animal. Men differ from animals in this respect, but it is just this capacity which men share that ought to be soft-pedalled rather than developed.

Such arguments show, I think, that the search for positive grounds for treating men equally is futile. If the general principle of equality of consideration were to depend, therefore, on the production of such positive grounds, there is little hope of justifying it. Does this mean, then, that it cannot be justified? If the appeal to intuition is ruled out is there no other way of justifying this fundamental principle? Is it merely a matter of taste or of how we have been brought up to see our fellow men?

2. THE JUSTIFICATION OF THE PRINCIPLE OF EQUALITY

The assumption underlying the attempt to justify equality of consideration to date has been that it is treating people alike that requires justification. But why should the problem be put in this way? Why should it not be assumed that it is treating people differently that requires justification? Suppose the principle were restated more negatively: 'no one shall be presumed, in advance of particular cases being considered, to have a claim to better treatment than another'. There would then be no need to look for positive grounds for treating people alike. The onus would always be on anyone who wished to treat people differently to produce grounds which might justify such treatment. Other things being equal, in other words, all people's claims should be equally considered.

This reformulation of the principle gets rid of the necessity for finding positive grounds for treating people alike; but it would amount to no more than a verbal trick if no reason can be produced for showing that this is the proper way to state the presumption. Unless it can be shown why the onus must be on those who want to treat people differently to produce grounds rather than on those who want to treat people alike, then this reformulation of the principle is a matter of arbitrary fiat. How then can this be shown? The only way to show this is to establish that the general principle of no distinctions without differences is a presupposition of practical discourse, or that it is presupposed in any attempt to determine what ought to be done.

The situation postulated is one in which any individual, possessed of a public language, asks the question 'What ought I to do?' There are alternatives open to him and he is asking for reasons for adopting one alternative rather than another. If he is going to choose one alternative rather than another as distinct from merely 'plumping' for it, there must be some discriminable feature of A which B lacks which constitutes a ground or a reason. A person who uses the discourse of practical reason seriously is committed to choosing rather than plumping, the notion of 'ought' being more or less equivalent to the notion of there being reasons for something. Basic, therefore, to the notion of acting with reason is the very formal principle of no distinctions without differences. What is called a reason for A rather than B is some aspect under which A is viewed which makes it *different* as a course of action from B. To use practical discourse seriously is to be committed to the search for such reasons. It is to be committed to choosing rather than to plumping. Without this presupposition the discourse would lack point. Of course the odd individual can ask whimsically what he ought to do without searching seriously for reasons in the alternatives before him. Or he could discover what he ought to do and then say that he was not going to do it. But this could not be the general practice or practical discourse could never have the function in social life which it in fact has. The general practice must be that people should have this function in mind when they employ this form of discourse.

The search for features of a situation which would justify one course of action rather than another presupposes that a reason for doing something cannot be constituted simply by the fiat of the individual. For if he is deliberating about the characteristics of A rather than B in order to choose, he must presuppose that there might be features possessed by either A or B which would make his choice correct or wise. This is to assume that there are principles in advance which distinguish in general between what is a good or bad reason for doing something. In deciding, for instance, whether to inflict corporal punishment on a pupil, one difference in the situation might be that this boy is the son of a political enemy. Without principles amongst which 'hurting children needs justification' does feature and 'one ought to try to hurt the children of one's political enemies' does not, there would be no way of ruling out as a reason for beating the boy the fact that he was the son of one's political enemy. If, therefore, a person is ever going to be able to say truly that a course of action has a given feature, and that this feature is a reason for or against choosing it, then practical discourse presupposes general principles giving relevance to reasons. Choice cannot be a matter of individual fiat if there is to be a possibility of its being shrewd, wise, correct, intelligent, or far-sighted. This is what any individual assumes who is seriously worried about what he ought to do. There must, therefore, be general principles on which he can rely in making his choices.

To say that a principle is general is to say that what ought to be done in any particular situation or by any particular person ought to be done in any other situation or by any other person unless there is some relevant difference in the situation or person in question. The mere fact that situations or persons are not identical must never be taken as a ground for making distinctions. If reasons hold in one situation then they hold in any other unless further reasons can be adduced which indicate a relevant difference.

We have now stated the formal principle of fairness or justice. This is not surprising; for we have been giving a formal analysis of what constitutes 'justification', which must have some root connection with the concept of 'justice'. Justice is quite a specific type of principle in spite of Mill's attempt in Chapter V of his *Utilitarianism* to make it synonymous with a whole range of virtues. It is really the principle that there should be principles. The notion basic to justice is that distinctions should be made if there are relevant differences and that they should not be made if there are no relevant differences or on the basis of irrelevant differences. The importance of the negative aspect of the principle (no distinctions without differences) has been fully realized both in relation to notions like that of equality before the law and in previous discussions of the principle.[1] The more positive aspect of the principle is less often emphasized though Aristotle drew attention to it when he pointed out that injustice arises as much from treating unequals equally as from treating equals unequally. In other words the making of categories on relevant grounds is as important as the impartial treatment of those falling within categories already made.

Both positive and negative aspects of the principle have to work with the notion of 'relevance'. This indicates its formal character as a principle for the creation and application of principles. In its positive aspect it lays down that if there is a relevant difference then there should be a rule for distinction in treatment. But the considerations which make a difference relevant cannot be determined by the principle of justice itself. Similarly the principle of justice itself cannot determine the grounds which make it proper to make an exception to a rule already in existence.

Another way of bringing out this second-order character of justice in relation to other principles is to note that there is never an issue of justice if a situation is not in some way rule-governed. It assumes that there is a rule other than that of justice stipulating that people generally ought to have something or be treated in some way or another. This other principle gives application to talk of relevant differences in cases of creating rules and of relevant grounds for exceptions in the case of administering rules. If it is a situation which is not rule-governed, then talk of justice is not appropriate. This can easily be shown in cases which are candidates for distributive justice where the situation is not at the moment rule-governed, perhaps because of unlimited supply of the commodity in question or because of infinite opportunities for the manner of treatment. There are, for instance, at the moment, no rules and hence no questions of justice in relation to the breathing of air. Similarly whether a man fixes his eye on one girl in the street rather than

[1] See Benn, S. I., and Peters, R. S., *Social Principles and the Democratic State* (London, Allen & Unwin, 1959), Ch. V.

another is not a matter of justice, whatever its status in the sphere of manners. This is because the distribution of glances is not rule-governed in the same way as the distribution of food. Under certain conditions, however, if, for instance, air became scarce, or if the man were the last male member of a decimated population left amongst a multitude of women, the distribution of air or of the man's glances might be made very much matters of social justice.[1]

Justice then is a limited principle and acting on it is a virtue of a limited character. It is a principle regulating the operation of rules, which stipulates the desirability of categories to be made on relevant grounds and the undesirability of exceptions made on irrelevant grounds. That the principle of justice cannot be sufficient for any moral system (though it is obvious that it is necessary) can be deduced from its character as a principle regulating the operation of rules. For there must always be a question about the desirability of the rule that is to be discriminatingly and impartially administered. Whether or not people in distress ought to be helped is not a matter of justice. What is a matter of justice is whether some forms of help ought to be given to some categories of people and others to others and whether there are grounds or not for making exceptions to the rule. Manifestly, too, a torturer could exercise his art on his victims with fine discrimination and impartiality. He would be just, though a torturer. The rule relating to torture, which he acts on with such eminent justice, is wrong but not necessarily unjust. Questions of injustice would arise in relation to torture or to the relief of distress only if the distinctive form of treatment involved could be related to some relevant difference that would constitute the basis for a category.

The argument is now complete for showing that the principle of justice is a presupposition of any attempt to justify conduct or to ask seriously the question 'What ought I to do?' For it has been demonstrated that no answer which is better or worse than any other could be given to this question unless there were principles for accepting or rejecting reasons on grounds of relevance. In other words, without such principles giving relevance, moral discourse could have no application. Once the necessity for general rules is admitted the principle of justice

---

[1] Cf. Hume's argument that but for the competition for scarce resources there would be no point in the concept of justice. (Hume, D., *A Treatise of Human Nature*, Book III, Part 2.) Hume, however, had a much narrower concept of justice than that here defended.

follows; for it is an explication of what is built into the concept of 'general rule'. 'Justice' is thus built in as the basic principle presupposed in any attempt at justification that is to have application. To refuse to accept the principle of justice is to refuse to make any attempt at justifying conduct. Any man who does this is putting himself in a very queer position. For if he supports his refusal by saying or thinking 'One ought not to make the attempt to justify conduct' he is using practical discourse in order to advise against its use. He is therefore presupposing the principle of justice in order to ban its use. This is a position which is logically indefensible. If, on the other hand, he says or thinks 'Never think or talk about what you ought to do!' or if he shoots anyone who does, he escapes logical inconsistency; but why should anyone pay any attention to what he says? In social situations governed completely by irrational fiat rational men may, of course, have to listen to commands or to significant exclamations in order to adjust themselves as best they can. But they are not situations to which the probing of the philosopher has much relevance. It is no use employing logical arguments with a maniac, a hysterical woman, or an enraged Nazi. But, it is to be hoped, such people are rare in the teaching profession to whom this book is addressed.

This form of argument for the principle of justice is not open to the charge of arbitrariness made against intuitionist and emotive theories of ethics. For it has been argued that it is a principle that must be accepted if practical reasoning is to have point and application. Justification is a specific form of human activity which is tantamount to the demand for reasons. The demand for reasons in the sphere of conduct is the demand to base distinct forms of conduct on relevant differences discriminated in the possibilities which are open. If there is to be serious deliberation in relation to such possibilities there must be principles picking out relevant aspects. These principles must be general; otherwise they could never fulfil this function of providing criteria of relevance in advance of a decision being made. The principle of justice prescribes the making of general rules for distinctive forms of action where there are relevant differences and, once rules are made, making no exceptions to them unless there are relevant differences in the situations or persons to which they are presumed to apply. The principle of justice in its negative and positive aspects is, therefore, a presupposition of the activity of justifying or searching for reasons for conduct. Far from it being an arbitrary principle it is the very principle that condemns arbitrariness.

For 'arbitrariness' involves either acting without searching for reasons or making rules which are not based on relevant differences.

Rational grounds have therefore been produced for showing that the principle of no distinctions without differences is not arbitrary. This was what had to be shown to justify restating the principle of equality of consideration in the form: 'no one shall be assumed, in advance of particular cases being considered, to have a claim to better treatment than another'. It has also been shown, however, that the use of practical reason always presupposes the demand for making categories where there *are* relevant differences. So both aspects of the principle of distributive justice have been justified. What has now to be examined is what the implications of this principle are for education. It can be inferred in advance that very little of a substantive sort is implied. For the arguments for the principle of justice have also shown both that this principle is only operative when a situation is rule-governed and that the principle of justice itself cannot supply the content of such rules. As such rules are basic to supplying criteria, both for making rules on relevant grounds, and for making exceptions to rules, the inference is not difficult that very little can follow from this principle alone about the details of educational provision. Other principles must be invoked to supply content to the abstract form laid down by the principle of justice. These general points must now be substantiated by considering more carefully some of the concrete problems of equality in education.

3. APPLICATIONS OF THE PRINCIPLE OF EQUALITY

Education is not a commodity like food. Problems of its distribution are, therefore, much more complex. Before considering them, therefore, it may help to indicate their general contours by taking some simpler examples, namely the case of equality of the sexes in relation to voting and the problem of a 'just wage'. It goes without saying, first of all, that both these situations are rule-governed. In both something of value is to be distributed and there is a real possibility of people being deprived of it. The voting case is one where the dispute is about whether there should be any grounds for denying access to it. Equals, it might be argued, should be treated equally. The second is a case where it is admitted that there should be categories, that unequals should be treated unequally; the problem is to determine not whether there should be categories but on what grounds categories are to be created.

In both cases talk of 'fairness' remains vacuous until more is said about what is at stake. What sort of activity, for instance, is voting and what is the point of it in a society? What is 'earning a wage'? What function does it have in society? In the absence of a rationale of this sort further discussion is impossible. For how can the 'relevance' of grounds for making exceptions or for creating general categories be determined without reference to such wider considerations which give point to the activity? To act as guides for action reasons deriving from such wider considerations must fall under principles. But which principles? Presumably in both cases considerations of personal good and of the public interest are involved. Voting is thought to be important as a device either for furthering the public interest or for protecting the interests of those who vote. Or it is thought in some way to be an affront to the dignity of a person for matters to be decided affecting his or her welfare about which he or she has no say. Similarly arguments about wages are related to considerations both of the public interest in so far as it is essential for a community to attract and train workers in certain skilled occupations. Or they are related to considerations of individual welfare and self-development. The arguments for criteria determining relevance will depend upon the importance attached to these underlying considerations which fall under principles.

In the case of voting, for instance, anyone who is prepared to argue the case will never base his proposals purely on the fact that women are women. There are, of course, those who have a completely irrational attitude. For them women may simply be classed as inferior beings. But argument is pointless with such people and it is a nice point to what extent arguments in spheres where people are subject to such irrational attitudes are much more than corks tossed to and fro by undercurrents of prejudice. This can only be determined by going through the arguments actually produced.

If, however, a person is really prepared to argue he will produce reasons related to principles such as those of the consideration of people's interests or respect for persons. He will connect 'being a woman' with other properties such as being ignorant of public affairs, or being influenced too much by emotion or by the opinion of her husband, which are relevant to what he considers to be the point of the activity. He may also point out that children and imbeciles are not permitted to vote. Presumably this is because it is thought that matters of private and public interest are not well promoted by the votes of those who lack a knowledge of public affairs. Or it may be thought that they are not fully 'persons'. Are women, therefore, in these respects, which are accepted as relevant, different from men? But supposing women *are* ignorant. Supposing it is argued that the illiterate should be excluded from voting as well as women for more or less the same reasons. The issue is not yet settled. For what of their dignity as persons? Should not their point of view be taken account of even though it is not a well-informed one? And how is their point of view to be taken account of if they have no opportunity of expressing it?

In cases such as this, arguments deriving from the consideration of interests clash with those deriving from respect for persons. There is no rule for determining which reasons are most relevant when the reasons fall under different fundamental principles which conflict in a particular case. Judgment is required, not a slide rule.

The case of a 'just wage' illustrates the clash of underlying principles even more clearly. It is usually granted in this case that there shall be different categories. But if the matter of wages is not to be left entirely to the market and to threats and pressures, what criteria should determine the level of wages? Should considerations of merit based on the value of the work done to the community be paramount? Or should allowance be made for the needs of individuals both in regard to their needs as private individuals—e.g. as supporters of large families—and as functionaries, e.g. as requiring to entertain others to expensive lunches? If both types of considerations are considered to be relevant in fixing wages, what relative weight is to be attached to them?

There is a further complication in such discussions. It may be argued that, though the right to vote or a fair wage has formally been granted, the realities of the situation militate against justice being done. For instance, employers of illiterate labourers or husbands of ignorant women may put pressure on them either not to vote at all or to vote in accordance with their authoritative demands. Or though, formally speaking, the right to a fair wage has been conceded, there is in fact a shortage of jobs or of money which prevents its implementation. Or, to take another case, it is often pointed out that although, formally speaking, everyone has equality before the law in the sense that no discrimination is made against a man in the courts on irrelevant grounds, in fact, if a man is wealthy, he can employ a good barrister which will in fact influence unfairly the treatment which he actually gets in comparison with a poor man who cannot afford such a luxury. To what extent, in cases such as these, are formal arrangements to be extended to minimize the influence of such actual inequalities?

It is obvious enough that if equality was all that was valued in a society there would be almost no limit to the demand for such an extension of formal arrangements. In elections, for instance, not only would everyone be protected at the polling booth by detailed legislation; transport would also be made available to ensure that everybody could get there in comfort. But this would only be tinkering with the problem; for, because of discrepancies in wealth, voters would have had unequal opportunities of learning what was at stake. So everybody would have to be provided with the necessary books, television sets, etc., to ensure equality in this respect. But, also, because of education and early upbringing, people would in fact be differently equipped to profit from such information. To remedy this it would not be enough to insist that they all went to the same sort of school; they would all have to come from the same sort of home. Actually the size of a family as well as the degree of harmony existing between parents may well be very important determinants of the ability to learn. So arrangements would have to be made to remove inequalities in such family factors. But even this would not be enough because of genetic differences. Careful attention would therefore have to be paid to breeding to ensure that individuals were not born with marked differences between them.

A thorough-going equalitarian would be interested in removing all such actual differences between people from another point of view as well. For as long as such marked actual differences exist between people, it can always be argued that with regard to some types of provision they constitute relevant grounds for making categories. A thorough-going equalitarian regards such categorization as obnoxious. He would, therefore, be in favour of measures which minimize relevant grounds for constructing categories; so he would have an additional reason for proceeding along the lines sketched above.

At some point in this imagined programme towards minimizing actual inequalities most equalitarians would in fact protest. Such a stand would not be taken on grounds of equality; for what would be said is that the implementation of such a programme would involve infringements of liberty, or that people would suffer or that their point of view as persons would be disregarded. In other words the pursuit of equality would be at the expense of the implementation of other principles which are thought to be important. As a matter of historical fact most equalitarians have seldom advanced such a generalized plea for equality. They have agitated against the existence of particular injustices arising from irrelevant grounds for making distinctions. The movement, for instance, for equality between the sexes was not a general movement for making women as much like men as possible. It was directed against the denial of access to various things thought desirable on the irrelevant grounds that a person was a woman. Also most equalitarians have believed strongly in other principles as well which have imposed limits on their pursuit of equality.

4. EQUALITY IN EDUCATION

The simpler cases of wages and of voting have been taken to illustrate some important general points about the application of the principle of equality. The first is that considerations of equality alone cannot determine what ought to be done in any concrete case of distribution where there is a dispute about whether exceptions should be made or categories created. At best the principle lays down a presumption. But if it is challenged relevant considerations must necessarily fall under principles other than that of equality. Voting is a case of equals being treated equally, wages of unequals being treated unequally; but in both cases the point of the activity has to be picked out in terms of general principles before relevant criteria can be produced either for claiming that difference in treatment is grounded on irrelevant distinctions, or for setting up categories on the basis of relevant distinctions. This is because, though voting and earning a wage are thought to be desirable, they are not usually thought to be desirable in themselves. Their value derives from fundamental principles other than that of equality. As in each case more than one fundamental principle is involved in addition to equality, irreconcilable disagreements may arise owing to the different weight given to the different fundamental principles determining the relevance of criteria, e.g. of desert rather than of need. Justification is required, therefore, of principles other than that of equality, and judgment is required to assess their relative importance as applied to a concrete situation.

Secondly these simpler cases have been used to make the contrast between a formal analysis of a situation in terms of what is prescribed by law, custom, or morality, and what actually happens. This raises the question of the extent to which formal arrangements should be extended to minimize the influence of actual differences. Again other principles are involved because objections to the pursuit of positive equality usually are based on other principles which are infringed in the process. These general points can now be made in relation to the more complex case of education.

Education is unlike voting and earning a wage in many respects, but especially in respect of its intrinsic value. It was argued in the first part of this book that education involves initiation into what a community considers to be worth while, and that it is impossible to represent it in terms of taking means to a worth-while end or bringing about a worth-while product by methods which are morally neutral. Being 'educated' marks a group of achievements which are internally related to a family of tasks. Nevertheless it was also pointed out that an educational *system* or a school can be regarded from an external point of view as a method of preparing people for jobs in a community. It can also be regarded, by the individual, as an avenue to power and prestige in a community. Indeed it is now becoming the chief mode of social ascent.[1] Obviously enough, therefore, questions of access to it and of its distribution are some of the most explosive issues in the modern world. How, then, is the principle of equality to be applied in this sphere?

(a) Interpretations of the principle in USA and England
In some countries, e.g. the USA, education at any rate up to high school level is regarded almost as a kind of commodity to which all have an equal right. It is rather like the right to vote, a case where the explicit presumption is that equals should be treated equally. Selection is delayed and works rather like a free-market economy on the basis of the survival of the fittest. It approximates to what Turner calls a 'contest' system in which all can have a go and see how far they can get.[2] The wastage is high; but as there is plenty of room at the level above the high school, and as the country is very rich, this is not disastrous. By the time the fittest struggle through to their PhDs some are very well educated, and a large percentage of the population pick up some sort of a training as well as a modicum of knowledge about many things.

In such a system agitations about equality centre round the injustice

[1] See Turner, R. H., 'Modes of Social Ascent through Education: Sponsored and Contest Mobility' in Halsey, A. H., Floud, J., and Anderson, C. A., *Education, Economy and Society* (New York, Free Press, 1961), Ch. 12.

[2] See Turner, R. H., op. cit.

done to those who are, for irrelevant reasons, deprived of their right to what is available for all. In the USA this amounts largely to the segregation issue. The general presumption in favour of all getting the same provision up to high school level is interpreted as meaning that all who live in a certain area should go to the same school, even if this means increasing the size of the school to over 2,000. In some states of the USA, education being universally administered on a state basis, separate schools have been established for negroes, who are banned from the schools reserved for whites. It is claimed that these schools are inferior in staff, equipment, and in prestige to the white schools. So the negroes are denied access on irrelevant grounds to a quality of provision which should be available to all.

In such a system there is provision, of course, for differences in aptitude and ability. American high schools usually have at least three types of courses, college, technical, and commercial. But the students have the right to opt for whichever course they want, to try and see how they get on. Naturally enough the general provision tends accordingly to cater for the 'average' child. There has recently been a widespread revulsion against this 'levelling down' of educational provision with the neglect of 'excellence' that it entails. Advanced placements schemes have therefore been started, by means of which the courses of able children can be supplemented so as to accelerate their development. Another significant trend has been the mushroom-like growth of private schools which claim to provide an education of a better quality for those who can pay for it. These trends are accompanied by arguments much more familiar in English education.

In the English system, at any rate in the decades preceding and succeeding the 1944 Act, the necessity for different categories of education was generally accepted. There was not the presumption that children should all go to the same school. The situation was more like the case of the 'fair wage' than of the right to vote. Differences in educational provision were accepted; the problem was to determine relevant grounds for assigning children to different schools. The system was more like what Turner calls a 'sponsored' system. There was much less room at the top and far smaller resources to be spent on education. The problem was that of determining relevant grounds for recruiting people to positions of authority and prestige in the community. As is well known the old scholarship examination, by means of which children from elementary schools were sorted out as being eligible for a grammar or central school, was elevated into the 11+ examination. On the basis of this examination, which included tests in English and mathematics, as well as an intelligence test and teachers' reports, judgment was made on the basis of the age, aptitude, and ability of children, and they were dispatched to their destiny in a grammar, technical or secondary modern school.

This, it was argued, constituted a substantial move towards remedying existing injustices. Secondary education, at least up to 15, was proclaimed to be the right of all. Access to the appropriate type of education was granted on what were thought to be relevant criteria. It could no longer be argued that lack of money could deprive a person of the type of education that a grammar school or independent school (such as Eton) could provide. It was admitted that the wealth of parents was an irrelevant consideration. No one now, with the relevant qualities, need be deprived of the most suitable type of education for him. This was part of the general new deal for the underprivileged which was characteristic of legislation generally at the end of the Second World War.

It would be very difficult to maintain that abstract considerations of justice, in the main, determined these main lines of educational provision in both countries. This, in fact, depended on a great number of contingent circumstances. The Americans, for instance, are so averse to children from the same community going to different schools that they are prepared to tolerate mammoth-size institutions in defence of this interpretation of the maxim that equals should be treated equally. This is not because of any deep-seated love of uniformity; for there was a time when the Americans were highly individualistic. Nor is it due purely to their fear that if their neighbour's child goes to a different school he may in fact be getting a better start in the race. It is also to be seen in terms of the school's historic role of helping to make a nation out of immigrants with a great variety of cultural backgrounds. This combination of contingent circumstances leads to the insistence that differences in provision must be made within the same school, whatever the differences in educational aims.

The English, on the other hand, have assumed that it is reasonable that unequals should be treated unequally. But they have also been led to assume that there are three different types of education—grammar, technical, and modern—which suit different types of children, and that these should be provided in different types of schools. Again this interpretation is not to be seen as due purely to a love of diversity or to the

Platonic vision of administrators who imagined that they were dealing with the three classes in *The Republic*. It is to be seen rather in terms of the historic evolution of the grammar schools, senior schools and central schools and the practical means that were available, on limited resources, of raising the school-leaving age to 15.

In neither the USA nor in England have agitations about equality in education taken the form of abstract pleas for ideal systems in which education is to be distributed in accordance with clear-cut criteria derivative from unitary aims. In both countries interpretations of the principle have to be seen in terms of these contingent circumstances, and arguments advanced in terms of it have almost always been related to particular injustices, to distinctions made on the basis of irrelevant differences. In the USA, as has been already explained, the main issue is the plight of the negroes. In England it used to be and still is, in the case of the privileged position of those attending independent schools, the injustice of a system that denies the best forms of education to those without wealth. It has now shifted to the new injustices created by the implementation of the 1944 Act which was in part designed to remedy the old injustices connected with wealth. A new problem, too, is looming rather like the American problem, which is due to the influx of immigrants.

When such agitations develop they are always complicated by disagreements not only, as would be expected, about the aims of education, but also about what education is. This dimension of disagreement makes arguments about voting and wages straightforward in comparison. For instance it can be argued that devices for distribution distort education and deprive it of its intrinsic value. On the one hand it is argued that an efficient system of selection by examinations may transform education into a matter of 'knowledge to be acquired and facts to be stored'. On the other hand it is claimed that attempts to distribute education 'equally' in a large school, on the basis of individual interest and aptitude, turns a school into a sort of supermarket with all the attendant losses in quality. Education, it is argued, can only really take root on an apprenticeship basis; a supermarket type of institution renders such a relationship very difficult to contrive.

If an educational system could be thought of in purely instrumental terms, like a wages system, discussions would be much more straightforward. Michael Young, for instance, in his satire entitled *The Rise of the Meritocracy*[1] imagines a community devoted whole-heartedly to

[1] Young, M., *The Rise of the Meritocracy* (London, Thames & Hudson, 1958).

economic productivity, in which positions in the community and training for them are determined solely on the criterion of merit. Schools in such a community become training institutions. The problems of selection are purely technical; for the criteria determining what is 'fair' are agreed and unambiguous, namely those to do with ability to contribute to the community's good, defined in terms of increasing productivity.

The flaws in such a conception, which the satire was written to expose, are obvious enough. No community has or could set itself such a limited end as increase in productivity; for what quality of life is such an increase intended to sustain? In so far as schools are concerned with education, and not simply with training, they are concerned with initiating children gradually into this quality of life. The forms of knowledge and awareness into which they are initiated are not just convenient vade-mecums for operatives, technocrats, and bureaucrats. The rights of individuals to such a quality of life can therefore be set against their duty to contribute to the state, with all that is implied in the way of training. Furthermore, even at the level of mere training, the skills necessary to run a rapidly changing industrial society change so rapidly with it that the notion of 'vocational training' has only limited application at the school level under modern conditions.

But included in the general notion of 'a quality of life' are different values on which different emphasis is placed in disputes about the aims of education. Some emphasize the supreme importance of individual choice; others emphasize the importance of mastery of certain forms of knowledge or skills; others emphasize the training of character; others stress the need for all-round development. All such aims must be set alongside the state's requirement for training in essential skills and in 'citizenship'. They are not necessarily incompatible; but differences in emphasis will suggest differences in educational provision and, perhaps, different criteria of access. Supposing, for instance, that a person is much impressed by the community's need for industrial development and for the pool of technicians and statisticians that goes with it. He will tend to stress the importance of training in educational institutions and the importance of mathematics, science, and technology. In a time of limited resources he may advocate criteria of selection related to these priorities. His proposals may be backed by someone else who values precision and rigour of thought as a cardinal educational value, irrespective of its benefit to the community. Someone else, however, may be led by his stress on the importance of individual choice, to deprecate selection and to advocate a situation where individuals are given the maximum opportunity to discover for themselves what they want to explore. He may be supported by another who thinks that 'wholeness' is important and who therefore deprecates any form of selection which will lead to premature specialization.

Such possible types of disagreement could be multiplied indefinitely; but there is no point in labouring the obvious. Enough has been said to substantiate the main claim that discussions about the fairness of the distribution of education are different in at least two ways from discussions of the distribution of simpler commodities. Firstly the nature of education can be seriously influenced by its manner of distribution; secondly it is something which is of intrinsic value, although what goes on in educational institutions can also be viewed instrumentally in relation to the needs of the community or purposes of the individual. As, however, there are different intrinsic values involved in the quality of life that is passed on in educational institutions, and as these can be seriously affected both by its manner of distribution and by the determination to relate this to the extrinsic ends of the community or of the individual, the possibilities of disagreements deriving from different values are endless.

It is obvious enough, therefore, why disagreements about what is 'fair' in education depend upon other values which a person has, which provide criteria for determining relevance in matters of distribution. Most people would admit that the wealth of parents is a completely irrelevant criterion. But there is not a corresponding measure of agreement about the criteria of aptitude and ability that have in England been substituted for it. Lack of agreement about the relevance of such criteria does not derive solely from the difficulties actually encountered in the attempt to categorize children in accordance with these criteria. Rather it reflects basic differences in emphasis about what is vital in education and about the extent to which what goes on in schools should be closely related to the extrinsic requirements of the community.

There is also a further basic source of disagreement, which relates not so much to what is fair but to the importance to be attached to fairness in relation to other principles. This usually happens when the pursuit of equality comes into conflict with liberty or with the demands for a quality of life. Defenders, for instance, both of the grammar school and of the independent schools often take their stand on these two principles. They argue for the right of parents to have their children educated at schools of their own choosing, especially if this entails paying large fees. They also argue that it takes many years to build up educational institutions which actually succeed in initiating children into the forms of thought and awareness, with their built-in standards of excellence, which are constitutive of a quality of life. There is a danger, they argue, that well-meaning ideologues should be driven by their unbridled passion for equality into dismantling schools which have achieved the rare distinction of knowing how to educate people. They also point out the great service done to education by pioneers such as Arnold and Froebel who used this liberty to carry out experiments in independent schools and to the standards set by grammar schools within the state system. They ruefully note that the modern Levellers are bent on making the English educational system as much like the American system as possible at a time when enlightened Americans are becoming profoundly disturbed about the inadequacies of their own system.

(b) The formal and the actual

Modern agitations about 'equality of opportunity' in the USA and England are also related in part to the contrast between formal arrangements and what in fact happens. Here again the important question arises, which has just been raised, about how far the claims of equality are to be pressed. How far are formal arrangements to be extended in order to minimize actual inequalities?

In the USA, for instance, realities make the plight of the negroes one facet of a more general problem. The standard of educational provision differs considerably in the different states as well as in different neighbourhoods. As there is a widespread ideological insistence on children going to the same school as their neighbours, this means that the type of educational provision in fact varies according to contingent circumstances prevailing in different states. Furthermore, as neighbourhoods differ widely in standards and cost of housing, and as the local community contributes considerably towards the cost of education, this means, in effect, that wealth can indirectly buy a more lavish type of education. American professors debate whether they are to invest their money in a cheap house in a poor area and spend the income so saved on a private school, as the standard of public education in the neighbourhood is so deplorable; or whether they are to spend more money on a house in a better class area where the quality of education is suitable for their children.

137

Similarly in England the 11 + examination is not in fact an objective test; for its standard varies according to different localities depending on the number of grammar and technical places available. It is even different from year to year in the same locality. Furthermore though, formally speaking, everyone is competing on equal terms, evidence shows that IQ score is very much affected by socio-economic class, especially by the speech habits of the family to which the child belongs.[1] The plight, therefore, of culturally deprived children, is unenviable; for they suffer from cumulative obstacles in attaining the level necessary for success.

Perhaps most serious of all has been the unintended plight of many children attending secondary modern schools. The intention of those who devised the 1944 Act was that the secondary modern school should provide a different, not an inferior, form of education which was meant to be suited to the distinctive ability and aptitude of those who attended them. Headmasters were encouraged to experiment and to devise a new form of exciting 'modern' education. This seldom happened.[2] Children who went to such schools felt that they were inferior as they had 'failed' the test. They could no longer claim, as they used to be able to claim under the old system, that they lacked education because their fathers could not afford it. They now had had their chance and had been found 'wanting'. The schools that they attended were often poorly equipped and housed in antiquated and lavatory-like premises. The staff were often disgruntled because they had failed to find employment in grammar or technical schools. Few attempts were made to develop a distinctive curriculum which was adapted to the ability and aptitude of the children. Courses of a vocational nature were, of course, laid on but, with the growing tendency for children to stay at school longer, the curriculum became increasingly a watered-down version of that of grammar and technical schools. This tendency was strengthened by the demand of employers for some objective sign, which meant in effect an examination, by means of which the attainment of school-leavers could be assessed. In brief a variety of social pressures combined to stultify the intentions of those who framed the 1944 Act with regard to the secondary modern school. The system has turned out to be so manifestly unfair in the way in which it actually works that various schemes are in train or in mind for revising it.

[1] See Bernstein, B. B., 'Social Class and Linguistic Development: a Theory of Social Learning' in Halsey, Floud, and Anderson, op. cit.

[2] See Taylor, W., *The Secondary Modern School* (London, Faber, 1963).

(c) Remedying actual inequalities
In the light of this experience most English educationists now query
the basic presumption that unequals should be treated unequally, if this
is interpreted as entailing attendance at a different school from the age
of eleven onwards, the type of school being determined by a crucial test.
It is argued that, if there is to be selection, it should be delayed as long
as possible and be made less irrevocable in its probable consequences.
Over and above this common measure of agreement there exists a
splendid variety of alternative proposals. Some argue that the difference
in provision should be provided within vast comprehensive schools to
be attended by all from a given neighbourhood from the age of eleven
upwards, as in the American high school system. Others argue that all
should attend the equivalent of the American junior high school from
the age of nine to thirteen and then pass on to different types of school.
Others argue that there should be 'comprehensive' education for all up
to fifteen and that there should be different types of provision after that.
There are disputes, too, about whether parents should be allowed to
choose to which of such multifunctional schools they send their children
or whether they should be compelled to send them to a school which is
arbitrarily fixed for them on a neighbourhood basis.[1]

Arguments for adjusting institutions in order to remedy such obvious
sources of injustice depend upon contingent factors which are more the
concern of the social scientist and psychologist than of the philosopher.
They only get philosophically interesting when a question of principle
is raised about the limits to which equalitarians are prepared to go in
order to remove such actual sources of inequality. Most enlightened
Americans are prepared to support Federal intervention in order to ensure that negroes are not in fact debarred from good schools and universities. But to what extent are they prepared to support Federal intervention in order to redress actual inequalities existing between the
different states in terms of educational provision? To what extent are
they prepared to agitate against housing regulations which ensure that
only people with a certain level of income can live within a given
district?

English equalitarians are never tired of stressing that being brought
up in a working-class home in fact imposes all sorts of handicaps on
children. Are they then prepared to advocate compulsory attendance at

[1] For discussion of alternatives see Elvin, H. L., *Education and Contemporary
Society* (London, Watts, 1965), Part II.

nursery schools (supposing that this were economically feasible) to make up for this? Are they prepared for the state to intervene in order to regulate other crucial factors, such as the size of families, perhaps by refusing to grant family allowances for more than three children? If they are prepared to admit the claims of liberty and of quality of life at this level why do they seem so oblivious of them at other levels?

Lieberman[1] suggests two meanings for 'equality of educational opportunity'. One is that A and B have it when 'they live under conditions which do not provide either person with any material advantage over the other in selecting or pursuing his educational goals'. He argues that such equality is almost non-existent, though many imagine that it exists. The other is that A and B have it 'when the material advantages which one of them possesses over the other in selecting or pursuing his educational goals cannot be removed without endangering other important values'. Because 'other important values' vary from person to person, so also does the interpretation of 'equality of educational opportunity'. This second meaning, however, is a sham. For people have not got it in any actual sense and are not prepared, for reasons which have nothing to do with equality, to take the steps necessary to ensure that they have it. To call the second state of affairs one in which 'equality of educational opportunity' prevails is to misrepresent the facts of life in order to retain a shibboleth. The plea for 'equality of opportunity' is more properly understood as either an attack on irrelevant aids to opportunity (e.g. wealth) or as a demand for replacing unreasonable by reasonable grounds for providing access to opportunities.

The obvious fact is that, descriptively speaking, there is no equality of opportunity and never can be unless equalitarians are prepared to control early upbringing, size of families, and breeding. Without taking such steps there will always be ineradicable differences between people which will affect how any system works in practice. Were there not such differences the principle of equality would have little point. For, as has been argued, an equalitarian is not necessarily committed to any factual assertions about men, but only to the determination to treat people the same unless the differences between them can be shown to be *relevant* to how they should be treated. What makes differences relevant is, as has been shown, a very complex matter which necessarily in-

[1] In 'Equality of Educational Opportunity' reprinted in Smith, B. O., and Ennis, R. H., *Language and Concepts in Education* (Chicago, Rand McNally, 1961), p. 142.

volves recourse to other principles. To extend the meaning of 'equality of opportunity' in the way suggested by Lieberman has the effect of soft-pedalling the importance of such other principles in discussions of educational provision. It is to fall in with the modern fashion of assuming that the only moral issues involved in educational provision are issues of equality. This chapter has attempted to demonstrate, not only that this is not so, but that it necessarily cannot be so.

Mill argued in his essay *On Liberty* that the only legitimate ground for interfering with individual liberty was that others were harmed by it. In other words he saw that one principle, that of the consideration of people's interests, sets limits to the pursuit of liberty. In a similar way it has been argued that other principles such as liberty and the development of a quality of life (which is involved in the consideration of interest)[1] both set limits to the pursuit of equality and, in the case of education, provide content for what is to be justly distributed. But it has not been claimed that philosophical analysis or argument can show at what particular points such limits are to be set. This depends upon practical judgment which has to be exercised in the light of a multitude of contingent circumstances. Philosophers can only map the contours of such arguments; they cannot pronounce upon the details of the view.

5. SOCIAL INEQUALITY

Often when people complain of 'inequality' they are referring not so much to the type of provision made but to the social attitudes that go with it. It is possible for a system to be fair, in that differences in treatment are grounded on relevant differences between people, and yet to be permeated by attitudes of contempt and deference which seem thoroughly objectionable. This is often the result of categorization where 'different' is generalized to 'worse' or 'better'. Many argue that such attitudes are developed by the English educational system in which failure at the 11+ examination is not interpreted just as implying worse at certain types of performance but generally worse as a person. Similarly secondary modern schools are not thought of simply as different; they are thought of as being worse schools. And so the attitudes of contempt and rejection build up.

It is questionable, as a matter of fact, whether such attitudes in England are the product of the present system of categorization. It is more likely that this system simply provides clear-cut channels through

[1] See Ch. VI, Sec. 1.

which existing class-attitudes can flow; for in England the old class-consciousness has not disappeared. Its basis has merely shifted from birth and wealth to occupation and education. It is questionable, also, whether any society can exist without such attitudes developing. In America a great virtue of the educational system is alleged to be that anyone can rub shoulders at school with a potential President. But the attitudes of contempt on the part of those who are successful in the scramble for wealth and prestige to those who are failures is much more virulent than those of the remnants of the landed gentry in England to labourers who work on their estates. In any social system some people are better at doing jobs than others and some are capable of doing jobs requiring skills that are beyond the capacities of others. There must inevitably be, too, some authority system which puts some in a superior position in a hierarchy to others. A process of generalization, a kind of halo effect, accompanies such stratification. 'Better at' is generalized to 'better' without specific qualifications; superior in rank is generalized to generally superior. It is argued by some[1] that such class attitudes are the inevitable product of living in any social system which necessarily requires differentiation of function within an authority structure. This may well be so. But what is lacking in such a situation is not necessarily lack of equality in any distributive sense but lack of respect for persons.

Lack of respect for persons seems consistent with treating people fairly. Civil servants can be scrupulously fair in dealing with cases; but they can think of the people whose affairs they administer merely as 'the public'. They can consider people's interests with fine impartiality and with a genuine regard for what is good for them. But they may have contempt for them as persons. They may be unmoved by the thought that they are dealing with *people* who are unique centres of consciousness, who have peculiar idiosyncratic wants and aspirations, who are subject to strange feelings and emotions, who are bound up with and take pride in their own achievements, however puny, and who all mirror the world from a distinctive point of view. They see people only under a certain description, as belonging to a certain category. This is what justice requires of them. Respect for persons requires much more. What it requires and how such an attitude can be justified will be left for fuller consideration in Chapter VIII. Enough has been said to distinguish this attitude from unfairness with which it is often confused.

[1] e.g. by Dahrendorf, R., in 'On the Origin of Social Inequality' in Laslett, P., and Runciman, V. G., *Philosophy, Politics and Society* (Oxford, Blackwell, 1962).

CONCLUSION

The purpose of this chapter has been not simply to exhibit a form of argument by means of which an attempt was made to justify the principle of justice, but also to examine the working of this principle both in general and in the particular field of education. One of the main points made about this principle was that, as it only applies when something of value is at stake, and as it only embodies the formal demands that distinctions shall only be made when there are relevant differences, it can of itself supply no more than a necessary, never a sufficient, moral basis for educational policy; for the value of what is to be distributed and the criteria of relevance for making distinctions must derive from other principles. There is also the ever present possibility that the pursuit of equality may conflict with adherence to other principles. The importance of these general considerations in the discussion of equality in education has been demonstrated.

The discussion, therefore, of 'fairness' has served as little more than a preliminary. It has made clear, it is to be hoped, a form of argument that can be used to justify other fundamental principles such as liberty. It has also shown the imperative need for the justification of *other* principles from which derive both the value of what is to be distributed and criteria by reference to which systems can be condemned as being unfair. Of crucial importance are questions of value relating to the content of education; for there is only an issue about fairness because of the assumption that what is to be distributed is valuable. Arguments, however, must be produced to show why what is passed on in schools and universities is valuable. The ethical foundations of the curriculum must therefore now be examined.

CHAPTER V

WORTH-WHILE ACTIVITIES

INTRODUCTION

Education, it has been argued, involves the initiation of others into worth-while activities. The curriculum of a school or university may be operated with a principle of options, which encourages the individual to choose some activity which is suitable to his ability, aptitude, and interest; but this choice is between a range of activities that are thought to be worth passing on. Science, mathematics, history, art, cooking and carpentry feature on the curriculum, not bingo, bridge and billiards. Presumably there must be some reason for this apart from their utilitarian or vocational value; for it has been argued that though most of these activities can be viewed instrumentally, to regard them as having educational value is to rule out such considerations. It would require, also, a considerable stretching of the concept of 'use' to hold that there was much use in learning poetry if a reason is to be provided which is somehow extrinsic to the values inherent in the appreciation of poetry. How then can the pursuit of such activities be justified?

Before tackling the question of the justification of such activities it is important to remove certain misunderstandings which often confuse the discussion of this topic and which load teachers with a quite unnecessary feeling of frustration, guilt, and inadequacy. I am maintaining only that there must be good reasons for pursuing these sorts of activities rather than others. This does not imply that there are equally good reasons for saying that some activities included on a curriculum are more worth while than others which are also on a curriculum. It might be possible, for instance, to show why history and literary appreciation are more worth while than bingo and bridge; but it does not follow that there must also be reasons for saying that history is more worth while than literary appreciation. Still less does it follow that a student will grasp what these reasons are before embarking on the worth-while pursuit in question and take to it because he sees the reasons.

I would hazard the guess that such advocacy is pretty ineffective to those whose view of such activities is an external one. Enthusiasm for them is caught rather than engendered by argument. I have heard education likened to a vast conspiracy. People are told that they ought to go to a university, for instance, because it will equip them for a job. If they were told the real reasons for going to a university, and if their going were dependent on accepting such reasons, my guess is that many would not go. But once they have got to a university, for some reason or other which is largely beside the point, the hope is that they will gradually come to see or to sense the proper reasons. I have sympathy for the professor of philosophy who, when being pressed to agree with the suggestion that students come to universities in order to become good citizens, replied that this sort of thing often had to be said in order to persuade hard-headed businessmen that universities were a good national investment, but that it would be a most regrettable state of affairs if university teachers themselves became victims of their own propaganda!

In all social movements, whether they be religious, political or cultural, there is always the problem of the majority who do not care. Perhaps a man has been brought up within a religious movement; the problem of converting the indifferent is one which he has heard discussed on many occasions. Perhaps his religion gradually slides away from him or he wears it as a more loose-fitting cloak. His affiliations change and he finds himself working with people who have, perhaps, a somewhat broader or more humanistic conception of the good life. But, lo and behold, again he finds himself in those familiar discussions about how others can be induced to join. Again he hears it said that the 'broad mass of the people' remain outside the movement in question.

The explanation of this familiar phenomenon, as well as of the inefficacy of advocacy, is not far to seek. The majority of men are geared to consumption and see the value of anything in terms of immediate pleasure or as related instrumentally to the satisfaction of their wants as consumers. When they ask the question 'What is there in this for me?' or 'Where will this get me?' activities like science and art have no straightforward appeal. For they offer sweat and struggles rather than immediate delight and their instrumentality to the satisfaction of other wants is difficult to discern.

I. JUSTIFICATION IN TERMS OF WANTS

Such features of worth-while activities present obvious limits to the effectiveness of advocacy. But do they also rule out the possibility of justification in terms of wants? Is there nothing in Mill's argument that activities which are qualitatively superior can be justified because on the whole and in the long run anyone who tries them as well as the life of ambition or of sensuous enjoyment will admit that these are superior in terms of quality and permanence of satisfaction?

There is an obvious difficulty about this form of argument, however it is stated, which is the general difficulty of naturalism. For it cannot be argued in general that if people on the whole want something and continue to pursue it, this is equivalent to showing that it is worth while. It would, perhaps, be a very odd state of affairs if something was worth while, yet no one wanted it; but establishing that it is wanted is not sufficient to establishing that it is worth while. Indeed a cynic might say that whereas the trouble with some people is that they cannot get what they want, the trouble with others is that they in fact want just what they get.

A difficulty more specific to Mill's argument is as follows. Supposing his hypothesis was put to the test and a man who had tried sensuous indulgence, the pursuit of power, and the accumulation of riches were persuaded to try science and painting pictures. Supposing that after a year or so he was asked what he thought about them and replied that he could see nothing in them which was worth the effort. Would we then say that Mill's hypothesis was refuted? Surely not. We would say that he had not really understood what science was about or that he had not mastered painting sufficiently to appreciate its finer points. To put the point more concretely: if we spend years trying to get children going on science, art, and history and they return, after our efforts, to bingo, billiards, and eating bananas, do we say that this shows that these activities are not worth while? Don't we rather say that there is something wrong with our teaching methods or that the children have been immunized against education before they came to us? In other words for some reason or other they have not come to grasp what there is in these activities.

In the case of such activities a strong case can be made for Socrates' view that if a man does not pursue or at least feel drawn towards what is good then he does not really understand it; for the activities in question all have some general point which must be sensed by their participants and they all have standards of correctness and style built into them which give rise to characteristic appraisals. For a man to grasp what these activities are he must be on the inside of them and be sensitive to these aspects of them. Could a man really understand science, for instance, who was unmoved by the passion for truth and the concern about evidence and clarity? What sort of a mathematician would a man be who cared nothing for neatness or elegance of proof? And could a man begin to understand what philosophy was if he welcomed contradictions, delighted in obscurity, and thought cogency in argument a bourgeois fad? You might as well call a man a real golfer who was pleased when he topped a ball up to the hole! The truth in the Socratic saying that no man wittingly pursues what he believes to be evil derives from the fact that the sort of knowledge that is required in these pursuits is not purely a matter of intellectual understanding. It has a 'feeling' side to it, which is exhibited in appraisals which are related both to the point of the activity and to the standards of skill, efficiency, and style which characterize it. That is why we could and always would say about a man who seemed to refute Mill's hypothesis that he could not have understood what the activity was about. For to understand is to be committed in some way to its pursuit. Of course such a man might understand and still be more attracted to something else of comparable quality. A mathematician might find himself drawn more to music and philosophy. But it would be odd if, in his right mind, he took up sweeping the streets, unless there was some special explanation or background for the sweeping, e.g. he was doing it as emotional release or to the glory of God.

These objections to Mill's argument make it clear that what is crucial is not the fact of wanting but the character of what is wanted. The question then is whether anything general can be said about the character of such activities and whether any good reason can be given why they should be regarded as more worth while than others.

2. PLEASURE AND PAIN

Attempts have been made to give some general characterization of the content of such activities by introducing notions such as those of 'pleasure' and 'happiness'. There are notorious difficulties about such attempts. In the case of 'pleasure', for instance, such a characterization is usually held to be unhelpful for at least three reasons. The first is that to maintain that something should be chosen or done simply for the sake of pleasure, or because of the pleasure it gives, or because it is enjoyable, is simply to characterize it as being one of the type of activities with which we are here concerned; it is to say, in other words, that it is not to be done out of duty or for any other further reason. It is something that an individual might want to do just for what is involved in it.

Secondly all sorts of activities can be indulged in just for what they are, which might be thought trivial or even undesirable, such as lying in the sun or eating opium. Thirdly whatever such activities have in common which leads to the talk of 'pleasure' in relation to them, *in addition* to their being done for their own sake, it is impossible to characterize this without reference to the characteristics of the activity in question. The pleasure of swimming or of conversation is impossible to characterize without a further description of what is involved in swimming or conversation. So we are back where we started with the characterization of activities. For the question can always be asked 'Why go for the pleasure in this activity rather than that?'

The same sort of conclusion would be reached if an analysis were attempted of the more difficult and elusive concept of 'happiness'; for whatever points are made about the connection between 'happiness' and notions like permanence, absence of anxiety about the future or regrets about the past, it must involve reference to a pattern of activities which are both intrinsically absorbing and mutually compatible. For happiness is inconsistent with continual frustration and conflict.

These arguments dispose of the suggestion that reference to notions such as 'pleasure' and 'satisfaction' are sufficient to characterize what it is about worth-while activities that constitutes a reason for pursuing them. But it does not show that such characterizations are not necessary. Indeed there are good reasons for thinking that they are; for to say that activities are indulged in for the pleasure or satisfaction which they afford is, at least, to put them in the class of activities that are pursued for their own sake. It is to class them as intrinsically and not just as instrumentally desirable. But is this the *sole* function of terms such as 'pleasure' and 'satisfaction'? Is not the logical function of phrases such as 'for the pleasure it gives' or 'for the satisfaction got out of it', which put activities into the class of being done for what there is in them, derivative from something in them which terms like 'pleasure' and 'satisfaction' pick out? Is there not some important truth in hedonism, in the context of reasons for action and choice, which this rather formal account of the function of phrases such as 'for the sake of pleasure' omits? I think that there is and intend now to explicate briefly what seems to be missing.[1]

---

[1] This discussion is indebted to Kenny, A., *Action, Emotion and Will* (London, Kegan Paul, 1963), Ch. 6, in spite of the fact that the position here adopted is rather different, as well as to A. Phillips Griffiths.

It would be difficult, if not impossible, to understand what could be meant by the notion of a reason for action unless we had also notions like those of 'pleasure' and 'pain'; for actions bring about states of affairs and if there are to be grounds on which one state of affairs rather than another is to be sought it must be in virtue of some feature it possesses which is in some way agreeable or disagreeable to a human being. For how else could such a difference ever be one that could get people to seek or avoid it? 'Pleasant' and 'painful' are the two most general terms which we have for picking out such features of situation. Of course the pleasure involved in getting a sum right is quite different from that involved in lying in the sun. But unless both had some sort of a 'feeling' side to them it is difficult to understand why anyone would choose them as a way of spending his time, assuming that he was not forced or bribed to spend it in this way or that it was not regarded by him as a duty.

The concept of 'reasons for action' is learnt *pari passu* with that of 'pleasure' and 'pain'. For there are certain respects in which human beings are more or less the same, which provides a solid basis for these concepts to get a grip on people's behaviour, and to guide their conduct. At the level of sensation it is a general empirical fact that there are pleasures such as those connected with the stroking of the erotogenic zones of the body and pains such as tooth-ache. At the level of activities and actions eating and drinking are pleasant for someone who is hungry; being frustrated in attempting to satisfy such wants is unpleasant. Mastering obstacles is accompanied by feelings of satisfaction; so is the creation of order. Failure is painful; feelings of insecurity, of lack of order, are unpleasant. There are more complicated emotional states, such as joy, which involve thrills of pleasure and others, such as fear and anxiety, which involve unpleasant feelings. And so on. It may well be that in all these cases 'pleasure' and 'pain' name no specific unitary type of feeling; the feelings of 'pleasure' and 'pain' may be inseparable from the complexes in which they occur. But that there is a recognizable 'feeling' side to these sensations, states, actions, and activities, no one would deny.

It is in relation to such universal pleasures and pains that the concepts of 'pleasure' and 'pain' as well as that of reasons for action are learnt. For 'wants' emerge from 'wishes' when children begin to grasp that means can be taken to bring about or avoid such pleasurable or painful conditions. And with the emergence of 'wants' the notion of 'reasons' emerges as well. For a 'reason for action' is that end, for the sake of attaining or avoiding which, means can be devised. Were it not for the 'feeling' side of what came to be typically regarded as 'ends' why would anyone ever go for or avoid one state of affairs rather than another? It is impossible, perhaps, to characterize this 'feeling' side in any other way. We have to take examples of the complexes in which it occurs and to appeal to anyone's introspection. How else, for instance, would one explain what is meant by tooth-ache? And we would not know really what to say to a man who knew in this way what 'pain' was and who did not also want, other things being equal, to avoid it or get rid of it. Without these very general concepts of 'pleasure' and 'pain' the concept of 'reasons for action' would be almost unintelligible. Unless, too, there were paradigm cases of pleasure and pain, which were pretty universal amongst language users, how could anyone learn to *apply* such concepts?

Once a person has got the concept of 'pleasure' and 'pain' it is possible for him to use logically derivative expressions. In the first place he can speak of things being done 'for the sake of pleasure' or 'for the satisfaction that there is in it'. Such phrases deny the instrumentality of what is being done in relation to some further end or deny that it is being done out of duty or for any type of consideration extrinsic to the activity itself. They class the activity as a 'pleasure'. It may, however, be the case that the person engaged in the activity in question is not in fact experiencing any of the feelings characteristic of 'pleasures'. People who dig their gardens for pleasure are not necessarily experiencing a thrill whenever they push the spade in the soil. But the denial of instrumentality goes along with the suggestion that the activity has features of this sort which are usually associated with activities termed 'pleasures'.

In the second place phrases such as 'finding things pleasant', 'enjoying doing things', 'taking pleasure in' can also be used. Their function is not so much to rule out the suggestion of extrinsic reasons in particular cases as to draw attention to the predilections of the individual under discussion. What is being picked out is the sort of thing which he, perhaps idiosyncratically, does for its own sake. Again such phrases can be used without having to verify whether the individual does have any of the characteristic feelings. It would be very odd if he never had them; but we can say that a person enjoys a game of golf without having to find out about his feelings when he hits the ball.

These arguments establish something of relevance to the justification of worth-while activities; but they do not establish nearly enough. They only show that such activities must belong to the general class which we call 'pleasures'. Otherwise they could not be intrinsically good. But nothing has yet been said which provides grounds for singling them out of the general class of 'pleasures' and spending a vast amount of time and money on handing them on to children. 'Pleasures' include sensations and emotional states as well as activities. We are here only concerned with activities. But the point already made still stands: what is it that curriculum activities have which other activities, which also rank as pleasures, lack, in virtue of which they are thought to be more worth while than others? In order to tackle this crucial question something must first be said about activities in general.

3. ACTIVITIES[1] AND THEIR JUSTIFICATION

An activity, needless to say, implies first of all an agent who is active rather than passive. Pain, warmth, and anxiety are not activities. But more than this is required; for not all the things which people can be said to do are activities. Sneezing and coughing, for instance, are not activities unless they are done with some sort of skill or effort, or according to certain conventions. Normally we either sneeze or we don't; we don't do the job with more or less skill or concentration. Activities, in other words, involve rules and standards and they usually have some kind of point. But again not all the things we do which conform to these criteria can be called activities. Cutting the Gordian knot, for instance, is not an activity any more than killing a man is, or discovering a secret.[2] These are performances which take time but do not, like activities, go on for a time. To be an activity something must go on for a time as well as involve skill and effort. Activities are things like combing one's hair, hunting for a stud, eating one's dinner, making love, writing a book, and watching a play.

Activities can be more or less interesting, absorbing or fascinating depending on the dispositions and competence of the agent and the characteristics of the activity in question. Fishing, for instance, is more absorbing in one respect for a man who depends on fish for his meals or livelihood than for one who does it for sport; but in another respect the interest depends not so much on the urgency of the objective as on the skill there is in it. The more occasions there are for exercising skill in

[1] See Griffiths, A. P., 'A Deduction of Universities' in Archambault, R. D. (Ed.), *Philosophical Analysis and Education* (London, Kegan Paul, 1965).

[2] See Kenny, A., *Action, Emotion and Will* (London, Kegan Paul, 1963), Ch. 8.

dealing with the unexpected, the more fascinating it becomes as an activity. Some activities are absorbing because of their palpable and pleasurable point, such as eating, sexual activity, and fighting. But erected on this solid foundation of want is often an elaborate superstructure of rules and conventions, which make it possible to indulge in these activities with more or less skill, sensitivity, and manners. Such activities become 'civilized' when rules develop which protect those engaged in them from brutal efficiency in relation to the obvious end of the exercise. Eating could consist in getting as much food into the stomach in the quickest and most efficient way—like pigs at a trough. Civilization begins when conventions develop which protect others from the starkness of such 'natural' behaviour. The development of rules and conventions governing the manner in which these activities are pursued, because of the joys involved in mastery, generates an additional source of interest and pleasure. Duelling can be delighted in by those who have no intention to kill; elaborate and witty flirtations can be conducted by people who would regard reference to the obvious end of such an affair as in very bad taste; the care of the home can completely transcend utilitarian considerations.

When a city becomes civilized and rises above the level of what Plato called 'the necessary appetites' activities develop which require great skill and which are strictly rule-governed, but which have no obvious point. Games develop in which the 'end' has to be invented in order to provide a focus for skill. To get a small ball into a small hole counts little *sub specie aeternitatis*; but think of the ulcers generated by the effort to manage it in as few shots as possible. Objects of beauty are created to give concrete and permanent expression to this striving for standards. Noises are made in most complex and complicated sequences by instruments in which animal, vegetable, and mineral are joined together in an amazing variety of combinations. Language itself can come to be used not to get others to do things, not to serve as an instrument for self-display or for the humiliation of others, but to create a common impersonal world of conversation which those gathered together build up by their personal contributions.

It is one thing to point to characteristics of activities that are usually thought to be worth while; it is quite another to show why these sorts of characteristics make them worth while. For it is obvious enough that not everyone who asks the question 'What ought I to do?' chooses a course of action which is likely to maximize opportunities for the pursuit of these sorts of activities. Not all men who devote themselves to a life of sensuous indulgence do so on impulse; not all pursuit of material gain springs from the unreflective following of a tradition. Indeed the jibe is often made that it is only people committed to a life of theorizing like Spinoza, who come out as whole-hearted defenders of the 'good for man' as conceived in this way.

Philosophers such as Plato, Aristotle and Spinoza who have attempted to justify this form of life have usually had recourse to the doctrine of function. Man's differentia, they have argued, consists in his use of reason. The good of everything in nature consists in developing that which it does better than other species or that which it alone does. Therefore man's good must be to indulge in those activities which involve the use of reason. There is some truth in this doctrine in so far as the behaviour of men is only *intelligible* if account is taken of man's reason, which is exhibited in the assessment of ends and in the choice of means to ends, and in the imposition of values and standards on desire; but this is not conclusive as a consideration which can be used to *justify* such a form of life. Indeed it shares the defects of all naturalistic arguments.[1] The argument from function, in other words, would only be valid if the principle were accepted that man ought to develop that in which he differs from animals. And how could this principle be justified?

The doctrine of function has many other difficulties about it which add to its implausibility as an argument. Nevertheless in its classical form it was on the right lines in attempting to justify the good life for man by an argument which appeals to man's use of reason; its defects as an argument derive from the attempt to fit the use of reason as content into a naturalistic form of argument. The proper way in which it should feature is as the starting place for some kind of transcendental argument, which attempts to make explicit what a person is committed to who makes use of his reason in attempting to answer the question 'What ought I to do?'

If anyone asks this question seriously, as has been argued before,[2] he must assume that there are general principles of some sort that make reasons relevant. Most of them will be of an interpersonal sort which limit one man's pursuit of good or of what he wants in relation to the demands and claims of others; but giving content to this interpersonal system of rules are judgments about the interests of the individuals

[1] See *supra*, Ch. III, Sec. 2.
[2] See Ch. IV.

concerned. Without such a content of interests there would be nothing for interpersonal rules to regulate.

The notion of 'interests', as will be shown later, is complex.[1] It combines a judgment about something being good or worth while with a judgment about its suitability to the individual in question. Things, of course, can be good in the sense that they are instrumental to or lead on to other things that are good. Similarly many answers to the question 'What ought I to do?' advise on policies and courses of action which will promote what is good or what is in the interest of a particular individual. We are not here concerned with such instrumental or technical judgments but with judgments about the activities or states of affairs which are intrinsically good, from which instrumental or technical judgments derive their normative force. That there must be such judgments about ends is obvious enough. Otherwise giving reasons for actions would be an endless paper-chase. It is with judgments such as these, which are answers to the questions 'Why do this rather than that?' when instrumental considerations are ruled out, that we are here concerned. In the next chapter we will touch briefly on instrumental judgments about means.

What has to be shown, therefore, is why a person who asks the question 'Why do this rather than that?' must pick out activities having certain characteristics rather than others. The first step must be to make explicit what seriously asking this question presupposes; for such reflection about activities is surely something that some do in varying degrees and others scarcely at all. The obvious point to make, first of all, is that asking this question seriously presupposes that the questioner is capable, to a certain extent, of a non-instrumental and disinterested attitude. He can see, in other words, that there are considerations intrinsic to activities themselves which constitute reasons for pursuing them, as distinct from considerations connected with what such activities might lead up to which usually relate to the satisfaction of what Plato called the 'necessary appetites'. It is surprising, as a matter of fact, how many people are strangers to this attitude. This type of probing is not pushed very far by the majority of men. Their way of life over and above those things which they do because of their station and its duties, because of general social rules, and because of palpable considerations of their interest, is largely the outcome of habit, social pressure, sympathy and attraction towards what is immediately pleasurable.

[1] See Ch. VI, Sec. 1.

What considerations, then, could there be which would induce a man to choose one activity rather than another once he has achieved the degree of disinterestedness and detachment necessary to pose this as a serious question? The answer must be that considerations must derive from the nature of the activities themselves and the possible relations between them within a coherent pattern of life. In so far as he is capable of asking this question of his life generally he must also be capable of appreciating that particular activities can be appraised because of the standards immanent in them rather than because of what they lead on to. For how else, in general, could this attitude of disinterestedness be learnt save by participating in activities which had their own built-in standards of excellence? It is significant that the Greeks, when they asked this question of their life, turned naturally to the analogy of the arts. They looked at their lives as a whole in ways made familiar to them by engaging in artistic creation and appreciation, which are paradigm cases of disinterested activity. It is, therefore, not surprising that the good life for them was the supreme example of an art. Aristotle's man of practical wisdom is the man who is an artist in shaping his own conative tendencies and giving expression to them in an appropriate manner on the appropriate occasion. One of Socrates' most telling criticisms of Thrasymachus in the *Republic* was his contention that, if knowledge is involved in the life of the superman as well as the mere pursuit of power, then there must be, taking the analogy of other practical arts, limits and standards determining right and wrong ways of doing things. If a man is going to be an artist even in something as limited as self-aggrandizement, there must be standards defining skilful and appropriate ways of bringing about even this end which are important to him. Machiavelli obviously admired the 'virtue' of the Prince which he displayed in inviting all his enemies to supper and putting them all to death in one masterly stroke.

It has been argued already that to understand characterizations such as elegant, ingenious, shrewd, appropriate, neat and cogent from the inside is, in a sense, to be positively inclined towards doing things in some ways rather than others. Such considerations must have an appeal to a person who is capable of appraising activities purely from the point of view of what is involved in them. They pick out the pleasures characteristic of these activities. But there are other dimensions of such activities. To ask the question 'Why do this rather than that?' cannot be divorced from questions of time and commitment. An activity must go on for a time and if one is deciding to spend time in one way rather than another surely questions relating to boredom must be relevant. From this point of view there must be some kind of preference for activities which are capable of holding a person's attention for a certain span of time, and which provide constant sources of pleasure and satisfaction. Washing glasses requires a certain amount of skill and attention; but the thought of spending hours at it must surely appal any reflective person if it is regarded as something which is intrinsically worth while rather than as necessary for health or domestic harmony. But blowing glass is quite another matter. Glass is resistant and full of surprises when it has to be shaped in ways in which it is not when, in its finished form, it has to be washed. Anyone, therefore, who is thinking seriously about how to spend his time cannot but go for activities which afford rich opportunities for employing his wits, resources and sensitivities in situations in which there is a premium on unpredictability and opportunities for skill—and a sense of the fitting. Activities based on the satisfaction of the necessary appetites will thus become transformed. Eating will be transformed into elaborate dinners where great skill and taste can be shown in the selection of dishes and drinks and in the opportunities afforded for conversation; sex will become transformed into an elaborate display of skill and sensitivity in the art of courting and making love. Both will be invested with all sorts of skills and standards and both will be spun out to circumvent their transience. And both, of course, can degenerate into highly civilized perversions.

Another dimension involved in asking the question 'Why do this rather than that?' must be that of mutual compatibility. This is where talk of happiness, integration, and the harmony of the soul has application. The question is not whether something should be indulged in *for the sake of* something else but whether indulging in some activity to a considerable extent is compatible with indulging in another which may be equally worth while. A man who wants to give equal expression to his passions for golf, gardening, and girls is going to have problems, unless he works out his priorities and imposes some sort of schedules on the use of his time. And there may be some worth-while activities that simply cannot be combined in a coherent pattern of life—athletics for instance, and observing the nocturnal habits of animals. The coherence theory of goodness has obvious application when this dimension of the question 'Why do this rather than that?' is opened up. The appeal to coherence, however, may be necessary; but it cannot be sufficient. For trivial activities could be combined in a coherent pattern of life, and it gives no ground for grading activities which might be mutually compatible.

4. THE CASE FOR CURRICULUM ACTIVITIES

This defect of the coherence theory might be regarded as a general defect of the argument to date. For no reason has yet been produced to show that the pursuit of science or art is any more worth while than playing golf or bridge, which share the character of being disinterested, civilized, and skilful pursuits. Yet it is the former rather than the latter types of activities which feature on the curriculum of schools and universities.

To justify the special importance of curriculum activities considerations could be produced relating to their point; reference could also be made to the opportunities provided for discrimination and skill. In relation to the first type of consideration philosophers have usually produced strong arguments for theoretical activities. They have claimed, not altogether convincingly, that the objects of most activities have certain obvious disadvantages when compared with the pursuit of truth or the creation of beauty. The ends of eating and sex, for instance, depend to a large extent on bodily conditions which are cyclic in character and which limit the time which can be spent on them; there are no such obvious limitations imposed on theoretical activities. The objects, too, of the life of the politician, of the businessman, or of the philanderer are necessarily competitive. If one man acquires power, riches, or a mistress like Aspasia, this means that others are disappointed; but in theoretical activities, although there are acute rivalries and although fashions exert a terrible tyranny, it is absurd to conceive of the object of pursuit under the aspect of ownership or possession. It is absurd for a man to be jealous of another philosopher in the same sort of way as he might be jealous of his wife's lover, or of a business rival. Questions of scarcity of the object cannot arise either; for no one is prevented from pursuing truth or painting pictures if many others get absorbed in the same quest. There is no question either, as Spinoza argued so strongly, of the object perishing or passing away. To get attached to pets, people or possessions is a bad bet *sub specie aeternitatis*; for there is one thing that we know about them—they will die or become worn out with use and age. No such fate awaits the objects of theoretical activities; for as long as there is an order of the world there will always be further things to find out about it. To love the world under this aspect is to have a permanent object which is safe for ever.

Theoretical activities could also be defended in respect of the unending opportunities for skill and discrimination which they provide. Most

157

activities consist in bringing about the same state of affairs in a variety of ways under differing conditions. One dinner differs from another just as one game of bridge differs from another. But there is a static quality about them in that they both have either a natural or a conventional objective which can be attained in a limited number of ways. In science or history there is no such attainable objective. For truth is not an object that can be attained; it is an aegis under which there must always be progressive development. To discover something, to falsify the views of one's predecessors, necessarily opens up fresh things to be discovered, fresh hypotheses to be falsified. There must therefore necessarily be unending opportunities for fresh discrimination and judgment and for the development of further skills. The quest has begun to falter when it gets in the hands of those who are wedded to a rigid methodology. Scratch golfers often get bored with the game because they have mastered it. It seems pointless to pursue excellence in many spheres beyond a certain point. But it is inconceivable that anyone could get bored in the same sort of way with science or philosophy. The nature of the pursuits precludes any such finality with its linked sense of mastery.

Some of these are quite good arguments for pursuing science or philosophy as if they were what we call games or pastimes; but they are unconvincing because science or philosophy or history manifestly are not just pastimes, and it is from the character which they share over and above what they have in common with games and pastimes that the strongest arguments for them derive. The first is the nature of their cognitive concern. In so far as knowledge is involved in games and pastimes, this is limited to the hived off end of the activity which may be morally indifferent. A man may know a great deal about cricket if he is a devotee of the game; but it would be fanciful to pretend that his concern to find out things is linked with any serious purpose, unless the game is viewed under an aesthetic or moral aspect. Cricket is classed as a game because its end is morally unimportant. Indeed an end has almost to be invented to make possible the various manifestations of skill. What a cricketer or onlooker knows is therefore harnessed to his intention of playing or judging cricket. If, however, he is interested in cricket as a sociologist or psychologist might be, then his interest is really in the behaviour of men as exemplified in cricket, not in judging or playing cricket for its own sake.

It may well be that people in fact come to understand each other better, to co-operate better with them, and to develop fine moral characters as a result of playing cricket. It may, too, be of great social value in the integration of a community.[1] Games may thus be of educational value; indeed play generally may be regarded as an important vehicle of education because 'serious' things may be better assimilated when they are not taught primarily under this aspect. Cricket, too, when seen through the eyes of a Neville Cardus, may acquire an aesthetic dimension. But if the participants in games come to *look on* games as exercises in morality, aesthetic grace, or in understanding others, they cease to be merely games. Often in golf people have to be reminded that it is 'only a game'. This is tantamount to saying that playing it supremely well or badly, or winning or losing, should not be regarded as significant from the point of view of the universe, or made significant because of a suggestion to play for £5 rather than 5s. Conversely when people say that politics has become 'merely a game' they imply that an end has been set up like the maintenance of power which has become morally adrift and arbitrarily set aside and isolated from the moral concerns of a community.

Curriculum activities, on the other hand, such as science, history, literary appreciation, and poetry are 'serious' in that they illuminate other areas of life and contribute much to the quality of living. They have, secondly, a wide-ranging cognitive content which distinguishes them from games. Skills, for instance, do not have a wide-ranging cognitive content. There is very little to know about riding bicycles, swimming, or golf. It is largely a matter of 'knowing how' rather than of 'knowing that', of knack rather than of understanding. Furthermore what there is to know throws very little light on much else. In history, science, or literature, on the other hand, there is an immense amount to know, and if it is properly assimilated, it constantly throws light on, widens, and deepens one's view of countless other things.

Some games in which skills are systematized, such as bridge and chess, have considerable cognitive content; but this is largely internal to them. Part of what is meant by calling something a 'game' is that it is set apart from the main business of living, complete in itself, and limited to particular times and places.[2] Games can be conceived of as being of educational importance only in so far as they provide opportunities for acquiring knowledge, qualities of mind and character, aesthetic grace and skills that have application in a wider area of life. Their importance for moral education, for instance, is obvious enough. For virtues such as

[1] See, for instance, James, C. L., *Beyond a Boundary* (London, Hutchinson, 1963).

[2] See Huizinga, J., *Homo Ludens* (London, Kegan Paul, 1949), Ch. I.

courage, fairness, persistence, and loyalty have to be exhibited in a pre-eminent degree in many games—especially those that involve teamwork. Others give scope for judgment, coolheadedness, and insight into other people's motives. The presumption of those who believe in the educational importance of games is that the situations which they present, and in which virtues have to be cultivated and exercised, are relevantly similar to situations in life of a less self-contained character.

Science, history, literary appreciation, philosophy, and other such cultural activities are like games in being disinterested pursuits. They can be, and to a large extent are, pursued for the sake of values intrinsic to them rather than for the sake of extrinsic ends. But their cognitive concerns and far-ranging cognitive content give them a value denied to other more circumscribed activities which leads us to call them serious pursuits. They are 'serious' and cannot be considered merely as if they were particularly delectable pastimes, because they consist largely in the explanation, assessment, and illumination of the different facets of life. They thus insensibly change a man's view of the world. A man who has read and digested Burke finds it difficult to look on Americans in quite the same way; his concept of jealousy develops overtones after seeing Othello. If he is also a trained scientist he scarcely sees the same world as his untrained contemporary; for he is being trained in modes of thought that cannot be tied down to particular times and places. A man who devotes himself to a game, on the other hand, does not thereby equip himself with a cognitive content that spills over and transforms his view of other things in life. He may, of course, regard other activities such as war or politics as if they are games of cricket on a large scale. This may shape his attitude to other activities. But it will not transform his understanding of them in the way that a study of psychology, social science and history should. It may well be that those who stood their ground resolutely at Waterloo learnt to do something very similar on the playing fields of Eton. But they did not learn to reason why there, nor to see in such a battle what Tolstoy saw on the fields of Borodino.

The point, then, about activities such as science, philosophy and history is that, although they are like games in that they are disinterested activities which can be pursued at set times and places, they can never be hived off and confined to such times and places. A person who has pursued them systematically develops conceptual schemes and forms of appraisal which transform everything else that he does. It is possible to conceive of what is being done in an almost infinite number of ways. A

Marxist, for instance, who is stirring up strife in a factory or selling horses on a farm in order to buy a tractor, does not see himself as just doing these things; he probably sees his actions as moments in the dialectical progression of historical change. There are at least two truths contained in the slogan 'Education is for life' depending on how it is interpreted. One is that if people are properly educated, so that they want to go on when the pressures are off, the conceptual schemes and forms of appraisal, into which they have been initiated in schools and universities, continue to develop. Another is that 'living' cannot be separated from the ways in which people have learnt to conceive and appraise what they are doing.

Enough has been said, then, to indicate the main characteristics which distinguish activities like science and philosophy from less serious pursuits such as games and pastimes. Why, then, must a person who asks seriously the question 'Why do this rather than that?' be more committed to these sorts of activities which have this special sort of cognitive concern and content built into them? The answer is obvious enough, namely that these sorts of inquiries are all, in their different ways, relevant to answering the sort of question that he is asking. If his question is concerned, as has been shown, with the nature and quality of the possible activities which he can pursue, he has really embarked upon a difficult and almost endless quest. For the description of disinterested activities, and hence the discussion of their value, is not a matter of mere observation. They depend on how he has learnt to conceive them. He cannot simply engage in such activities; he has to see what he is doing in a certain way. This will depend very much on how he has been taught to conceive it, on the concept of what science, art, or cookery is in his culture. This has been formed in the main by the differentiated forms of understanding that have been developed. Is the historical or religious or moral dimension to what he is doing emphasized? Is his concept of himself as an artist or a scientist one which emphasizes pleasure or social responsibility or cosmic piety? Does he think of science or art as an ideological superstructure growing out of an economic base or as the expression of unrecognized sexual strivings? Or has he been encouraged to think of such activities as somehow self-contained and unrelated to the rest of his experience as a sentient being? What a man thinks of science, or history or art *as* will thus depend upon his general conceptual scheme which is formed by the cross-fertilization of such inquiries with practical experience conducted in the light of deposits of previous inquiries, however embryonic they may be. To regard such inquiries or creative activities, therefore, as merely pastimes is to ignore the fact that they are the main determinants of the conceptual schemes picking out all other pastimes as well as of what is to count as a pastime.

It might be argued that this is a bit far-fetched; for cannot a man be just doing science or creating a work of art as he might be just raising his arm? There are two answers to such an objection. Firstly what is it just to raise one's arm? Presumably this description rules out either the suggestion that the arm is just rising, like a facial twitch, or that it is being raised for some other reason, such as to attract attention. Even this minimal notion is only intelligible within a conceptual scheme for the description and explanation of actions. Secondly 'doing science' or 'writing a poem' are not actions but activities. This makes a great difference to the determinateness of description. Because of the obvious connection with bodily movement the claim that a person is just raising his arm is intelligible; but 'just doing science' or 'just writing a poem' are not closely connected with any particular actions or bodily movements. The suggestion, therefore, that a person is 'just doing science' may be intelligible in so far as, negatively speaking, it constitutes a denial that a person is trying to bring about some other end by scientific activity; but positively it is open to manifold interpretations. For, in what does 'doing science' consist that corresponds in any way to the determinate bodily movements involved in raising the arm? If a person claims that he is 'just doing science' the only appropriate answer is a request for a more specific characterization of what he conceives of 'science' as. In providing this he will involve himself in a story to which history, philosophy, social science, aesthetic sensitivity, morality, and other such forms of knowledge and awareness are inescapably relevant. It may indeed transpire that he regards it rather like writing a poem.

In so far, therefore, as a person seriously asks the question 'Why do this rather than that?' he can only answer it by trying this and that and by thinking about what he is doing in various ways which are inseparable from the doing of it. When he stands back and reflects about what it is that he is doing he then engages in the sorts of activities of which the curriculum of a university is largely constructed. He will find himself embarking upon those forms of inquiry such as science, history, literature and philosophy which are concerned with the description, explanation, and assessment of different forms of human activity. It would be irrational for a person who seriously asks himself the question 'Why do this rather than that?' to close his mind arbitrarily to any form of inquiry which might throw light on the question which he is asking. This is presumably one of the basic arguments for a 'liberal education'. It is presumably, also, the logical outcome of Socrates' claim that the unexamined life is not worth living.

The force of this argument for curriculum activities might be admitted, but it might be said that introducing this further feature of their cognitive content, in virtue of which any rational man who seriously asks 'Why do this rather than that?', must grant their superiority over games, provides an argument only for their *instrumental* value. It does not show that they should be pursued for their own sake, particularly if they are rather boring. This argument, too, also shows the great importance of physical education. For without a fit body a man's attempts to answer the question 'Why do this rather than that?' might be sluggish or slovenly. So it provides, it seems, a transcendental deduction of the principle of physical fitness. The seeming correctness of such a deduction does not establish that physical exercise is worth while in itself. It shows why a rational man ought to engage both in physical exercise and in theoretical activities; but it does not show that he must necessarily regard the latter as any more worth while in themselves than the former. And palpably many rational men do find theoretical activities worth while in themselves but do not take the same view of physical exercise, whatever status they accord it as being instrumentally valuable.

Is there, then, no further argument which could support the worthwhileness of theoretical speculation or aesthetic explorations?[1] Does their value depend solely either on their instrumentality to answering the question 'Why do this rather than that?' or on their possessing to a more pre-eminent degree characteristics such as skill and complexity, which they share with games and in virtue of which they are better *as* games or pastimes? The answer is partly to question the appropriateness of the notion of instrumentality in this context. Thinking scientifically for instance, is not exactly instrumental to answering the question 'Why do this rather than that?'; for it transforms the question by transforming

---

[1] Aesthetic activities involve special difficulties for this argument. There is, first of all, the difference between the creative and appreciative aspects of them. There is, secondly, the difference between the arts in respect of their concern for truth. It might reasonably be argued that literature and poetry, for instance, are developments of a dimension of awareness of the world, while other arts, like music, may be creating, as it were, another world to be aware of. The latter would, therefore, be more like games than like science or history. Obviously it would take a very full discussion of the different forms of aesthetic activity to settle such questions, which is beyond the scope of this book.

how 'this' and 'that' are conceived. It is built into asking the question as well as into answering it. It is not surprising that it should do this; for this is derivative from a further feature possessed by theoretical activities and not by games or pastimes. This is their 'seriousness' in a sense rather different from that already used to bring out a difference between games and theoretical activities. This sense must now be explicated.

Games have to date been regarded as not serious because, as it were, they are hived off from and contribute little to the 'business of living'; they are not usually pursued on grounds either of morality or prudence. But they are not 'serious' in another slightly different sense. They are hived off from man's curiosity about the world and his awe and concern about his own peculiar predicament in it. Any reflective person who asks the question 'Why do this rather than that?' cannot arbitrarily limit the context in which this question is asked. If he asks this question seriously he must answer it in the consciousness that there are regularities in nature, one of them being his own mortality as a man. Whitehead gave expression to this point in his own way when he said: 'Religion is what the individual does with his solitariness. . . . In its solitariness the spirit asks, What, in the way of value is the attainment of life? And it can find no such value till it has merged its individual claim with that of the objective universe. Religion is world loyalty.'[1] A man's consciousness of possibilities may be highly differentiated in scientific, aesthetic, historical and religious forms of awareness. Or these possibilities may be only obscurely intimated in an undifferentiated way. But in so far as he can stand back from his life and *ask* the question 'Why this rather than that?' he must already have a serious concern for truth built into his consciousness. For how can a serious practical question be asked unless a man also wants to acquaint himself as well as he can with the situation out of which the question arises and of the facts of various kinds which provide the framework for possible answers? The various theoretical inquiries are explorations of these different facets of his experience. To ask the question 'Why do this rather than that?' seriously is therefore, however embryonically, to be committed to those inquiries which are defined by their serious concern with those aspects of reality which give context to the question which he is asking. In brief the justification of such activities is not purely instrumental because they are involved in *asking* the question 'Why do this rather than that?', as well as in answering it.

[1] Whitehead, A. N., *Religion in the Making* (Cambridge University Press, 1926), pp. 47 and 60.

This attitude is not simply one of curiosity, though this may provide some sort of natural basis for it in the way in which sympathy for others may provide a natural basis for respect. It is rather the attitude of passionate concern about truth that informed Socrates' saying that the unexamined life is not worth living. It lies at the heart of all rational activities in which there is a concern for what is true or false, appropriate or inappropriate, correct or incorrect. Anyone who asks seriously the question 'Why do this rather than that?' must already possess it; for it is built into this sense of 'serious'. It is impossible to give any further justification for it; for it is presupposed in all serious attempts at justification. It is thus the motivational linch-pin not simply of the ethical system here defended but of any system that is based on discussion and argument.

The old contrast between reason and passion is therefore quite out of place. For, as has already been argued, rational activities all have their distinctive forms of appraisals such as cogent, precise, elegant, relevant, and consistent, which provide motivations which are internal to the forms of thought in question. Furthermore such activities will only be seriously engaged in by those who have a serious concern or passion for the point of the activity, which is the ascertaining of what is true, valid, appropriate and correct. Such a passion is different from that of the dogmatist who is attached to particular truths rather than to the overall concern for truth together with the principles of procedure, such as liberty and tolerance, which are necessary to implement it. (See Chapter VII *infra*.)

Any rational man, therefore, who is also a teacher, must have an abiding concern that this sort of attitude should be passed on to others. For without it the basic motivation will be lacking for teaching, in a proper sense, to be effective. 'Teaching', to repeat what Scheffler suggests[1], 'requires us to reveal our reasons to the student and, by so doing, to submit them to his evaluation and criticism.' But this presupposes that the student is disposed to listen to reasons and to submit seriously to the conditions of discussion. How is such an attitude developed? It certainly is not universal. Indeed it is rare to find people who really listen to what other people say. Rarer still is the humble determination to take account of objections. This determination certainly is not innate; for, as Bacon pointed out, the willingness to look for negative instances, which count against one's cherished opinions, goes against the inveterate tendency of the human mind to generalize on the basis of a few instances and to

---

[1] See *supra*, pp. 39, 40.

believe what one wishes to be true. It is mainly caught from those who are already possessed of it, who exhibit it in their manner of discussion and in their teaching. But unless what was so intimated were absorbing it would be difficult to account for its strength and persistence in those who acquire it; for mannerisms and more evanescent attitudes are also picked up in this sort of way. Such an attitude is surely in some way called forth by man's predicament as a thinking being in a universe whose local conditions have made thinking possible. The teacher helps to awaken an awareness of the manifold aspects of this predicament; he indicates in some way how things are and the appropriateness of conducting life on the basis of such considerations.

CHAPTER VI

THE CONSIDERATION OF INTERESTS

INTRODUCTION

The treatment of what is worth while has been somewhat selective so far because of the cardinal importance of showing that there are reasons for choosing some forms of activity rather than others as ends in themselves. This is of importance for ethical theory generally and of particular importance for the thesis about education put forward in this book; for it has been maintained that education is concerned with initiation into activities which are worth while in themselves and which have certain cognitive features. If no reasons could be given for the pursuit of such activities the main thesis of the book would lack a solid ethical foundation. It is hoped that satisfactory reasons have been given. Other questions must now be discussed without which the treatment would be decidedly lop-sided.

It was stressed in the Appendix to Part One that, though education is of the essence of a school, schools must also fulfil functions of a more instrumental nature. On the one hand they must act as orphanages for children with parents. On the other hand they must have regard to the need of the community for citizens who are trained in specific ways. They must, in other words, consider the interests of children and what is in their interest and have regard also for the public interest. These notions must now be briefly examined and their ethical foundations made explicit.

1. THE CONCEPT OF 'INTERESTS'

The concept of 'interest' is a very ambiguous one. It is worth dwelling on it for a moment not only to make clear what it is that has to be justified in this chapter but also because much educational talk about having regard to children's interests is bedevilled by crucial ambiguities.

The trouble arises from the fact that there are both normative and psychological uses of 'interest'. In the psychological sense[1] we speak of what people are interested in, meaning what they are disposed to attend

[1] See White, A. R., 'The Notion of Interest' in *Philosophical Quarterly*, Vol. 14, No. 57, 1964.

to or take notice of; we also speak of interests in a more dispositional sense when we wish to refer to people's hobbies, or those activities in which they will tend to be interested in a more permanent sort of way. In the normative sense 'interests' is used both in a legalistic sense to speak of spheres of action or activity to which a person has a right[1] and in a more general sense[2] to speak of those things which are both worth while and in some way appropriate for the individual in question, i.e. beneficial to him. When we speak of considering a person's interests we are using 'interest' in this latter normative sense. This is the sense of 'interest' which is being used when it is said that the school must be concerned with the interests of individual children. A teacher, like a guardian in relation to a ward, who is mindful of children's interests, is not necessarily exercised about what they actually want or are interested in, psychologically speaking, or in their hobbies; he (or she) is concerned either about protecting them in what he thinks they have a right to pursue or with ensuring that they pursue what is both worth while and suitable for them, i.e. beneficial for them. He therefore has to consider not only what in general is worth while pursuing but also what the potentialities and capacities are of the particular children for whom he is responsible.

Very often when a person is exercising himself about such problems on behalf of another it is said that he is concerned about what is *in* that person's interest. Needless to say people are also most exercised about this question in relation to themselves. A judgment about what is *in* a person's interest is slightly different from one about a person's interests in that it introduces instrumental considerations as well as considerations of individual differences in the enjoyment of what is worth while. It indicates some policy or course of action that will promote an end which is assumed to be desirable. For instance, it might be said to a man bent on being a headmaster that it was not in his interest to divorce his wife or that it was in his interest to go to church regularly. Alternatively such judgments may relate to general policies which are thought manifestly to promote the pursuit of a number of ends which are constitutive of a person's style of life. When, for instance, a person is told that his tendency to associate with beatniks is not in his interest the suggestion is that it militates generally against his way of life. It is imprudent.

[1] See Lamont, W. D., *The Principles of Moral Judgment* (London, Oxford University Press, 1946), Ch. III.

[2] See Benn, S. I., ' "Interests" in Politics' in *Proc. Aristotelian Soc.*, Vol. LX, 1959–60.

Such judgments, however, about what is in a person's interest are not entirely relative to the individuals to whom the advice is offered. For it is generally assumed that there are certain courses of action and policies that are in no individual's interest such as the impairment of his faculties. It is assumed that the promotion of health and security enhance any man's pursuit of good, whatever it may be. It is assumed in other words that, whatever a person's interest may be, health and security will help him to achieve it and that pain, disease and insecurity will militate against it. Therefore, there are some judgments about what is in a man's interest that are not relative to any particular individual; for there is some general advice relating to general conditions that will maximize his opportunities for pursuing his interest, whatever it may be, and others which will militate against it. Hobbes, for instance, was justified in thinking that the constant threat of sudden death was in no man's interest, according to ordinary standards of thinking. For obviously such a threat would hamper and distract him in doing most of the things which he might think desirable.

There are some who think that such judgments about what is in a person's interests are instrumental judgments related to the actual wants of individuals or to what they are interested in, psychologically speaking.[1] But a return to the Hobbesian example, I think, refutes this view very quickly. For it could very easily be replied to anyone, who was impressed by Hobbes' point of view, that the pursuit of good activities would be enhanced by the constant threat of sudden death; for if men had to live each day as if it were their last they might take more seriously the question 'Which activities are worth pursuing?' Therefore, it could be argued, it is in every man's interest to live under the constant threat of sudden death. This objection to Hobbes' position, which is not fanciful for those who have lived with death as a constant companion, brings out the point that judgments of what is in a man's interest cannot be regarded as relative purely to the sorts of things he happens to want or to be interested in pursuing. For the objection is not on the grounds that the prediction is false that removal of the constant threat of death will enhance a man's opportunities for pursuing those activities which as a matter of fact interest him; it is rather that he tends to pursue things that are not worth while. The removal of the constant threat of death will

[1] See Barry, B. M., 'The Public Interest', *Proc. Aristotelian Soc.*, Suppl. Vol. XXXVIII, 1964, Section II, who puts forward such a naturalistic analysis that is rejected here.

maximize his opportunities for doing what he wants; but, alas, he wants to do all the wrong things.

Considering people's interests, therefore, or considering what is in their interest, cannot be equivalent simply to determining what ought to be done either on the basis of what people actually want or on a basis of what will maximize opportunities for doing what they want to do. For, as has been previously observed, though we think it regrettable that some people cannot get what they want, we also think it regrettable that other people want just what they get. In other words judgments are passed on people's wants in deciding what is in their interest.

The concept of the 'public interest' is a difficult one to elucidate.[1] Some interpret it as a blanket term used to justify policies that are difficult to defend in a more determinate way. But it is possible to give more specificity to it by pursuing two notions that are intimated by it. The first is that of pursuing a policy that is not obviously biased in favour of any particular private or individual interest. If the NUT is beseeched to have regard to the public interest, the force of the injunction is to get them to consider the interests of people in the community other than teachers, not to look at their proposals purely in terms of a sectional interest. This is the negative interpretation of the concept of the 'public interest'. A more positive notion is that of the promotion of policies that are in any man's interest, whatever form his individual pursuit of his interests may take. The supply of food, the provision of conditions of security, health and transport services would be in the public interest if this more positive interpretation is adopted.

In both senses of 'the public interest' the school is obviously concerned with promoting it; for the training of technicians, typists, and countless other forms of skilled workers is necessary to the viability of the economy of an industrialized society. Unless the wheels of industry keep turning the conditions will be absent which will allow any man to pursue a multitude of individual interests. And keeping the wheels of industry turning is a policy that favours no particular sectional interest. This is what leads economists to speak of money spent on schools as a public investment.

2. THE QUESTION OF JUSTIFICATION

The last chapter was mainly preoccupied with arguments about the

[1] See Barry, B. M., op. cit., whose explication of 'public' is more acceptable than his explication of 'interest'.

content of people's interests. The normative notion of 'interests' combines judgments about what is worth while or desirable (judgments of content) with judgments about individual capacity and potentiality. The attempt was made to provide a rational foundation for the former type of judgment, but no attention was paid to the question 'Whose interests should be promoted?' As yet no argument has been given for refusing to limit the enjoyment of worth-while activities to an *élite* whose psychological capacities equip them pre-eminently for their pursuit, or to any individual who asks the question 'Why do this rather than that?' Why should not a community be arranged so that only he could enjoy such activities for what they are in themselves?

Why, in other words, should not a man who asks the question 'Why do this rather than that?' limit consideration of possible ends of action to those that affect only himself? Why should he not ask 'What ought I to do considering only myself?' Normally, in posing this question, we take account not only of the character of the activity in question and its compossibility with other activities which we might want to engage in; we also think that the damage it might do to others is an important consideration, whatever the intrinsic worth of the activity. Kant's claim that the development of the good will is the only unconditioned good rested on the obvious fact that all worth-while activities could be pursued for ignoble ends; it is also true that in certain circumstances their pursuit might be at the expense of others. But why should a rational man consider the interests of others? Anyone concerned with promoting the public interest has obviously to face this question.

The answer is surely that consideration of the interests of others is a presupposition of asking the question 'Why do this rather than that?' seriously. This question, as has been already pointed out, is a question in public discourse. It presupposes a situation in which men are concerned with finding answers to questions of practical policy, in which they need the help of other men. In entering into such a discussion any rational man must assume not only that there are worth-while things to do but also that he might want to engage in such worth-while things. If he thought that, having discussed such matters with his fellows, his stake in such a worth-while life was going to be completely ignored, it is difficult to conceive how he would ever take the step of engaging in such a public discussion. As a rational man he must see, too, that what applies to him applies to any other man engaging in such a discussion; for how could he think that he alone has any claims?

171

There is one question, then, about the worthwhileness of the alternatives which present themselves; there is another question about the limitation of the pursuit of such activities to some individuals rather than others. If men generally thought that no consideration was going to be given to their desire to engage in such activities, this form of discourse would lack point. As a public activity it could never get off the ground.

It is not, of course, being argued that the interests of some cannot, on any particular occasion, be shown to be more important than the interests of others. The argument is only that this has to be *shown*. The presumption relates to the consideration of interests, not to the consideration of any particular interests. Neither is it being maintained that unscrupulous men do not use the conditions of public discussion for the ruthless pursuit of their own interests. In the same way unscrupulous people trade on the presumption of truth-telling, which may well be another fundamental and independent principle presupposed by the pursuit of truth,[1] in order to practise their private deceit and exploitation. Individuals too, however rational, may be overcome by the psychological strength of other ways of looking at any particular situation. None of this is being denied. All that is being maintained is that the principle of the consideration of interests is presupposed by the general practice of discussion directed towards discovering what is good or what ought to be done, and that any individual who seriously engages in such a practice must, to that extent, do so under the conditions imposed by such a principle. Private ploys are parasitic on public practices in the same sort of way as, more generally, a private language presupposes a public language, with all the principles (e.g. non-contradiction) that are necessary for it to have meaning or point and to be applied. This is the truth embedded in the more specific and less defensible claim of writers such as Toulmin who claim that moral discourse must be distinguished by its function of *reconciling* the independent aims and wills of a community of people.[2] It follows, therefore, that reasons have to be produced for limiting consideration of interests either to those of oneself or to those of others. In other words the question is not 'What ought I to do considering only

---

[1] See Winch, P., 'Nature and Convention' in *Proc. Aristotelian Soc.*, Vol. LX, 1959–60. Winch relates this principle to the more general possibility of communication. A stronger case can be made for it as presupposed by forms of discourse whose point is to find out what is true, correct, good, etc., not by language in general.

[2] See Toulmin, S. C., *An Examination of the Place of Reason in Ethics* (Cambridge University Press, 1950), esp. Ch. 10.

myself?' Indeed, if the first principle of justice is accepted, some further reason would have to be given for limiting considerations of good produced to those which affect only the questioner.

It may be that, psychologically speaking, people are much more prone to take more account of self-regarding than of other-regarding alternatives. But psychologically speaking they may also be more inclined to go for alternatives that are immediately attractive than for those that have qualities in virtue of which they are worth while. To correct such psychological proclivities is one of the basic tasks of moral education. For as Butler put it, the trouble with most people is not just that they lack benevolence but that they lack prudence also.[1] But the strength of such psychological tendencies is no ground for either refusing to ask the question of practical reason or to limit it, when asked, to possibilities that can affect only the questioner. The question is 'What are there reasons for doing?', not 'What are there reasons just for me to do?' Given that there are things that there are reasons for doing, questions of distribution are further questions.

So also are questions about the psychological capacities of individuals which fit them for doing some things rather than others. The school, assisted by advice from psychologists, is very much concerned with these latter questions. The growth of counselling services in schools, to supplement or replace the old system of careers masters and visiting psychologists, is evidence of the growing realization that such judgments are very complex. Whether such an institutionalization of prudential advice is a desirable development is a further question which raises considerations beyond the scope of this chapter.

3. BASIC RULES

Anyone who considers seriously questions to do with the public interest must come to the conclusion that not only commodities such as food and raw materials are necessary to it, but also the observance of a minimal code of basic rules which are in any man's interests to observe and have observed. For without such a framework of order and security no one will be able to pursue for long either what he wants or what is good—allowing for the probability that these two do not always coincide. Such a minimal system of rules is manifestly justifiable as being in the interest of any man asking the question of practical reason.

[1] See Butler, J., *Sermons on Human Nature*, Sermon I.

These 'basic rules' of social life are not presuppositions of practical discourse like fundamental principles; for they are contingent upon certain very general empirical facts about men and their situation upon earth. The most basic fact is the one to which Hobbes gave such prominence—man's indisputable mortality and his universal desire, other things being equal, to remain alive, and his universal aversion to pain. To be alive, needless to say, is the general condition necessary to satisfying any other desire or policy; so whatever a man's attitude to the pain and awesomeness involved in death, it must be in his interest to remain alive as a condition of either satisfying any other desire or of implementing any answer whatever to the question 'What ought I to do?' Another universal fact is man's vulnerability to attack from others[1] and approximate equality in this respect in relation to other men. Even a child can kill a man if he can catch him asleep. Another such fact is man's need of other men, if he is to survive, and his limited social feeling with regard to them, which may only extend to his family or tribe. There is, in addition, the limited supply of food, shelter, etc., which are necessary for man's survival.

This concatenation of general empirical conditions makes a limited number of basic rules imperative, the acceptance of which is necessary for any form of social life, man and his environment being what they are. Indeed acceptance of such rules by a number of individuals almost constitutes a definition of a 'society'. There must be rules of some sort covering injury to life and property and permitting interchange and transfer of goods. Unless, too, the question of interest is going to be arbitrarily confined to the doing of what is worth while by one individual or to the butterfly-like existence of a group of people with no intention of perpetuating the pursuit of what is worth while beyond their lifetime, there must also be rules of some sort regulating reproduction and the care of the young. When rules develop in clusters in such cases there exists what is known as an 'institution' such as property or marriage whose function it is to put members of a society under specific forms of obligation. The details of such obligations depend, of course, on contingent circumstances and vary from society to society; but that there must be rules which create obligations in these areas is obvious enough if impartial consideration is given to what is in the interest of any man under the general conditions of his mortality.

[1] The details of this account of basic rules owes much to Hart, H. A. L., *The Concept of Law* (London, Oxford University Press, 1961), Ch. IX, Sec. 2.

In brief, a strong case, in terms of the consideration of interest, can be made for basic rules which are universal such as those prohibiting murder, theft, and the breaking of contracts which are quite compatible with different interpretations of these types of practice. Such rules can be justified without entering into the difficult discussion, in which we were engaged in the last chapter, of what the characteristics must be of those worth-while activities which are underpinned by the basic rules which have been outlined.

4. PRACTICAL ACTIVITIES

Any school which is conscious of its social function must supplement the family in equipping children with such basic rules which are equivalent more or less to social hygiene just as it must also give some kind of training in basic skills, which are instrumentally necessary for the economy of a society. This, of course, can take the form of moral education rather than of some narrowly conceived type of indoctrination, just as technical training can be conducted in such a way that it is also of educational value.

What, however, is to be said of those who emerge with a burning zeal to promote the public good, who devote their lives to a practical form of life in politics or social work just as others devote themselves to business, farming or to medicine as activities. They may do so out of duty or out of necessity. On the other hand they may do so because of the pleasure that is in it. Are such activities any less worth while than theoretical pursuits?

To answer this question the same point must be made as was developed in the context of a person who was imagined as 'just doing science'.[1] What there is in politics, administration, or business depends to a large extent on what a person conceives of himself as doing when he engages in them. A politician or an administrator is, properly speaking, concerned with the promotion of the public interest. This is an endless pursuit; for in political life there is no definite terminating point or secure resting place. Its promotion can also involve endless skill, finesse, and enterprise. Its structure as an activity, however, will depend very much on the cognitive development of its participants. Both Caesar and Pompey were engaged in politics in the dying days of the Roman Republic. But the differences in grasp and conception between these two contemporaries were so staggering that they were scarcely engaged in the same activity. This was because Caesar was a man of action with wide-ranging theoretical

---

[1] See *supra*, pp. 161, 162.

175

interests. His passion for order and his sense of the ways in which concrete objectives could be fitted into a general plan was enlivened by an understanding almost unparalleled amongst his contemporaries. The obvious enjoyment and sense of achievement which he derived from both politics and war were related to the level at which he conducted both types of operation.

An example such as that of Caesar suggests two obvious points. The first is the absurdity of supposing that theory can be confined to studies and that practical activities can be engaged in without being conceived of in a certain way depending on the theoretical understanding of the person concerned. The second is that the implementation of practical policies need not be conceived of as a succession of things done out of duty or necessity. They can take the form of activities and, as soon as they are conceived of in this way, standards and their accompanying skills begin to creep in, and what began as a series of instrumental acts can come to be delighted in for its own sake as an absorbing activity. This, presumably, is how housewives convert duties into pleasures.

What then is to be said about the moral standing of such activities? They are obviously similar to games and pastimes in that they can be delighted in for the skill that they require and for the sense of achievement that they make possible. But they are also obviously superior to games; for they are not just done for pleasure. They are serious in a way in which games are not as they fall under the principle of the consideration of interest. They are concerned with conditions of order without which the pursuit of what is good would be impossible. In this respect they are like eating and drinking which are pleasures but which are also activities necessary to the maintenance of any form of good life. They are also serious in that they are concerned with the promotion of forms of society in which other moral principles are also institutionalized— e.g. justice, equality, freedom, respect for persons. Because, however, they are partly instrumental in respect of their justification, and because they are partly dependent, in respect of their quality, on the level of understanding that goes into them, their degree of worthwhileness must depend in part on the pursuit of truth in its different forms which they sustain and by which they are transformed.

This, of course, is not to deny value to activities which have a limited cognitive content. This is extremely important when questions are raised about the education of children who are neither very intelligent nor very interested in the more theoretical types of pursuit. Cooking, for instance, is obviously an activity which is necessary for the maintenance of a way of life. But it can be done just as a tiresome chore, or it can be delighted in for the opportunities for skill and ingenuity which it affords. It can become an extremely absorbing and worth-while pursuit. It will, of course, be enhanced as an art if understanding develops about its underlying principles and if it is not just conducted on a rule of thumb basis. But in so far as it tends to become pursued for its own sake, for the values intrinsic to it, rather than purely instrumentally, it can come to contribute substantially to a quality of living.

It was argued in the first part of this book that 'education' implies both cognitive content and the disinterested pursuit of what is worth while. If activities such as cooking come to be practised in such a way that they satisfy the second criterion but the first only to a limited extent, they should not be despised on that account. It is desirable, of course, that cognitive perspective should also be developed in relation to them. But if it cannot be in the case of some children, that is no reason for concluding that such activities have no educational value. It has been argued before that, though education necessarily consists in the transmission of what is worth while, the coat of what is worth while must be cut according to the cloth of individual aptitude, which is often best assured by building in a principle of options into a curriculum. The development of understanding is not an all or nothing affair. In other words it is a question of how far the individual child can go in developing a theoretical structure for practical activities rather than a question of which children can do this and which children cannot. But for every child there are things which he or she can learn to do which involve skill and which can be engaged in with love for what they are, rather than purely instrumentally. Of obvious importance in this context are the enjoyment of personal relationships and conversation, physical prowess, dexterity, taste in clothes and in the arrangement and decoration of rooms, and the cultivation of a variety of skills which are necessary for turning a house into a place where people can live with some kind of grace and dignity.

The implication of this emphasis on the duty of the school to consider the interests of children is emphatically not that duller children should be simply encouraged to build boats, make guitars, do cookery and metal-work, whereas more intelligent children should be excluded from such practical activities and provided with a more academic curriculum. For on the one hand, one of the defects of grammar school education is, perhaps, that insufficient attention is given to practical and creative activities. On the other hand duller children are quite capable of appreciating simpler forms of activity that are often dubbed 'academic'.

It was argued in the Appendix to Part One[1] that at the early stages of education simpler forms of what is valuable are all that is possible for children. A dull child of twelve, who has a mental age of eight, is therefore in the position of an average eight-year-old in relation to his capacity for enjoying various forms of what is valuable. This is not, however, confined to practical activities. Simple stories and poetry can be appreciated, for instance, by duller children. They may never be able to reach the stage when they can appreciate fully Browning, T. S. Eliot or Henry James; but there are simpler examples of these art forms which are well within their grasp. The Bible and Homer, for instance, provide long-standing examples of poetry and stories that are well within the reach of most of the population. The pity is that nowadays horror comics and strip cartoons, which lack the qualities of simple works of art, seem to be more widely read. This general point, which has been exemplified in the field of literature, can be made equally well within the field of music, elementary science, history, and moral awareness.

In brief, education is not simply for the intelligent. It is not a question of some being capable of it and others not. It is a matter, rather, of how far individuals can progress along the same avenues of exploration. It may be that a boat is an exciting centre of interest that will provide an incentive for sustained effort. But the effort need not be directed simply towards building better and better boats. It can also be directed outwards towards history (e.g. the Sutton Hoo burial mound), towards literature and poetry which abound with tales of boats, and to elementary science which provides theories about the tides, winds, and oceans which constitute the relevant environment. The fact that some can progress further along these avenues of exploration and appreciation than others does not entail that the others can proceed no distance at all. A quality of life is not the prerogative of an intellectual *élite*.

[1] Sec. 3(a).

CHAPTER VII

FREEDOM

INTRODUCTION

So far arguments have been produced for the principles of justice and of the consideration of interests. But adherence to such principles is quite consistent with benevolent despotism; for a man could arrange the lives of others with scrupulous fairness and concern for their interests without permitting them freedom. Indeed many teachers have behaved precisely in this way towards children long after the time when they are capable of directing their own lives to a considerable extent.

It might be argued, of course, that freedom is to be justified on the grounds that it tends to promote people's interests; it maximizes their opportunities for doing what is worth while. But it is only too apparent that both men and children often choose what is bad and sink further and further into a state of degradation as their choices proceed. Parents and teachers are often put in the dilemma of choosing between letting children decide things for themselves, when what they decide will almost certainly be against their best interest, and insisting that they do what is in their manifest interest. A parent whose brilliant daughter is clamouring to marry an elderly rake rather than take up her place at a university is in just this sort of predicament.

It might be replied that these are exceptional cases and that in general the enlargement of people's freedom tends to promote their interest because it provides more opportunities for the discovery of what is good. This argument is plausible if it is confined simply to a limited choice between a variety of things that are good, e.g. a curriculum which permits many options. It is a more doubtful argument if it is extended to include bad or indifferent things as well, e.g. if children were allowed to choose drug-taking or bingo rather than art and arithmetic. It also has to meet the formidable sociological case developed by writers such as Eric Fromm[1] who argue that the development of freedom may occasion psychological strains and insecurities which induce men to fall back into a more limited, womb-like form of life. Conversely anyone who believes

---

[1] Fromm, E., *The Fear of Freedom* (London, Routledge, 1942).

in freedom would be reluctant to admit that his approval of it must be subject to the demonstration that it in fact tends to maximize good activities in the world. He would be more inclined to argue that it is desirable that men should be free rather than slaves irrespective of the consideration of such consequences. Such a conviction requires an independent argument which shows freedom to be desirable without making its desirability contingent on its tendency to promote people's interests.

A person who believes in freedom as an independent principle is not of course committed to it as an absolute principle. He may also believe in justice and the consideration of interests. He is committed to such principles subject to the condition that in any situation other principles may be more pressing. For instance, a believer in justice may have to modify claims deriving from this principle on the grounds that too rigid adherence to it may be manifestly against people's interests. Similarly a believer in freedom may have to modify his demands for it if they involve obvious harm or unfairness to others. Mill made this point very forcibly when he argued that the sole warrant for interfering with people's liberty was if its exercise involved manifest harm to others. In other words there is a presumption in favour of allowing people to do what they want. Reasons must always be given for interfering with people, not for allowing them to do what they want. To be free means that there are no constraints on people in doing what they might want to do. What has to be justified is the erection of this state of affairs into a moral presumption which requires that reasons have to be given for placing restrictions on the exercise of people's wants. The position of the principle of liberty is similar, in other words, to that of equality. It constitutes a presumption. Reasons have to be given for interfering with people just as they have to be given for treating people differently. But, as again with the principle of equality, the rationality of putting the presumption in this way has to be demonstrated.

I. JUSTIFICATION OF THE PRINCIPLE OF LIBERTY

The fundamental arguments for putting the presumption in favour of freedom derive surely from the situation of practical reason. If a person is asking seriously what he ought to do or what there are reasons for doing he must obviously demand absence of interference on doing whatever there are reasons for doing. Reasons for interference may, of course, derive from other principles; but other things being equal he must demand to be allowed to do what there are reasons for doing. Otherwise his deliberation about alternatives would have no point. Now such deliberation is not something that grows out of his head like a plant from a bulb. It mirrors a social situation into which he has been initiated in which alternative courses of action are suggested and discussed. In such deliberation assessments such as 'wise' and 'foolish' are applied to suggestions in the light of public criteria which are built into the form of discourse.

Given, then, the public character of the situation out of which practical reason develops and which gives meaning to the terms in which it is assessed, it would be strange and paradoxical for a person, who has taken this sort of discussion into his own mind, to hive it off permanently from the public deliberation from which it derives its very existence and meaning. Purely on grounds of prudence, too, if a person is genuinely concerned about what he ought to do, he would be very foolish to shut himself off from other rational beings who also have views about what there are reasons for doing. It would be even more foolish to impose constraints on others so as to prevent them from giving him advice. Spinoza argued that there is nothing more useful to man than other rational men;[1] for conversation with other men is the most obvious means the individual has of increasing his understanding of the universe. The same point applies to the enhancement of an individual's judgment about the alternatives which present themselves in the practical sphere. The conclusion of this argument must surely be that freedom of expression—at least of other rational beings—must be demanded by any rational being who is genuinely concerned with answering the question 'What ought I to do?' as well as possible. For on a matter such as this, which is a matter not of private taste but of public criteria, he would be very stupid if he deprived himself of access to considerations which others might offer.

The argument, however, need not be based simply on the manifest interest of anyone who seriously asks the question 'What ought I to do?' For the principle of liberty, at least in the sphere of opinion, is also surely a general presupposition of this form of discourse into which any rational being is initiated when he laboriously learns to reason. In matters where reason is paramount it is argument rather than force or inner illumination that is decisive. The conditions of argument include letting any rational being contribute to a public discussion. For, as

[1] Spinoza, *Ethics*, Part IV, Prop. XXXV. Corollaries 1 and 2.

Mill pointed out long ago, truth must be the sufferer if opinions are stifled.[1]

So far the presumption in favour of the principle of freedom has only been established in the sphere of opinions. The presumption in favour of the principle has also to be justified in the sphere of actions. This is not very difficult to do; for the opinions expressed in practical discourse are intimately connected with actions. They are attempts to answer the question 'What ought I to do?' As has already been pointed out anyone asking this question must demand freedom of action for himself to do what there are reasons for doing; otherwise his deliberation would be pointless, a rehearsal without a play to follow. But must he also demand such freedom for others?

The same sort of considerations surely apply here as in the justification in the previous chapter of the principle that one ought to consider the interests of others. If a person joins with other rational beings in trying to answer questions of practical policy and if, as a rational being, he must demand freedom of action for himself to do what there are reasons for doing, how can he engage in such discussions with other rational beings and yet deny to them what he rationally must demand for himself? If they are beings like himself who are rational enough to be concerned with the question 'What are there reasons for doing?' and if, as rational beings, they must make a prima facie objection to being interfered with in carrying out what there are reasons for doing, how can anyone treat others as rational beings in so far as their contributions to a discussion may be extremely pertinent and yet, at the same time, refuse to treat them as rational beings by interfering with their freedom without good reason? Because, therefore, in the sphere of practical reason, there is such a close link between discussion and action, in the sense that a rational man who asks the question 'What ought I to do?' must demand for himself freedom to do what there are reasons for doing, freedom of action as well as freedom of thought can be shown to be a general presupposition of practical discourse in so far as it is a public activity to which rational beings contribute.

2. CONCRETE IMPLEMENTATIONS OF THE PRINCIPLE OF LIBERTY

So far a very abstract account has been given of the principle of liberty in order to produce rational grounds for maintaining that the presump-

[1] See Mill, J. S., *On Liberty*, Ch. II.

tion must be in favour of freedom. Even within this rather abstract realm, however, the distinction had to be made between freedom of thought and expression and freedom of action. In concrete situations, where actual arguments about restraining people occur, the need for such distinctions is paramount. For 'free' is a term like 'equal'; its commendatory force is not matched by its determinateness in application. Politicians make much play with both terms; for they both are terms of commendation and as quite different states of affairs can be commended by using the same term, they are obviously very useful for obtaining consensus or arousing indignation. When Churchill entered an election with the slogan 'Set the people free' he awakened a response amongst many listeners. But his listeners imagined themselves to be victims of very different types of restriction, e.g. on private building, foreign travel, access to unrationed food. And what did his slogan have in common with Rousseau's announcement that mankind was born free but everywhere is in chains?

It is obvious enough why there must be such ambiguities inherent in the general use of the term 'free'. Roughly speaking it suggests that there is a lack of impediment or constraint on a person doing what he might want to do. As wants are multifarious and as there are many different types of impediment and constraint, it is not difficult to see why general remarks about freedom are capable of diverse interpretations. Very often the context makes clear how the term is being applied. If a man is going to prison or is in the middle of divorce proceedings he will know how to interpret queries about when he will be free. But if a lecturer stopped in the middle of his exposition and asked one of his listeners whether or not he or she was free, it would be difficult to grasp quite what was being asked. This is not just because of the many possible wants people might have which might be subject to constraint; it is also because questions about freedom usually only arise when there is some consciousness of constraint. Just as movements for equality have generally not been movements towards making everyone as alike as possible but have been agitations against irrelevant grounds for making distinctions between people, so also movements for freedom have not usually been generalized demands for the removal of constraints; they have been agitations against particular types of constraint that have appeared obnoxious or unjustified. Thus there is little talk about freedom in spheres where interference with others is very difficult or in spheres of indifference. There are no movements for the freedom to dream, twiddle one's thumbs, or to grow vegetables. In spheres like choice of wife or employment, foreign travel, speaking in public, and publication, the situation is very different. For it matters very much what people do in these spheres and it is not difficult to stop them doing what they want.

To make talk about 'freedom' concrete, therefore, it has to be made clear what it is that people might want to do and what or who is hindering or preventing them. Because people differ in their wants and because there are many different ways of constraining them there are, therefore, very different applications of the concept of 'freedom'. In this country, for instance, people value very much being able to speak their mind in public and to criticize the Government. We therefore think of a people as not free who are prevented from doing this. The Russians, on the other hand, perhaps do not set so much store by this. They, however, tend to think of a people as 'not free' whose desire to work and to have basic economic necessities is arbitrarily interfered with by private individuals who own capital. Similarly in this country there have been agitations for different rights at different periods, depending on the important spheres of conduct that were interfered with. Habeas corpus, the right to worship as one pleases, the right to combine for a purpose other than that of trade, and the right to withdraw labour are obvious examples.

One has, therefore, first of all to look at the wants whose satisfaction or expressions are being interfered with. But equally important is a consideration of the possible types of constraint or impediment. These can very roughly be divided into two main categories, the impediments of nature and the constraints of men. The former may be external to man like those imposed on the satisfaction of his wants by the sea, ice, and air. People sometimes say that they are not free to jump in the air, or to play golf in the snow. No one of course is stopping them; but they imagine the natural world as a concatenation of constraints. It would be more precise to say that in such cases a person is not able to do what he wants, because of facts about the natural world. But if these impediments are pictured as constraining a man, then there is talk of not being 'free'. Some of such impediments are due to facts about our own nature. Because of certain facts about ourselves not all of us are able to become poets, mystics, or administrative civil servants. Again such limitations are often exalted into constraints and people talk of not being 'free' to do what they really want. This conception of 'freedom' becomes more plausible when the mind of the individual is pictured as if it were a miniature society in which the 'self' or 'real will' of the individual is prevented from doing what it decides by recalcitrant passions which obstruct it or deflect it from its course. It is often thus argued—e.g. by Plato—that the man who is truly free is the man who is in control of his passions. This exalted conception of 'positive freedom' is then contrasted with the more mundane conception of those who think that it is only men who are free and not their 'wills' or 'true selves' and that 'freedom' properly denotes the absence of constraint on their actions by others. The notion of the 'positive freedom' of the rational men, the latter would argue, is a dangerous extension of a notion that has proper application only in a social context.

A consideration of the appropriateness or inappropriateness of this extension of the concept of 'freedom' would require full discussion of the issue of 'free-will'[1] with which we are not here concerned. The term 'free' is much more properly used in the context of constraints set by men, where it has its natural home, and it is with these that we shall be concerned in this chapter. Such constraints are not all of a piece; for the arbitrary constraints of the bully or tyrant must be distinguished from the subtle pressure of constraints set by the law, which is the most effective and far-reaching type of social control yet devised by man.

At different periods in the history of England different types of constraint have seemed to be the most obnoxious form of oppression. In the seventeenth century, for instance, John Locke proclaimed that the greatest evil of all was 'to be subject to the inconstant, uncertain, unknown, arbitrary will of another man'.[2] He was protesting against the arbitrary despotism threatened by the Stuarts who were trying to extend the sphere of the king's prerogative. At other periods of history the constraints of custom and public opinion have seemed particularly oppressive. It was against constraints such as these, which we now associate with Victorian England, that J. S. Mill made his moving and reasoned protest in his essay *On Liberty*. The modern version of such constraints are those which we associate with 'keeping up with the Joneses', with the 'organization man', and with the 'teen-age culture'. Then, of course, there are the constraints of the law itself which are

[1] For further discussion of this issue and references to main works in this field see Benn, S. I., and Peters, R. S., *Social Principles and the Democratic State* (London, Allen & Unwin, 1959), Ch. 9.
[2] Locke, J. *The Second Treatise on Civil Government* (Ed. Gough, J., Oxford, Blackwell, 1948). Ch. IV, Sec. 22.

often attacked for limiting individual initiative, and enterprise. In discussing freedom concretely, therefore, it is important to discover what types of constraint are thought to be oppressive in any given context. There is no one problem of freedom any more than there is one problem of equality.

3. THE PARADOX OF FREEDOM

It is one thing to agitate against the tyranny of arbitrary men or of public opinion; it is quite another to take practical steps to be rid of the constraints which they impose. For here we are confronted with what Popper has called the 'paradox of freedom',[1] which is that too much freedom leads to too little. In realms which are not either those of indifference or those where interference is almost impossible, if people are allowed to do what they like, what tends to happen is that the strong impose arbitrary constraints on the weak. In such spheres individuals are only in fact free to do or say what they like if they are protected from arbitrary interference by law or public opinion or both. The unpalatable lesson of history is that it takes a constraint to catch a constraint.

There are many who have yearned for a life where men would be able to do what they want without rules and regulations, without people in authority to give them orders. But such a state of nature is not a state where there are no constraints; it is a state where the constraints are arbitrary. Such constraints do not vanish into thin air by men being transformed into angels; they gradually cease if another less obnoxious and more levelling type of constraint is developed to protect the weak. No doubt many men would be decent enough, under favourable conditions, not to interfere with others. But laws are not made primarily to restrain those who follow the moral law within; they are made to protect ordinary people against those who acknowledge no such code or who abide by it only haltingly. 'For liberty', as Locke put it, 'is to be free from restraint and violence from others; which cannot be where there is no law.'[2] This is the theme of so many stories of the brief period when the West was being opened up, when the land was overrun by arbitrary adventurers. In such a state of nature the weak were

[1] See Popper, K., *The Open Society and Its Enemies* (London, Routledge, 1945), Vol. I, pp. 225–6.

[2] Locke, J., op. cit., Ch. VI, Sec. 57.

oppressed by the strong until the rule of law was established. Similarly in the economic sphere unfettered free enterprise was fine for the few; but it was only when the countervailing constraints of the trade unions on the few became effective and when laws were introduced governing wages and conditions of employment, that the economically weak ceased to be grossly exploited by the strong. In the sphere of freedom of speech, too, we can only speak our mind in public because the law, backed by public opinion, protects us.

The individual, therefore, in order to have his freedom in some sphere guaranteed, has to accept a less obnoxious, more levelling, sort of constraint which protects him and which also constrains him from interfering with others in a similar way. The example of voting illustrates this very well. The act is simple—just the recording of a cross on a piece of paper. But a most elaborate system of electoral law has been found necessary to make sure that the voter is in fact free to record his vote as he pleases. In the early days of full adult suffrage all kinds of pressures were put on people to vote as someone else required. The system of electoral law was devised to protect the individual, to ensure his freedom in a field which is of vital importance for parliamentary democracy.

Some political philosophers have grasped clearly this 'paradox of freedom' and have drawn quite mistaken inferences from it; for they have argued that it demonstrates that 'freedom' means not doing what one wills without restraint but accepting the law or the 'real will' of the community. This is to confuse what looks like a general empirical condition of 'freedom' having concrete application with the meaning of 'freedom'. It may well be the case that, men being what they are, they will not in fact be free to do what they please in a certain sphere unless they are prepared to accept constraints prohibiting others from interfering with them, and them with others, in this sphere. But this does not show that 'freedom' *means* the acceptance of constraint. To take a parallel: it may be the case that men cannot think without brains; but this does not imply that 'having a brain' is part of the meaning of 'thinking'. Those who have confused such a general empirical condition of freedom with its meaning have often been led to do so because they have also been advocates of 'positive freedom', in which the passions of the individual are thought of as having been mastered so that his 'will' is free from internal constraints. As many such thinkers (e.g. Rousseau) have equated the 'real will' of the individual with the laws of the community working through him, these two strands of thought have become intertwined and the doctrine has emerged that the true freedom of the individual consists in obeying the laws of the state and that the individual may have 'to be forced to be free'.

Those who live in the modern world would need little reminding that the law, which is the most far-reaching and effective form of constraint yet devised by man, can oppress people as well as safeguard their liberties. The state can become a Leviathan as depicted by Hobbes or an instrument of an oppressing class, as depicted by Marx. It is a strange irony, however, that some political philosophers, who have favoured this intrusion of the state into the private life of the individual, have argued for such a condition by claiming that 'real freedom' demands it.

4. THE FORMAL AND THE ACTUAL

The contrast between considering a system in terms of formal principles and in terms of what actually happens can be made in the case of freedom, as it was in the case of equality. The paradox of freedom just considered exemplifies the sort of steps that have to be taken to ensure that the discrepancy between the formal and the actual is not wide. In a state of nature men are formally free in the sense that no rule prevents them from doing what they want. But such a condition can only obtain in fact if a formal system is developed so that other rules, backed up by effective sanctions, ensure that individuals will not in fact be interfered with in certain respects.

There are, however, other ways in which major discrepancies can exist between the formal and the actual. It may be the case that a formal system exists not only prescribing but guaranteeing non-interference in certain spheres of action, but people do not avail themselves of the opportunities which it offers. The law may safeguard, for instance, their right to say what they like in public or change their employment or start a business of their own; but actually, for some reason or other, they do none of these things. This may be because public opinion or religious pressure in fact prevents them. Such a case is similar in its main outline to cases falling under the paradox of freedom already considered, but intimates that legal safeguards are not always effective. A different type of case is that where an individual wants to do something where his freedom is guaranteed, but is not able to do what he wants because of, e.g., lack of money or time. In such cases it is often said that he has no 'actual freedom'—only 'formal' freedom. Suppose, for instance, that a person wants to go abroad, or to educate his children privately in a country which permits such things, but has not the money to pay for his fare or to pay the fees. Certainly such a man would not be able to do what he wanted, but would it be appropriate to say that he is not free to do this? For who is stopping him? To take a parallel: is the truth of the statement that in America anyone is free to become President contradicted by the observation that many lack the ability required? Is the actuality of the freedom of all, as distinct from the lack of conditions formally excluding anyone, affected by the lack of ability of many? Is the ability to do something a necessary condition of being free to do it? It is so surely only in the general sense that this must be in general something that people are thought to be able to do. Unless this were so, talk of their being free to do it would be pointless. But the general notion of people being free to do certain things is quite consistent with the empirical fact that not all are able to do them.

Such a state of affairs may be objected to, of course, on grounds of equality. It might be thought unfair that some people so obviously have advantages in respect of freedom which others lack. But it could only be objected to on grounds of lack of freedom if the inability in question were conceived of as being not simply the product of some artificial social arrangement which was alterable and hence a candidate for an equalitarian 'social engineer', but also one which had been rigged in the interest of coercion or constraint. A Marxist, for instance, considers inequalities of wealth to be contrived somehow in the interests of the exploiting class. A person, therefore, who is unable to do what he is free to do, because of his lack of financial resources, would be regarded by a Marxist as being a victim of oppression. Others would be thought of as indirectly preventing him from doing what he wanted. Because, therefore, of a special type of social theory, such inabilities would be regarded as cases such as those already referred to in the paradox of freedom, where some are actually not free because of their actual oppression by others. Without such a special theory the straightforward thing to say would be that such people are unfortunately unable to do what they are free to do. Such a situation might well be condemned on grounds of social injustice, but it seems unnecessary to condemn it for its alleged absence of freedom as well. For freedom is only absent, in an actual sense, when others in fact stop a man doing what he wants.

Different again from this type of situation is one where people are both able and free to do something, but do not do it because they cannot be bothered. It may indeed be the case that people positively shrink from doing what they are free to do, because of what Fromm calls their 'fear of freedom'.[1] The individual's sense of security may be undermined by the widening of the area of his discretion. He may be unable to tolerate the uncertainty involved in having to make so many choices himself and may welcome with relief some more womb-like type of existence in which things are decided for him. This type of explanation has been given of the ease with which modern man has given up his freedom and relapsed into the arms of authoritarian systems or into systems where the general will of the group determines his destiny. Psychologically speaking such relapses are explicable in terms of the tendency of the individual, when confronted by threat or insecurity, to regress to his earlier stage of infantile dependence, to recreate the conditions of his earlier feeling of security. There is another more sociological explanation, too, of this unfortunate proclivity.

The development of individualism, with its stress on individual initiative and liberty, has been accompanied, of course, by the vast growth of law as a predominant means of social control. In the old type of society social control was provided much more by custom and by the ties of the local community. With the development of physical and social mobility social control had to be exercised much more by law operating on a national scale and by the built-in conscience of the individual. This type of development, which was necessary for individual liberty, brought in its train the kind of depersonalization which is associated with life under any bureaucratic centralized system. In the small, face-to-face communities of the Middle Ages few men were free to do the sorts of things that are now thought worth while. It was difficult to rise in society through merit and initiative. Men regarded the social order as almost divinely ordained. There was little fairness, little choice on the part of individuals of their careers, rulers, religion, and marriage partners. But they had not only a feeling of security, in spite of the obvious insecurities which they had to face arising from violence, illness, and tempest; they also had a feeling of belonging, of kinship, which derived from their membership of the close-knit cohesive groups of family, church, and the local community where they were born, worked, married, and died. They had an appointed place in the world. With the rise of individualism, and the quest for individual salvation in religion, with

[1] Fromm, E., *The Fear of Freedom* (London, Routledge, 1942).

the development of achieved rather than ascribed status in society, something began to go out of the world in a way which Tawney has so vividly portrayed[1]—fraternity. Life began to look more and more like a race with a set of rules to protect individuals and to ensure fair play—a race in which Hobbes so graphically put it 'to outgo the next before is felicity, and to forsake the course, is to die'.[2] Artificial attempts have been made to fill this aching void left by the passing of fraternity. The great appeal of Marxism, for instance, has been that it feeds on an induced feeling of solidarity amongst the oppressed. Nationalism, too, trades on this need to feel that we are members of a group, that we have a place where we belong and function to perform as men had in the old city states.[3]

This rootless feeling of modern man has enhanced his feeling of insecurity and uneasiness engendered by the increased area of his discretion in determining the contours of his life. It is not surprising, therefore, that many who are formally free to do all sorts of things in fact avail themselves little of their opportunities, or voluntarily abdicate from some existing areas of discretion by joining organizations which decide things for them. But this does not show, as writers like Fromm have argued, that men lack 'positive freedom' which is as important as the more mundane concept of freedom here defended. All it shows is that to be free is not necessarily to be happy, that gains in freedom are often at the expense of security and fraternity, and that people can be free without much wanting to do the things which they are free to do. A man is free in so far as no one will stop him doing what he might want to do. To say that he is free does not entail that he actually wants to do what he will not be prevented from doing. It is true, of course, that agitations for freedom only arise when people actually want to do things which they are prevented from doing, e.g. attending a public meeting. But once such a freedom has been established, men do not cease to be free in this respect if they get bored with attending public meetings. In brief the concept of 'free' is to be explicated in terms of what people might want rather than in terms of what they actually want, though it is obvious enough that it is only thought to be important as a principle because there are occasions when actual wants are interfered with. The introduction of the notion of 'positive freedom' is unnecessary and misleading in this as in many other contexts.

[1] See Tawney, R. H., *Religion and the Rise of Capitalism* (West Drayton, Penguin Books, 1938), Part IV.
[2] Hobbes, T., *Human Nature*, English Works (Molesworth, Ed.),Vol. IV.,p. 53.
[3] See Ch. VIII, Sec. 2.

Behind this rather loose talk of 'positive freedom', however, is something slightly different which is very important, namely the value to be ascribed to the autonomy of the individual, to his determination to direct his own life according to thought out principles. In a situation in which little formal freedom exists, of course, he may be prevented from doing this. He may decide to marry someone of a different colour but may be put into prison when his decision is known. But, on the other hand, an individual may be formally free to determine all sorts of things like this himself, but may in fact always do what others tell him or may just drift along from day to day following his inclinations without any consistent policy. Obviously anyone who seriously asks the question 'What ought I to do?' is on the path to autonomy. But it is a further question whether or not he is free. This will depend on whether or not there are any constraints preventing him from doing what he has decided to do. The use made of freedom should not be confused with what is meant by being free to do something.

5. FREEDOM IN EDUCATION

So far an analysis has been given of the principle of liberty, an attempt has been made to justify it, and general problems of its application have been considered. Its application in the specific field of education must now be examined. The issues raised here are very different from those raised in the previous two chapters; for whereas they were concerned with the distribution and matter of education, questions to do with its manner have now to be tackled. There is, of course, an issue to do with the freedom of the parent in relation to educational provision, which is closely connected with the problem of its distribution; but the more perplexing problems relate to the freedom of the child and of the teacher. The problems are created by the differences in application necessitated by the fact that the principle has to be applied in an educational situation. We shall begin, therefore, with the freedom of the child, pass on to the freedom of the teacher, and end up with a few brief remarks about the freedom of the parent.

(a) The freedom of the child

It has been maintained that the concept of freedom joins together two main components: first the notion of possible wants or decisions and secondly that of the absence of constraints upon them. In applying this concept to a situation in which adults are involved, their possible wants are taken more or less for granted as brute facts about them. A question of freedom arises only when there is a possibility of their being constrained in respect of such wants.

In an educational situation, however, the application of the principle is not so straightforward. For, almost by definition, it is a situation in which constraints are imposed upon children's wants. To start with children are compelled to attend school which is not a promising start from the point of view of freedom. Some of them, of course, want to attend as well; but the combination of legal requirement and parental pressure do not readily intimate an area of free choice and action.

Secondly the conditions under which learning takes place make it imperative that something like the rule of law should be established within an educational situation. However much encouragement is given to children within a class-room to follow their own interests and to work at their own pace, there must be conditions of order sufficient to permit a large number of children to work at the same time in a small space. What such conditions are depends on the age and number of children, what is being learnt, and the amount of space available. But without minimum conditions of order a class-room would degenerate into a Tower of Babel, and the freedom of some would be exercised at the expense of others. Education could not go on.

Thirdly an educational situation involves essentially a contrived and controlled environment. Children may be encouraged to choose things and to follow their own interests in their study. Indeed emphasis may be placed on the desirability of spontaneity and autonomy. But such choice has always to be exercised within a range of what is thought desirable. Amongst the materials, with which they are encouraged to experiment, knives and liquid paraffin are not included. Horror comics and pornography do not adorn the shelves of school libraries. Sexual experimentation is not encouraged in the common rooms. Such controlled conditions act as general constraints on the wants of children. By means of them adults exert a steady, if mild sort of pressure.

This must be the case; for no educator can take the wants of children for granted, part of his business as an educator being the transformation of wants, both in respect of their quality and in respect of their stability. To effect such a transformation a background of constraints on children's wants is necessary. It may, of course, be possible within such a controlled environment to harness the worth-while content of education to existing wants either by developing understanding, skill, and a sense of standards in relation to existing wants as in activities like canoe building, making guitars, or dancing, or by using such existing wants as a means to developing new ones, as in the project method. But it may at times be necessary to exert pressure on children so that they master something irrespective of what they want. Many students, for instance, have been told to write an essay on something in which they were not at all interested and, as a result, have developed a new interest in something. Such possibilities open up wider empirical questions about intrinsic and extrinsic motivation as well as moral questions about the permissibility of various methods of changing people's wants. But the basic point remains: no educator can be indifferent to what children want. He cannot, as in an ordinary social situation, say that what people want to do is their own affair, provided that they do no damage to others or interfere with their liberty. To adopt this *laissez-faire* attitude in a school would be to abdicate as an educator. Caretakers, maybe, can adopt such an attitude, but not teachers.

The justification of such a framework of order does not fall, naturally enough, in the main under the principle of liberty. It falls under the principle of the promotion of what is good, with its subordinate principle of the consideration of what is in people's interests. Nevertheless a case can be made in terms of liberty for such conditions of order in school which illustrates the paradox of freedom very well. If the rule of law imposed impartially by those in authority is absent it simply is not the case that children are actually able to do what they individually want. They are subject either to the arbitrary will of a bully or to the tyranny of peer-group pressure. Progressive schools in which the staff, as a matter of policy, withdraw from their proper function of exercising a just and levelling form of social control, are notorious for peer-group pressure and the proliferation of rules administered with severity by the children themselves. Or something like a state of nature prevails, as depicted with ghoulish exaggeration by William Golding in his *Lord of the Flies*. I once asked a colleague why his parents took him away from one of these schools. He replied that it was such hell when the headmaster was not around because of the bullying that went on. The headmaster in question prided himself on the fact that the staff laid down no rules. What he had not grasped was that there are other ways in which adults can control situations, when they are there, without having to formulate rules.

In all such situations, when human beings are gathered together, it is completely unrealistic to suppose that men or children are ever, as a matter of fact, free to do what they like simply because of the inherent decency and good sense of all concerned. They are in fact free because some rule or other, in addition to the moral law, is effectively enforced which prohibits interference. The practical choice is never between simply doing as one likes and being constrained; it is rather between being subject to different types of constraint. From the point of view of freedom it is a better bet for the individual to accept a system of levelling constraints which limit his freedom of action but limit also the freedom of action of others to interfere with him, than to commit himself to a state of nature in which he runs the risk of being arbitrarily coerced or subjected to merciless group pressure. Adolescents who join in rejecting the authority of parents and teachers often make a dubious gain in terms of freedom; for they find that their opportunities for doing what they want as individuals are much more stringently curtailed by peer-group pressures.

The gist of the argument so far has been to show that because an educational situation is one in which an environment is specifically contrived so that what is good can be promoted and passed on, there are conditions of order which must obtain in order that this overriding aim can be implemented. As, however, freedom is an independent principle like justice it cannot be abrogated entirely for the sake of the promotion of what is good. The presumption in favour of it still holds. It has to be shown that restrictions imposed on children, even in this contrived situation, are essential in terms of the promotion of what is good. Rules for the sake of rules, or as expressions of a teacher's love of power, are anathema to any rational man. Some types of rules, it has been argued, can be justified in relation to the paradox of freedom, as well as because of their necessity for the promotion of what is good. But the fewer restrictions the better, and all such rules must have some point. What they are, how they are decided upon, and how they are enforced will depend upon all sorts of contingent questions to do with the age of the children, the size of the school, whether or not it approximates, as does a boarding school, to a 'total institution', and so on. Contingencies abound when such a concrete level of the implementation of general principles is reached. About such contingencies there is very little, philosophically speaking, to say; for common sense must not be passed off as philosophical analysis. Philosophy is only one component in educational theory. When it comes to the formulation of particular principles for implementation in particular schools the contribution of philosophy, in terms of abstract analysis and justification of principles, must be put together with that of psychologists, sociologists, and teachers, who have practical experiences of the particularities in question. Philosophy contributes to practical wisdom but is not a substitute for it.

There is, however, another aspect of the freedom of the child which is very relevant to the ideals of progressive schools; for often such schools are not much concerned with providing conditions in which education of what they derisively call an 'academic' sort can proceed. They are much more concerned with the moral rehabilitation of misfits, or with character development, and emotional maturity. They are particularly interested, perhaps, in the development of moral autonomy and independence. Children have to learn to make their own choices, to stand on their own feet; it is argued that this sort of permissive atmosphere encourages them to do this.

Anyone concerned seriously with answering the question 'What ought I to do?' will be equally concerned about implementing such a laudable ideal; for the search for reasons for action is the hall-mark of the autonomous person. He is not prepared to accept authoritative pronouncements and is unhappy about simply doing what others do without inquiring any further. He will thus be very concerned that people should be educated in a way which encourages independence of mind. But he will also hope that this can be done without too great a cost in terms of security and happiness—especially in view of the danger of a relapse into submission to authority or group conformity, because of the 'fear of freedom' already mentioned. He will be concerned that individuals develop who can make proper use of the areas of discretion permitted by a liberal society. Little, however, is yet known about the conditions which favour the development of such autonomy. Do children in fact learn to behave autonomously by being brought up from their earliest years in a very permissive atmosphere without a proper framework of order? This seems highly improbable both on general grounds and on the basis of the slender empirical evidence that there is about such matters. It would not be appropriate to enter into a detailed consideration of the empirical evidence, but the general grounds can be briefly mentioned as they make explicit considerations which are often forgotten in talk about children's autonomy and choice.

Autonomy implies the ability and determination to regulate one's life by rules which one has accepted for oneself—presumably because the reasons for them are both apparent and convincing. Piaget has shown that such an attitude towards rules is generally impossible before the age of about seven. Secondly there is evidence to suggest that the giving of reasons for action has little educative effect at an early stage. Yet long before this age children, for reasons both of their own survival, and for the welfare of others, must acquire in *other ways* a basic code of behaviour.[1] Thirdly they have to learn what it is to act on rules generally before the notion of determining their own code of rules for themselves can have any significance for them. If, too, such a choice is to be a real possibility for them rather than a lip-service to a shibboleth, they must have experience on the basis of which they can decide between alternatives. This is parallel to the problem of an 'elective curriculum'. What sense is there in saying that children should have 'choice' of what subjects they are to study unless they have been given some experience of such subjects on the basis of which they are in a position really to 'choose'? There is all the difference in the world between choosing between alternatives and 'opting' for alternatives on the basis of what is immediately attractive. I was once discussing with a girl her 'choice' of a College of Education. It transpired that she was inclined towards one college rather than another because of the picture of it on the brochure! Choice should not be confused with the way of opting for things which is encouraged by advertising agencies. For children to learn to choose in this real sense they must live in a fairly predictable environment so that they can learn to make realistic assessments of consequences. In human affairs the environment is mainly social, i.e. constituted by rules and standards. If predictability is not provided by something approximating to a rule of law how can the capacity for choice be developed in children? If rebellion and criticism are regarded as valuable something concrete must be provided to rebel against, so that children can learn to do this, knowing what is likely to happen. The virtue of a legal system, in relation to its encouragement of autonomy, is that it provides rules with determinate sanctions. Individuals who break the law do so with the knowledge of what is likely to happen if they are found out. They are thus put in a position where concrete probabilities are presented to

[1] For problems about such 'other ways' see Peters, R. S., 'The Paradox of Moral Education' in Niblett, W. R. (Ed.), *Moral Education in a Changing Society* (London, Faber, 1963).

them. If children are brought up without such stable conditions it is difficult to see how they can learn to make realistic choices.

Fourthly those who are staunch advocates of autonomy, such as Existentialists, draw attention both to the necessity and virtue of the choice between rules which conflict on particular occasions. It is seldom pointed out that such conflicts are only real if the individual already accepts the rules which conflict as binding on him. But if he has not been brought up in such a way that he has internalized a set of rules, how could such conflicts ever occur out of which his independence and strength of character begin to develop?

Fifthly although there is little virtue in order for its own sake, the fact is that human beings are beset by anxiety unless minimum conditions of order are provided. If they are anxious or insecure they will be an easy prey to all sorts of irrational pressures. They will submit readily to authoritarian regulation or peer-group pressure; they will dart to and fro between alternatives that offer easy gratification. They are in the worst possible condition to learn how to direct their lives autonomously.

The development of autonomy is a slow and laborious business. Young people have to learn gradually to stand on their own feet and direct their own lives. They are not likely to do this if they are not encouraged to take responsibility and make choices about important matters within their limited experience; still less are they likely to do it if they are pitchforked into an anarchic situation in which they are told that they have to decide everything for themselves. Rationality requires a middle course between authoritarianism and permissiveness. Above all what is required is a rational attitude to and exercise of authority on the part of parents and teachers. Further consideration of this must be reserved until Chapters IX and XI.

(b) The freedom of the teacher

The question of the freedom of the teacher centres mainly on his right to teach what he likes and to put forward his own views about controversial matters. This is usually defended by arguments similar to those used by J. S. Mill in his essay *On Liberty*. Truth, it is argued, is only advanced if people are allowed to voice their own opinions, however heterodox. For if the orthodox opinions are true their truth will be strengthened by being challenged by conflicting opinions. If, on the other hand, they are false, their falsity cannot be exposed unless challenge to them is permitted. To forbid freedom of thought is to presuppose infallibility. The pursuit of truth develops only by the progressive falsification of orthodox opinions.

Such arguments are more or less unanswerable in the sphere of what Locke had previously called 'speculative opinions' in his *A Letter Concerning Toleration*. The matter, however, is not quite so straightforward in the sphere of what he called 'practical opinions'. Neither is the position of the teacher in relation to both sorts of opinions quite so simple as that of a man publishing a book for an adult public or reading a paper at a scientific congress. The qualifications required by these differences must now be explored.

Mill distinguished in his essay between freedom of thought and freedom of action. The right to the former is absolute, the right to the latter conditional upon the possible harm done to others. A difficulty, however, arises with opinions which Locke called 'practical' which have a very close connection with action because of the harm that they may do to public order and to the enjoyment of rights by other individuals. Mill's failure to consider carefully the status of such opinions rather weakened his case for toleration. There are laws forbidding the expression of extreme forms of such practical opinions—laws against libel, slander, obscenity, and sedition. How far should such intervention be extended? What should the attitude be of someone who believes in toleration to opinions that are directed against a system that makes toleration possible? It is one thing to tolerate the Marxist interpretation of history, which is a matter of speculation; but what attitude should be taken to the promulgation of opinions about the tactics of revolution and to advice to party members about how to infiltrate into the main centres of control in the state? A rational course has to be steered between McCarthyism on the one hand and the feebleness of the Weimar Republic on the other. As this is a case where two fundamental moral principles conflict, that of liberty and of the consideration of people's interest, no hard and fast rule can be laid down. It is to be hoped that in a democratic society a balance in favour of toleration can be maintained, it being left to the good sense of individuals to combat such revolutionary or obnoxious opinions. There are such powerful irrational forces in man that sustain and magnify his intolerance that a bias in favour of toleration is justified. But there may come a time when sterner measures have to be taken. Race prejudice may fester and spread like a rash on a community. Insecurity and unemployment may make men disposed to listen to those who use the free speech afforded by a democratic society to suggest that the system which makes it possible is nothing but an instrument of class oppression. At what precise point the expression of such opinions has to be checked, and what form of safeguard has to be used, is a matter of judgment.

The teacher's position in regard to the expression of opinion is complicated both by his educational role and by the fact that he is dealing with people whose minds are immature, which imposes special responsibilities on him. At university level these complications are of less importance. University teachers have in the main a firm allegiance to the pursuit of truth, in its various forms, and usually feel some obligation to initiate others into it. They are bound, of course, to some extent by syllabuses and examinations which they help to construct; but their right to interpret such syllabuses in their own way is unquestioned. Their main concern is with the pursuit of truth and what Mill says about 'speculative' opinions applies pre-eminently to them. They feel little squeamishness, too, about presenting their own point of view strongly about controversial matters in their subject to students. For they know full well that there are others with different points of view to whom students can listen if they wish. They also know that many of their students have begun to acquire the manner of thinking which will enable them to sift, assess, and criticize their own views. Indeed if their students do not start producing attempted refutations of what they say they should consider that they are falling down on their job. There are, of course, too, some university teachers who have little interest in the wider educational or moral context of their activities; they are required to give lectures and accordingly conduct their private musings in public.

The situation in schools is somewhat different. To start with, though school teachers, like university teachers, should have a strong allegiance to the discipline in which they have been trained, they are concerned more specifically with education and less with developing the frontiers of knowledge than university teachers. They are subject to closer public supervision than university teachers and many of them have to prepare children for public examinations in accordance with syllabuses over which they have little control. Although headmasters in England have a very high degree of autonomy, assistant masters may often have to work very strictly in accordance with patterns prescribed by the headmaster or by the head of their department. Although their freedom to interpret such syllabuses in their own way is usually granted they often

200

have to be much more mindful than university teachers of the rather narrow requirements of examinations, and are very conscious of their dubious role as agents of selection in a system where there is too little room at the top.

No doubt many of the restrictions set on their freedom by such facts of life are thoroughly undesirable, but even without them there are aspects of their situation which should give them cause to ponder on the extent to which they are justified in plugging their pet theories. To start with they are very often the only competent exponent of the form of thought in question. Their students will not hear another point of view about the same matter from someone else. Secondly even in a sixth form their students are still struggling to acquire the procedures as distinct from the content of the form of thought. They are not therefore properly equipped to assess and criticize what a teacher tells them. A teacher, for instance, who plugs the economic interpretation of history in a sixth form will encounter few students equipped to dispute what he says. If he presents the Reformation purely from the Protestant point of view a Catholic in the class may be thoroughly disturbed but will lack the equipment to give expression to his inarticulate uneasiness. A scrupulous and competent teacher will know that different interpretations of the evidence are possible about such matters. His concern should not be to pump opinions into his students but to see to it that his students acquire the competence to form their own. For his basic task is not to teach his students what to think but how to think.

This does not mean, of course, that a teacher must sit as inscrutable as the Buddha and never commit himself to an opinion about anything. Children will usually glean where a teacher's sympathies lie, anyway, without his having to avow them. His attitude should rather be, if he is a rational man, that nothing depends on the contingent fact that he happens to hold a particular opinion. After all he may be wrong. The important thing to get at is what grounds there might be for him or anyone else to hold this opinion or a contrary one. He must be, to a certain extent, an authority on what he is teaching. If he is not, he should not have been appointed. But his claim to authority derives not from the particular opinions which he holds about any substantive issue but from his mastery of the form of thought by means of which such opinions are arrived at. This is what he has to impart to his students. He has to teach in such a way that his students can eventually dispense with him.

The discussion to date has only been concerned with speculative opinions that are handed on in the various school subjects. The responsibilities of a university teacher do not extend much beyond these, though there are some who think it also to be the function of a university teacher to induce some kind of moral commitment in his students. At the school level, however, the matter is again very different; for moral education is certainly a very important aspect of education at school. Here again the teacher has no right to use the special relationship in which he stands to children to parade his own idiosyncratic opinions. Maybe he is a vegetarian or a pacifist; perhaps he believes steadfastly in the virtues of nudity or of polygamy. His concern should not be to convert children to adopt such substantive positions because of their admiration for him, but to get them to see the reasons on which such positions are based; for his job is teaching, not indoctrination. He must get them to face squarely the question 'What ought I to do?' and lead them on to fundamental principles on which answers to this question must be grounded. Whether they come to agree with him on matters of substance is another matter.

About some moral rules, however, on which there is a broad consensus, his attitude must be rather different. These are what have been referred to above as basic moral rules[1] which are those which are in anyone's interest whatever his conception of the good life may be. Rules like those prohibiting injury to the person, theft, lying, and the breaking of contracts are necessary for the life of a school as well as for that of any other community. Any teacher must insist on the observance of such rules both from the point of view of the maintenance of necessary conditions of order in the school and from the point of view of moral education. But here again he should not be just content with enunciating that it is wrong to do such things; he should try to get children to see why it is wrong. And just seeing, of course, is not enough; they have to feel it as well. Otherwise such rules will not bite on their behaviour. How this can be done is, of course, another matter about which too little is known. Is such a deepening of moral consciousness much aided by discussions in a formal situation? Is it mainly a matter of what is imparted on concrete occasions? Does it depend much more on the peer-group than on the example of adults? These are all empirical questions with which philosophy is not concerned. Answering them, however, has little bearing on the question of the teacher's freedom in

[1] See Ch. VI, Sec. 3.

relation to such opinions, though it has very great relevance to his practical task as a moral educator.

In the sphere of more general religious and political opinions the position of the teacher is fairly straightforward. He is not employed as a missionary for any church or as a recruiting officer for any political party. It is his job, however, to initiate children into the skills, attitudes, and knowledge which are necessary for them to participate intelligently as citizens in the life of a democratic state. In so far as he deals with such matters in formal periods, e.g. in R.I. or Current Affairs, his main endeavour should be the deepening and informing of a religious and political consciousness rather than the defence of particular dogmas or programmes. If, of course, a teacher is an atheist or an agnostic, and is required to teach R.I., this is a different matter. Obviously he cannot teach religion *as* religion if he is unfamiliar with or antipathetic to the form of awareness on which it is based. He has, therefore, the alternatives of teaching something else under the aegis of R.I., e.g. history of the Hebrews, comparative religion, morals, or refusing, on conscientious grounds, to have anything to do with it. Little more can be said about this topic without detailed discussion of the nature of religion, of its difference from and relationship to morals, and of the anomalies and complications arising from the status of R.I. under the 1944 Act, which would require a chapter to itself.[1]

What the teacher does about his own beliefs outside school hours is, of course, his own business, provided that he does not implicate his employers in his activities; his activities are subject to law and public opinion like those of any other individual. The fact that he is a teacher does not deprive him of the normal rights of a citizen. He may have unusual and perhaps mildly outrageous views on many things; his political and religious affiliations may be very unorthodox; he may well indulge in bizarre 'experiments in living'—to use Mill's phrase. But unless these can be shown incontrovertibly to distort or bias his conduct as a teacher on the job or to influence children unduly by his public example, it is difficult to see why his employers, in a democratic society, should take active cognizance of such matters. To take a concrete case: a teacher may join some society in his spare time for the amelioration of the condition of homosexuals in society. Parents and indignant citizens might band together and start an agitation to have him dismissed

---

[1] See Hirst, P. H., 'Morals, Religion and the Maintained School' in *British Journal of Educational Studies*, Vol. XIV, No. 1, November 1965.

from his post, as a source of corruption. Another might drink overmuch or lead an irregular sex life, and it might be suggested that his competence was reduced as a result, or that children were corrupted by his example. What would have to be produced, however, would be concrete evidence of corruption or incompetence. General probabilities are not enough. If this demand were once abandoned the teacher's position in the community would become intolerable.

An exception, however, might be made in the case of commitment to practical opinions which must necessarily involve a particular attitude to children, if held sincerely. A man may have homosexual tendencies, but it has to be shown that these necessarily take the form of attempts to seduce small boys. Most 'normal' men have strong heterosexual tendencies; but in a co-educational school the girls in the class are not necessarily in a permanent state of moral danger. Hence the necessity for evidence that such tendencies take this concrete form of expression in a school situation. It might be the case, however, that a man who sincerely holds Fascist opinions must have a certain type of attitude to Jewish or coloured children in his class. It might be argued, too, that even if there was little evidence to support the assumption that such a man would in fact discriminate against Jewish or coloured children, the children in question might live in perpetual fear of him because of his known opinions. A similar argument might be advanced in relation to the probable attitude of an active Communist towards children of the bourgeoisie, though the connection in this case is looser. Such extreme cases might be cited as exceptions to the general principle that concrete evidence must be produced before the presumption in favour of toleration is abandoned. But such cases are mercifully rare in England at the moment.

(c) The freedom of the parent

The ground of a parent's right to educate his children as he thinks fit is not altogether perspicuous. It presupposes all sorts of things about the parent-child relationship which would take a long time to discuss. Some regard the parent's rights in this sphere rather like rights to property; others assimilate them to those of a trustee. But though the grounds of this right are obscure there are few in Britain who would question that the parent has such a right. Indeed in England the right of a parent to educate his child as he likes is one of the most long-standing rights of the subject. Burke, for all his attack on 'abstract rights', includes the right to 'the nourishment and improvement of their offspring' amongst the 'real rights' of the subject. Even Hobbes, thought to be one of the precursors of modern totalitarianism, presumed that the sovereign would not interfere with matters such as the subject's choice of vocation, choice of wife, and choice of education for his children. This right is of particular importance for those whose religion requires a special sort of education.

This right was established, of course, long before compulsory education for all was ever contemplated. Such compulsion was obviously enough an infringement of liberty in so far as parents were no longer free to exercise their discretion by not having their children educated at all. The arguments for such a limitation of freedom are obvious enough too. A highly industrialized society cannot be run effectively unless a certain level of literacy and numeracy is attained by all and a high degree of specialized knowledge and skill by many. Also without certain minimum conditions being insisted on, individuals would be deprived of the necessary conditions for attaining the quality of life in such a society which is handed on in a good educational system. Compulsion cannot force people to become educated. But without it many children would be deprived of their opportunities for entering into their cultural heritage. Such a limitation on freedom can therefore be justified both in terms of the interests of the community and the long-term interest of individuals potentially composing it. For matters as important as this cannot be left purely to the good sense of parents.

Since the development of state education the right of the parent has come to mean that of educating his children in a private school if he should wish to spend his money in this way. For most people such a right is 'formal' rather than 'actual'; for only a small minority have the money necessary to exercise it. Naturally enough the state cannot be expected to pay for such a luxury and naturally it is reasonable for the state to insist that a certain minimum standard of educational provision should be maintained. In this way the point of a compulsory system is retained without insisting on uniformity in implementation. For without this latter condition the children themselves might suffer as a result of the parent's exercise of their freedom of choice and so, derivatively, would the state.

There are few who dare challenge this watered-down prima facie right of parents in a democratic society. Arguments against the existence of private schools derive from a conviction that it is unfair that the possession of money should put some in a privileged position, especially as much of the wealth so used is inherited rather than earned by the parents in question. When so few have actual access to a formal right of this sort it is argued that there is a case for abolishing it. Fairness must take precedence over freedom—especially as the present division in the educational system tends to perpetuate class attitudes which encourage lack of respect for persons.

At this point another principle becomes relevant—that of the promotion of what is good; for one of the main reasons why parents, who can afford it, insist on exercising their right is that the quality of education provided in the best independent schools is very good indeed. Of course there are many exceptions. Some independent schools, especially at the preparatory level, are not very good, and some parents have predominantly social motives for exercising their right of choice at such a great expense. They do not want their children to mix with children from another social class; or they see that education at an independent school may enhance their children's prospects of high social status and good employment. But the fact is that there are many very good independent schools with long traditions which have built up by long experience and trial and error a system which successfully combines academic achievement with character-training. Historically these schools have been pioneers in many spheres of educational experiment and the state system owes an enormous amount to their example. It would be criminal folly to dismantle a system of education which contributes and has contributed so much to the quality of education in England. The real scandal is that both the major political parties and the public as a whole have cared so little about education in the past that they have never spent enough money either on schools or on salaries of teachers to cater adequately for the nation as a whole. They have, of course, paid lip-service to the importance of education; but when it has come to producing enough money to develop a really effective and fair educational system, other demands on the Exchequer have always seemed more pressing. The reply to this is obvious enough—that radical improvements will only be effected in the state system when the wealthier and more influential minority of the population have to send their children to the same schools as everybody else.

And so the debate proceeds over the status of independent schools with arguments deriving from liberty, equality, and the quality of life. It represents *par excellence* an issue where these basic principles conflict. Obviously some compromise which does not involve abandoning altogether the right of parents to educate their children as they think fit will have to be found. The point at which such a compromise can be found must depend on the ingenuity of practical men. It cannot be determined by philosophical analysis alone, though such analysis can do much to get clearer on what fundamental points decisions have to be made.

CHAPTER VIII

RESPECT FOR PERSONS, FRATERNITY AND THE CONCEPT OF MAN

INTRODUCTION

In Chapter II, when a general account of education as initiation was outlined, the criticism was dealt with that stress on the impersonal standards to which both teacher and taught must owe allegiance might be at the expense of personal relationships between teacher and taught. In answering this objection great importance was accorded to respect for persons and fraternity in the teaching situation; but nothing was said to justify the appropriateness of these attitudes.

Respect for persons was also seen to be crucial in the discussion of equality; for lack of equality, as a distributive principle, was distinguished from attitudes connected with snobbishness and social superiority which, it was claimed, denote lack of respect for persons. But again no arguments were put forward to suggest that respect rather than contempt for persons is an appropriate attitude.

There is also a gap in the account of fundamental principles so far put forward; for nothing has been argued about the attitude which is appropriate towards human beings whose conduct they are meant to regulate. Yet without some such attitude it is difficult to see how rational beings could be induced to act on such principles. This stress on attitudes, as was argued in Chapter III, is the strength of the emotive theory of ethics. What has to be shown, therefore, from the point of view of ethical theory in general as well as from the point of view of the highly selected aspects of it put forward in this book, is that there are some attitudes towards others that a rational man must have. The case, therefore, for respect for persons and fraternity must now be presented.

I. RESPECT FOR PERSONS

Kant held that respect for persons was derivative from respect for law. He argued that though respect is a feeling, it is not a feeling received through influence, but is 'self-wrought by a rational concept, and, therefore, is specifically distinct from all feelings of the former kind, which may be referred either to inclination or fear. What I recognize immediately as a law for me, I recognize with respect. . . . The object of respect is the law only, and that, the law which we impose on ourselves, and yet recognize as necessary in itself. . . . Respect for a person is properly our respect for the law (of honesty, etc.) of which he gives us an example.'[1] The difficulty about this view is that contempt for persons seems, prima facie at any rate, quite compatible with meticulousness in acting on principles. One could take careful account of a person's interests, for instance, as a guardian might that of his ward, and yet have and show contempt for him as a person. It does not look, therefore, as if the appraisal which goes with respect for law or principles necessarily either coincides with or implies that which is necessary for respect for persons.

Kant, however, had a distinctive concept of law, at least in the practical sphere, in that for him the thought of such laws was inseparable from that of the autonomous rational beings who created them. The principles of practical reason were not 'out there' to discover; they were not, as in Plato's system, principles permeating the nature of things which a rational being might discern; they were the creation of individuals possessed of reason and desire. Kant's conception of law was therefore inseparable from his belief in the activity, dignity, and worth of rational individuals who created it. For him the existence of individual rational beings was not just a fact about the world; it was a fact of supreme ethical importance. The notion of 'persons' picked out not simply the fact; it also bore witness to the ethical importance of the fact. And this fact was intimately connected with the activity of men as rational beings in deliberating about what they ought to do.

(a) The meaning of 'respect for persons'
There is much to be said for this doctrine of Kant in that the notion of being a person is connected with 'being on the inside' of those experiences which are characteristic of practical reason, of acting on principles and of determining the future in the light of knowledge of the past and awareness of what may be. Choice, which is intimately connected with the exercise of practical reason, is too narrow a concept; for it implies

[1] Kant, I., *Fundamental Principles of the Metaphysics of Morals* (Ed. Abbott, T. K., London, Longmans Green, 1940), pp. 22–3, footnote 2.

deliberation between alternatives. It does not cover such things as the grasp of rules, as the formulation and statement of intentions and the making of promises by means of.which individuals determine the future. Notions like that of 'endeavour' used by Spinoza to characterize a general tendency to persist in a form of being are too general; for they apply also to plants and other homeostatic systems which are not conscious of themselves or of the past and future. The notion is much more that of an assertive point of view; of judgments, appraisals, intentions, and decisions that shape events, their characteristic stamp being determined by previous ones that have given rise to permanent or semipermanent dispositions. The shaping of a pattern of life in this way is constitutive of what we call an individual person. When it is said that a man who brainwashes others, or who settles their lives for them without consulting them shows lack of 'respect for persons', the implication is that he does not treat others seriously as agents or as determiners of their own destiny, and that he disregards their feelings and view of the world. He either refuses to let them be in a situation where their intentions, decisions, appraisals and choices can operate effectively, or he purposely interferes with or nullifies their capacity for self-direction. He ensures that for them the question 'What ought I to do?' either scarcely arises or serves as a cork on a tide of events whose drift derives from elsewhere. He denies them the dignity which is the due of a self-determining agent, who is capable of valuation and choice, and who has a point of view of his own about his own future and interests.

The notion of a 'person', which is picked out by reference to such notions connected with being an assertive point of view, is narrower than the wider notion of being an 'individual'. For instance, the individual's awareness of pain, or his visual experience, is not necessarily a manifestation of his existence as a person; if it were so dogs and octopuses would be persons. Yet the principle of consideration of interests could be applied to dogs without ever treating them as persons. A policy would have to be pursued which took account of avoiding pain for them and maximizing their opportunities for satisfaction. This would be done without 'respect for persons'; for the dog's point of view about his forms of satisfaction would not be taken into account.

It is possible, too, for individual men and women to live together in society without any clear consciousness of themselves as persons. They might be thought of as having claims or interests as occupying a certain status; but their view of such matters as individuals might be totally disregarded. Societies are really nothing more than groups of individuals who are initiated into and who accept and maintain a public system of rules. Nevertheless it is quite possible for people to live in societies without any awareness of the determining role of individuals. Indeed they may not distinguish clearly between a social order and a natural order and may think that individual men are comparatively impotent in relation to both of them. Though we might say that they were *potentially* individual persons who had been conditioned to accept a rather womb-like existence, they might nevertheless have no consciousness of themselves as persons. They might be conscious only of their particular social roles and of their general kinship with other members of the society. They might have neither respect for persons nor consciousness of either themselves or others as persons in any important sense. Young children are in this position.

People only begin to think of themselves as persons, as centres of valuation, decision and choice, in so far as the fact that consciousness is individuated into distinct centres, linked with distinct physical bodies and with distinctive points of view, is taken to be a matter of importance in a society. And they will only really develop as persons in so far as they learn to think of themselves as such. The concept of being a person, in other words, is derivative from the valuation placed in a society upon the determining role of individual points of view. Individuals will only tend to assert their rights as individuals, to take pride in their achievements, to deliberate carefully and choose 'for themselves' what they ought to do, and to develop their own individual style of emotional reaction—in other words they will only tend to manifest all the various properties which we associate with being 'persons'—if they are encouraged to do so. They would be persons all right in the sense that the moral laws were true in virtue of which they had such rights; but if such rights were not recognized they would not be treated as persons, would not think of themselves as such. Even in a society which, because of the importance which it attaches to individual points of view, is permeated by the concept of a person, an individual who was systematically discouraged and sat on might have such a low opinion of himself that we might be inclined to say of him that he simply had not got the concept of himself 'as a person'. What we might mean is that he had the concept of a person but that, because of special circumstances, he was incapable of applying it to himself. Presumably, at certain periods, slaves have been in just this predicament.

In our society being a person matters very much. Individuals are encouraged to judge and choose things 'for themselves'; they are held responsible for the consequences of their actions as individuals and are praised and blamed accordingly; they feel pride for things well done and guilt and remorse for things badly done. They are encouraged to be the determiners of their own destiny and, to a certain extent, they *are* so because our society encourages this form of individual assertion. This consciousness of being an individual person rather than just a member of a group is therefore both exhilarating and sobering. The sense of mastery and making an impact on the shape of things is mingled with apprehension for the consequences of failure. Men, however, come to value it very much for what there is in it as distinct from the value attached to it by their society. Indeed, were it not the case that there is much in it to prize, it is difficult to see how societies would come to attach such overriding value to the assertion of an individual point of view.

This consciousness of being a person reaches its zenith, perhaps, in the experience of entering into and sustaining a personal relationship, which is based on reciprocal agreement, where the bonds that bind people together derive from their own appraisals and choice, not from any status or institutional position. They create their own world by voluntarily sharing together and mingling their own individual perspectives on and developments of the public life of their society. The obligations, mainly of a contractual nature, which sustain their relationship, are felt to be more binding than most duties simply because they are explicitly undertaken and because they create pools of predictability in a realm, which was previously subject only to the play of natural appetites and aversions, within a world marked out by impersonal traditions and institutional pressures.

A person who is conscious of his own agency in shaping events is also aware of the irksomeness of external forces that may prevent or impede him in doing what he wants. He has learnt, however, to come to terms with the confines of nature; for his concept of himself as an agent develops *pari passu* with the concept of a nature which is unaffected by human whims and wishes. It is only in the autistic thinking of the infant, or in magic, that the natural world is subject to human whims and wishes. But he is vividly aware of the irksomeness of constraints imposed on him by other men; for he knows that these are alterable and often unnecessary, as well as frustrating to his purposes. But most irksome of all is the refusal by others to let him determine his own destiny and order his own preferences in any major respect by conceiving of goals, deliberating about alternatives, and attempting to implement those of his choosing. To be treated as a moron or merely as an instrument of the purposes of other men, and to have his feelings completely disregarded, is intolerable for a man who is conscious of his own potentialities as a self-determining agent. It may not be so, of course, for a man who has always been a slave and who has no consciousness of what he might achieve as an agent; there is no reason to suppose that slaves were discontented with their lot as long as they viewed their situation as part of the order of things.

(b) The question of justification

It has been argued that, in so far as a man has the concept of himself and of others as persons, he must have been initiated into a society in which there is a general norm which attaches importance to the assertive points of view emanating from individual centres of consciousness. A man develops as a person as this concept of himself and of others develops. He also comes to value what is involved in being a person for what there is in it as distinct from the importance attached to it by the social norm. To ask him therefore whether persons ought to be respected is rather like asking a man whether he ought to be afraid of a dangerous situation; for the concept of respect is necessary to explicate what is meant by a person. If he has the concept of person and understands it fully from 'the inside' (i.e. not just as an anthropologist might 'understand', or fail to understand, a concept purely on the basis of external observation) then he must also have the notion that it matters that individuals represent distinct assertive points of view.

The explication of a concept, however, never settles a question of policy. The problem is to produce an argument to establish that any rational being must have the concept of a person and therefore respect others and himself as such. The procedure must therefore be to return to the situation of practical reason and to show that respect for persons is a presupposition that any participant in such a situation must accept. An argument must be advanced to show that it would be impossible for a man to take part seriously in the situation of practical reason who lacked this basic attitude to his fellow participants.

Such an argument is not far to seek. Indeed it has been implicit, as would be expected, if the lines of the analysis of 'person' are correct, in the various characterizations of what it means to be a person. Central amongst these are experiences connected with the individual being the determiner of his own destiny, and with representing an assertive point of view. These phrases are attempts to intimate the sort of presuppositions that any man must have about himself and about others if he is to enter into any rational discussion with them about what ought to be done. In the foregoing chapters on 'Freedom' and 'The Consideration of Interests' it was argued that any man entering such a discussion seriously must claim freedom from interference for doing what there are reasons for doing and must assume that consideration must be accorded to him in so far as he has interests whose nature he wants to determine. If he was going to be subject to arbitrary interference, and if no prima facie attention was going to be paid to his assessment of his interests, such a discussion would lack any point. He must presume, too, that what holds for himself holds also for any other man who seriously joins with him in trying to answer such questions. Within such a discussion, too, the principle of impartiality requires that he listens to what people say and assent to or dissent from contributions according to relevant criteria, e.g. the quality of arguments adduced, and ignores irrelevant considerations such as the colour of the eyes or hair of the contributors. These general principles governing the situation of practical reason are precisely those which safeguard the experiences which we most intimately associate with being a person, i.e. not being arbitrarily interfered with in respect of the execution of our wants and decisions and not having our claims and interests ignored or treated in a partial or prejudiced manner. Arguments for the justification of these principles have already been put forward in previous chapters; so there is no need to repeat them in order to justify respect for persons.

It may be found, of course, that particular people are inarticulate or stupid, or that they are dishonest in the manner in which they advance claims. All such factors are relevant to the attention paid to particular people on particular occasions. But the argument is not meant to show that anyone must do anything particular on any particular occasions. Rather it relates to prima facie principles which a man must *in general* accept if he is determined to settle things, in so far as he can, by discussion.

The norm of respect for persons, therefore, picks out as crucial those types of experience, which are a selection from the more varied range of experiences located at an individual centre of consciousness, which are of cardinal importance for those entering seriously into discussion with their fellows about courses of action or ways of living. 'Respect for persons' is therefore a principle which summarizes the attitude which we must adopt towards others with whom we are prepared seriously to discuss what ought to be done. Their point of view must be taken into account as sources of claims and interests; they must be regarded as having a prima facie claim for non-interference in doing what is in their interest; and no arbitrariness must be shown towards them as participants in discussion. To have the concept of a person is to see an individual as an object of respect in a form of life which is conducted on the basis of those principles which are presuppositions of the use of practical reason.

2. THE INFLUENCE OF FRATERNITY

It has been assumed to date that rational discussion must take place on the assumption that individuals are concerned about what is to be done in so far as it affects either themselves or other individuals. It is possible, however, to conceive of a group of beings discussing what ought to be done by the group as a whole without any concern for the stake of any individual in the future. They would not, it might be argued, enter such a discussion as individuals with claims and interests to be considered; only as members of a collective concerned about the destiny of such a collective. They could be knit together by a feeling of fraternity derivative from their common concern as seekers after what was desirable for the collective with no concern for the agonies, elations, or difficulties of any individuals. They might, too, be very conscious of what as a group they might accomplish in promoting what they thought desirable; but they might be oblivious of or unimpressed by the role of any individuals in such an undertaking. And anyone who was ineffective in group discussion or in carrying out his allotted task would be universally despised or 'shamed' into silence or effectiveness. In short, what would be lacking amongst such a group of rational beings would be any general notion of the importance of *individual* consciousness or the role of the *individual* in determining his own destiny.

It might well be said that such a group of beings would have in fact no concept of themselves as persons. Like Kant's rational beings they would have respect for law, which would be tinged with the consciousness that the law, demarcating what was desirable, had been arrived at by their own active deliberation and would only be implemented by their corporate striving. What they would lack would be the additional Kantian conviction of the importance of their own *individual* striving which would 'like a jewel, still shine by its own light' in spite of the 'niggardly provision of a step-motherly nature',[1] or the Utilitarian notion of the importance of their individual interest. They might have the concept of a quality of life; but this would be something discerned rather hazily in the order of things like a Platonic Form or an Aristotelian essence. Or it might be a classless society whose inevitable approach could only be accelerated or retarded by collective action. It would not necessarily be something which had to be formulated and kept in being by human agency like the moral law of Kant. The concept of the individual person, which carries with it the conviction that his experiences matter and that his dignity as a determiner of his destiny has to be respected, would not be crucial in their system of thought.

The question, however, is whether a being who deliberates with others about the 'good' of the collective to which he belongs, is guilty ultimately of some kind of incoherence or woolliness of thought if he thinks that there can be any such 'good' which is not that of the individuals who compose it. There are, of course, goods such as security which all members of a group have individually in common. There are, as has been shown, policies which are 'in the public interest' in that they favour the particular interest of no individual or section of society.[2] But how can such concepts ultimately be applied without reference to the consciousness of individuals? A group or collective has no consciousness or life apart from that of the individuals who compose it; so is not any conception of the 'end' or 'welfare' of a group that fails to do justice to this fact about the world doomed to ultimate incoherence? This was one of the cardinal points in Aristotle's criticism of Plato's *Republic*. He pointed out that it was no good depriving the Guardians of happiness and saying that it was enough that the state should be happy; for happiness can only be enjoyed by individuals.[3] The notion of the welfare of the state is therefore an incoherent one unless it is related to the quality of life enjoyed by its members. Without experiences such as those connected with pleasure and pain, it is difficult to see how an individual could learn to apply the concept of a reason for action for himself, let alone for the collective of which he was a member.

[1] Kant, I., op. cit., p. 11.
[2] See Ch. VI, Sec. 1.
[3] See Aristotle, *Politics*, Bk. II.

Nevertheless the feeling of fraternity generated by membership of a cohesive group can be so strong that even rational beings can be led to apply fundamental principles, whose proper sphere of application is to individuals, to collectives viewed as supra-individual entities. This thoroughly incoherent form of application bears witness to the strength of fraternity which may easily cloud and distort the judgment of rational men.

(a) The meaning of 'fraternity'[1]

The concept of fraternity has literal application only to people who are members of the same family, where the common fact of kinship generates a powerful feeling of oneness and belonging which transcends purely personal attractions and animosities. It would be strange for a larger association of men to imagine that they were literally kin, though Aristotle criticized Plato for confusing the unity appropriate to a state with that appropriate to the household. Love, he argued, will be 'watery' if the young think of all their elders as fathers. Nevertheless a small community, such as a city-state, could be sufficiently homogeneous to be permeated by such a feeling of unity and belonging. Members could be knit together by common traditions, by a common language, and a common religion; they could pursue cultural interests together and show an active common interest in agriculture, in trade, in defence, and in the government of the community.

In such a community men might think quite rationally together, and be staunch advocates of fundamental principles such as justice, equality, liberty, and the consideration of interests. But they might apply them very differently, as Plato did, because of their commitmemt to a common life rather than to the rights of individual persons. Justice might be interpreted as the principle of making distinctions only where there are relevant differences; but the supremely relevant differences would be the contribution made to the community as a whole by those occupying different positions in the community. Man would be considered only as a functionary, not as an individual with a distinctive point of view on the world. Liberty might emerge as the plea for the self-sufficiency of the community and absence of interference on the part of foreign powers. Or it might consist, as in Rousseau's attempt to recreate the ideal of the city-state, in relying on the 'general will' of the community

[1] I owe much of this section to an unpublished paper by Professor A. P. Griffiths, which I once discussed at length with him.

to free the individual from the tyranny of his own desires. Similarly consideration of interest would only take account of the common interest of the community, as in Rousseau's *Social Contract*, not of individual idiosyncrasies.

In the life of a city-state such as Athens, or even of a Swiss Canton, the attitude of fraternity is natural enough in applying the fundamental principles of social life. For traditions, common interests, and common concerns have concrete and palpable existence in the life of a face-to-face community. But it is possible for attenuated, though equally potent, expressions of this attitude to be attached to the life of entities whose manifestations, indeed whose very existence, are much more hypothetical. Cases in point would be the focusing of this attitude on the common life alleged to be shared by members of the same class and nation.

Many, pondering over the obscurities, absurdities, and plain errors in Marxist doctrine, must have wondered why such a fanciful doctrine could have encouraged such widespread allegiance. The explanation is partly to be found in the part played in it by the appeal to fraternity which it embodies, for which more individualistic doctrines give little scope. For the dynamic of Marxism has been built largely round an assumed common predicament and a fabricated common hope. The common predicament was that of the proletariat who everywhere had nothing to lose but their chains. They were united as fellow-sufferers, the victims of the capitalist system. This solidarity as a class would be and was increased as they became increasingly aware of their common predicament.

But this was only a negative dynamic which constitutes only half the appeal. The positive aspect of the doctrine consists in the vibrant conviction that it is only the proletariat who can have a common interest which will permit real fraternity, the much neglected ideal of the French Revolution. On Marx's view such a common interest is impossible within a capitalist state which embodies the exploitation of one class by another. Not only is such a state in a constant condition of disequilibrium because of this basic conflict of interest; the bonds which might bind men together are also non-existent. For, on his view, traditions whether cultural, moral or religious, are but superstructures, the appearances on the surface of the underlying and opposed interests of the warring classes. Fraternity is impossible, too, for the capitalist class, because the capitalist class, for all their common interest in exploiting the workers, are basically antagonistic to each other on account of the underlying logic that each one must maximize his own profits at the expense of his competitors. The working class, however, are not mutually antagonistic to each other. They have no possible interest in doing each other down. 'It is only among such as these,' said Marx, 'that the true brotherhood of man is to be found.' Only with the coming of the classless society when there is only one class, the proletariat, will a common culture, or a common morality, and political institutions working for the common good be possible. This vision of a classless society, in which true fraternity will at last be possible, is the fabricated hope which provides the positive dynamic of Marxism.

In such an ideal society, knit together by fraternity, fundamental principles would receive appropriate application in the light of its emphasis on fraternity. Distributive justice would be there all right; but it would be less important because there would be a condition of abundance of goods. With the consequent diminution of competitive features in a society there would be more preoccupation with common tasks. Man would be no longer alienated from his work or from his fellows. The relevant distinctions between men would be immediately their ability to contribute to the common good and perhaps, at some remote stage, their 'need', however that would be determined. Liberty would not be interpreted predominantly in political terms but in economic terms. Men would be free from the exploitation of other men, from wants which are partly due to such exploitation, and from the tyranny of nature from which science could set man free. True equality would exist with the removal of artificial social distinctions which created individual differences, there being only minimal differences in natural endowment. The consideration of interests would always focus on the common good which is identical with that of all individuals.

Marxists are committed to the doctrine that major social changes are brought about by changes in technology and that ideas are comparatively impotent save in so far as they are reflections of the underlying reality of economic change. One of the most obvious refutations of their thesis is the immeasurable influence in the modern world of the concept of a 'nation'. Yet this is one of the cloudiest concepts in the history of thought —even more cloudy than Marx's own concept of 'class' which was at least clear enough to be obviously inadequate. For what is a nation? It is alleged to be distinct from a state. Indeed Hegel, one of the most vociferous advocates of nationalism, regarded it as an important event in the development of a nation when it formed itself into a State. 'In the existence of a Nation, the substantial aim is to be a State and preserve itself as such. A Nation that has not formed itself into a State—a mere Nation—has strictly speaking no history, like the Nations, that existed in a condition of savagery.' Is a common language a criterion of a nation? It cannot be; for the Slavs and Indians speak many languages. Is a common religion essential to it? Surely not; for the Africans are not united in this respect. Must it have a common history? How can it when Arabs, Jews and Americans, who have a very variegated history, claim to belong to 'nations'. If a nation is constituted by the acceptance by a people of a common legal system this rules out many who claim to be nations, e.g. the Jews, and it is then very difficult to distinguish a nation from a state. And what could the claim amount to, so often made, that states should be based on the principle of national self-determination?

Could it not be that the modern belief in some hypothetical and extremely dubious entity called a 'nation' is a product of the thwarting of fraternity or of the need for a positive object on to which fraternal feelings can be attached? When the life of small communities is disrupted by conquest or by technological advance and especially when some common suffering (e.g. foreign oppression) is shared, is not the feeling of fraternity projected on to some entity, such as a nation, to which fellow-sufferers can all fancy that they belong? At the time when Hegel was writing, for instance, there was widespread dissatisfaction in Germany after Napoleon's conquests and a yearning to belong to some larger unit which could replace the small states, which were in a state of decadence and disruption. Hegel felt this yearning for participation, which he exalted into his famous 'philosophy of identity'. It had appealed to him from the first when he was inspired by Rousseau and the ideals of the common life of the Greek city-state. He poured these sentiments, shared by the German Nationalist movement, which he criticized, into the mould provided by the rise of the new Prussian state. The concept of a nation provided a richer fraternal filling for the more administrative concept of 'state'.

The interpretations of principles such as freedom, justice, and the consideration of interests through nationalistic attitudes are too familiar to need much exposition. 'Freedom' is interpreted as national self-determination, the individual's 'real freedom' consisting in service to the state. Justice simply is conformity to the laws of the state. The interests of the nation are paramount, those of the individual being identified with those of the nation or obliterated by the stress on his 'station and duties' as a citizen. Fundamental principles undergo far-fetched and fanciful transmogrifications when distorted through fraternal feelings attached to such a mystical entity as a nation. But underlying the ideological froth is a yearning for kinship which often issues in the most extreme forms of antipathy towards members of the 'out-group'. Indeed a myth like that of common blood or Aryan ancestry can be invented to satisfy this free-floating feeling, and can issue in the most appalling atrocities towards those who are alleged to lack this inner sign of kinship.

(b) Fraternity and respect for persons in Christianity
Examples have been given so far of systems of thought in which fraternity is the predominant prism through which the light of funda-mental principles has to be filtered, rather than respect for persons. It is possible, too, for there to be systems of thought in which there is a tension between these two attitudes. Such a tension exists in any system strongly influenced by Christianity, whose distinctive function was to articulate basic attitudes towards man and his destiny rather than a system of social principles.

The sayings of Jesus about the Kingdom of Heaven were central in his teaching but were open to diverse interpretations. It was possible to stress its inwardness, the suggestion that it is a state of mind that grows like a mustard seed and which works from within like leaven in bread; it was also possible to emphasize that it is amongst us rather than within us when two or three are gathered together in the name of Jesus. In the doctrine of the early Church there was both the stress on indivi-dual worth, immortalized by Jesus in his sayings about God's concern for each of his children and proclaimed loudly by St Paul in the doctrine of salvation, and the stress on the body of Christ manifest in the cohesive group of believers. 'For as we have many members in one body, and all members have not the same office; so we, being many, are one body in Christ, and everyone members one of another.'[1] The same was true of Luther.[2] The early Christians who laid aside the ties of family, con-sidered that they were bound together by spiritual ties which were more intimate and enduring than those of kinship and of blood. But they also

[1] Romans xii. 4, 5.
[2] See Wolin, S. S., *Politics and Vision* (London, Allen & Unwin, 1961), Ch. 5.

thought that every man must care supremely about the state of his soul; for every individual mattered in the sight of God.

In the history of Christianity these different attitudes, both of which are basic to Christianity, have received different emphasis at different times. R. H. Tawney was at his most eloquent when describing this contrast. In his brilliant chapter on 'The Puritan Movement' he puts the contrast as follows:

> Where they [Catholic and Anglican] had seen society as a mystical body, compact of members varying in order and degree, but dignified by participation in the common life of Christendom, he [the Puritan] saw a bleak antithesis between the spirit which quickeneth and an alien, indifferent or hostile world. Where they had reverenced the decent order whereby past was knit to present, and man to man, and man to God, through fellowship in works of charity, in festival and fast, in the prayers and ceremonies of the Church, he turned with horror from the filthy rags of human righteousness. . . . The moral self-sufficiency of the Puritan nerved his will but it corroded his sense of social solidarity. . . . A spiritual aristocrat, who sacrificed fraternity to liberty, he drew from his idealization of personal responsibility a theory of individual rights, which, secularized and generalized, was to be among the most potent explosives that the world has known. . . .[1]

The Christian concept of man has always veered between emphasizing his spiritual affinity with other men as members of one body in Christ and the ultimate loneliness of each individual in his quest for salvation.

A similar tension has existed in many movements of the western world which have been strongly influenced by Christianity. The Labour Party in Great Britain, for instance, has been fired by the Socialist vision of a society in which true fraternity is possible; it has preached the virtues of social solidarity and has attacked the 'profit motive' of an individualist system which makes work for the common good an impossible ideal save in a national emergency; on the other hand it has received the bulk of its support from those who think that each individual can only have an 'equal opportunity' to develop himself if wealth is more evenly distributed, and if the major sources of economic power are

[1] Tawney, R. H., *Religion and the Rise of Capitalism* (West Drayton, Penguin Books, 1938), pp. 228–9.

publicly owned and controlled. The public school system has tried similarly to inculcate virtues such as team-spirit, group loyalty and the traditional adherence to a common code; but it has also encouraged individual initiative and a sense of responsibility and has idolized those who stick to their principles in the face of community pressure.

(c) The question of justification

The justification of the attitude of fraternity is not quite on the same footing as the justification of respect for persons; for there never has been a race of men without some kind of fraternal feeling, whereas respect for persons is a comparatively rare phenomenon in the history of man. Also, whereas respect for persons is an attitude underwritten by a reasonably distinctive set of appraisals, fraternity, as has been already indicated, has many vicissitudes. The issue, therefore, with fraternity is usually not whether it should be felt but whether the type of 'kinship' to which the feeling is attached is a significant one.

There are all kinds of similarities, such as the colour of men's hair or eyes, which could generate a feeling of 'kinship'. But only some are emphasized in particular societies. This feeling of 'kinship' has a snow-ball effect, which is a particular case of the general sociological law that social beliefs beget social realities;[1] for if people feel that they are 'kin' or belong to some group with shared practices and ideals, they will tend to develop standard habits of thought and behaviour which multiply the grounds which there might be for regarding them as 'kin'. An obvious modern example would be the development of the 'teen-age culture'. The development of 'social classes' and 'nations' are other instances which have already been cited as major manifestations of the fraternal feeling. Often the obvious similarity, such as the colour of a man's skin, is but an outward sign of deep-seated resemblances in speech, beliefs, and a general way of life that already exists. It is dwelt upon as a significant similarity because of its palpability rather than because of its significance in itself.

There is one type of 'in-group' which is universal amongst men and which is the centre of fraternity in its literal sense. This is the family. Of course what constitutes a family and its internal structure varies enormously from society to society. But the existence of the family and the feelings of 'belonging' and loyalty which it generates are universal

---

[1] See Merton, R., *Social Theory and Social Structure* (Illinois, Free Press, 1949), Ch. VII.

in the species. The explanation is not far to seek; for at the moment men universally are introduced to society through membership of this 'primary group' and it is within this group that the fraternal attitude is first encountered and learnt. Indeed there is evidence to suggest that if a man does not have the opportunity, because of early deprivation, to acquire these attitudes at an early age within such a primary group, he will find it almost impossible to acquire them later.

Supposing, however, that a man is not moved by the knowledge that he is kin to other men in some respect—even as belonging to the same family—and cannot see why this contingent fact should constitute any ground for excitement. What could be said to demonstrate that his acknowledged 'kinship' should be something that is other than a matter of indifference to him? This is rather like asking what can be said to a man who has the concept of 'person' but does not think that persons ought to be respected; for in both cases the concept is norm involved. He can only properly be said to have the concept of 'person' if he thinks that the fact that he and others represent distinct points of view is a matter of importance; similarly he can only properly be said to have the concept of 'kinship' if the fact of his membership of some group is regarded as a matter of importance. But again, as in the case of respect for persons, such a conceptual explication cannot settle a question of policy. What has to be shown is that some group memberships are more important than others and hence justifiable as bonds on which the feeling of fraternity can get a grip.

How can such worth-while allegiances be picked out? The first step must surely be to distinguish important allegiances from the hypostatization of entities on the basis of them. Individuals may be members of the same state. As citizens they live under a system of law which prescribes rights and duties for them. This system persists even though they as individuals perish. It is possible, too, to speak of the 'will' of the state or of the acts of a state in so far as individuals decide or do things in accordance with properly constituted public procedures. These procedures persist and give continuity even though the individuals who operate in accordance with them change and pass away. It is the persistence of such authority relationships, and of the procedures defining what are legislative, administrative, and judicial acts that give content to the fiction of a corporate person. For any rational man the existence of such a framework of order is a matter of great importance; for without the rule of law it would be extremely difficult for him to enjoy those conditions of security which are necessary conditions both for his liberty and for the pursuit of what is good. He must therefore regard his duties as a citizen as important to him and his feeling of kinship towards others as fellow-citizens is one that is based on an important allegiance. For he is united to them by a common interest in maintaining a system that is of great importance to all alike. There is no rational warrant, however, for exalting such a system of rules into an entity which could exist without individuals to act on them.

The question, therefore, for any rational man is to consider his various allegiances in terms of the rules and purposes derivative from them and to assess them on that basis. In so far, for instance, as he is regarded as belonging to the 'middle class' in a society, should that be of much concern to him? If membership of such a class were defined in terms of some fairly arbitrary classification of occupations by the Registrar-General this might concern him very little. If, on the other hand, it were defined in terms of adherence to certain 'bourgeois' values such as honesty, enterprise, precision, hardwork, and fairness, it might concern him very much. Many allegiances do not permit of such wide interpretations. If a man joins the Society for the Propagation of Christian Knowledge, for instance, the focus for fraternity is pretty unambiguous.

It follows from this that there is one sort of kinship that must be appropriate for a rational being, whatever he feels about his loyalty to family, state, class, or club, and that is his kinship with other rational beings as persons. In so far as he is a rational being, and joins with other rational beings in seeking to discover what ought to be done, his kinship to them as persons, with points of view to be considered, claims to be assessed impartially, and interests to pursue without unjustified interference must be considered important; for this minimal type of kinship is a precondition of the situation of practical reason. The feeling of fraternity must therefore at least be attached to the kinship of being a person.

The power of the feeling of fraternity, however, does not necessarily follow the lines of its rational justification. The attachment of the feeling of fraternity to others as fellow participants in rational discussion must be, for a rational being, the most justifiable of all its possible objects; but it is not necessarily the form of attachment that moves an individual most. This is partly because the development of practical reason in the sense here outlined takes a long time and is superimposed on other more powerful and primitive layers of mind. An individual grows up in a family and internalizes a code of behaviour as a result of identification with one or other of his parents. He later acquires other codes of behaviour through peer-group pressure. Such codes of behaviour may or may not be rationally justifiable. An individual may emerge to a stage when he can rationally assess such rules and be moved by the thought of other rational beings who are in the same predicament as himself; but he may nevertheless be more moved by any reactivation of the old mechanisms by means of which he first acquired his code of behaviour. Fear of an authority, love for a leader, or the force of public opinion may swamp his respect for persons. The individual's sense of justice may be strong; but it may go under if more primitive pressures are put on him. Many rational beings capable of respect for persons have joined in the persecution of minorities.

There is also the fact that fellow-feeling for another as a person is a more abstract sentiment than the fraternity felt by members of a cohesive face-to-face group. Moral agents do not form special societies for discussions of moral problems; cohesive face-to-face groups are not constituted by their acceptance of fundamental moral principles. Neither is morality a code confined to a club, class, or state. Kant, it is true, conceived of rational beings as living in a 'kingdom of ends' whose laws were the objective principles formulated and accepted by rational beings; but this was a moral philosopher's version of the kingdom of heaven rather than an account of a concrete community. A 'moral community' is not therefore supported by those massive feelings of loyalty built up over years of constant association in common tasks that are so characteristic of face-to-face groups. Indeed to confront another simply as a person is to conceive of him as detached from his status and roles and from his natural affinities and associations. On the more negative side, too, a 'moral community', by definition, has no authority structure, no built-in appeal to consensus. By this is meant that the validity of moral rules is not determined by appeals to authority or to majority agreement as are the rules of states and clubs. There is therefore no palpable psychological or physical sanction that determines their enforcement. Their validity is determined by appeal to reasons and the psychological strength of a man's conscience does not always match its legislative supremacy. As Butler said of conscience: 'Had it strength, as it has right; had it power, as it has manifest authority; it would absolutely govern the world.'[1] It is not suprising therefore that rational beings frequently allow

[1] Butler, J., *Sermons Upon Human Nature*, II.

their feeling of kinship for others as rational beings to be overcome by more massive and primitive loyalties, and that systems of thought can issue from the pen of rational beings such as Hegel and Marx in which fundamental principles are interpreted with more emphasis on group-loyalty than on respect for persons.

3. EDUCATION AND THE CONCEPT OF MAN

An account has already been given in Chapter II, Section 4, of the ways in which respect for persons and the feeling of fraternity enter into an educational situation. It was also stressed that the teacher's respect for persons is overlaid with the awareness that he is confronted with developing centres of consciousness. He must be concerned with the development of each individual and his rational acceptance of the principle of freedom must dictate that a principle of options be permitted within a range of activities and modes of conduct that are desirable, whatever his own particular preferences.

In approaching the task of guiding the development of children towards what is worth while, it is not sufficient for the teacher to have a clear grasp of what is worth while, a concern for individual children, and a determination to follow the principle of liberty as far as he can. He must also be familiar with generalizations about motivation, learning, and child development; for an uninformed respect for children as persons is not likely to take the teacher very far in applying the moral principles which have been treated so laboriously in this section of the book. It might be thought, then, that all the teacher has to do is to turn to the works of psychologists in order to give content to his concept of the person whom he is determined to treat with respect. When, however, he turns to the psychologists he finds a bewildering variety of views about these matters. The differences are not based so much on disagreements about empirical findings but on different approaches to the development of children and different conceptual schemes for imposing order on what findings there are.

If, for instance, he consults any psychologist who has a Freudian orientation he will first of all get the strong impression that with children things are never quite what they seem. He may think, for instance, that a child has a genuine interest in exploring the physical properties of the natural world as exemplified in sand, water, or cylindrical shapes. He will soon have it explained to him that such manipulation or exploration is a substitute for playing with excrement, for manipulating the genitals, or for sexual curiosity. He will learn that the Freudian has a very definite notion of which types of activity are basic and which are derivative offshoots. Activities which he may think worth while such as sculpture or scientific research will be relentlessly traced back to their infantile prototypes. For they are not regarded as being 'natural' in the way that eating, sucking and sexual activity are 'natural'. If he is clear-headed he will realize that, even if this rather far-fetched story were true, it should not affect the worthwhileness of his cherished pursuits. For a story about something's origin need not affect the issue of its value. Nevertheless he will find his view of such pursuits insensibly altered.

The teacher will also find that in Freudian theory the development of the child is not charted in terms of his cognitive grasp but in terms of his emotional reactions, with special emphasis on sex, anxiety and aggression. At the basic oral, anal, and phallic stages the relevant zones of the child's body become sensitized and the child has to learn to deal with conflicts occasioned by the emergence of wishes that he is forbidden to translate into action. Relationships with parents and parent-substitutes are regarded as crucial and the child's character is thought to to consist largely of precipitates left by his struggles at the different stages. If the teacher studies this sort of psychology, therefore, he will tend to find little that is relevant to cognitive development or to the content of any curriculum. Instead he will find a great emphasis on the child's emotional life and on personal relationships in teaching, and the content of a curriculum will be looked at from the point of view of its suitability for this. He will find himself cast in the role of a parent or therapist. Motivation will be thought of as mainly extrinsic and his attitudes to children and to what he has to teach will be regarded as crucial; for on this theory most of the difficult things that belong to 'culture' are thought to be picked up by identification with authority figures.

If the teacher finds this account of child-development both disturbing and somewhat unhelpful to him in his task he may turn to Piaget's theory, which has achieved great popularity in recent times amongst teachers. Here he will find a much more congenial account of child development with the stages of conceptual grasp laboriously mapped in relation to school subjects—especially mathematics and physics. He will learn at roughly what stages the categorial apparatus of the Kantian mind develops; he will learn the age at which reversibility and seriation are possible mental operations for a child. He will also learn when children can emulate Aristotle in classifying and ordering the objects of the natural world and how they later can proceed to the hypothetico-deductive form of thinking so characteristic of Galileo. He will also learn logical truths dressed up in psychological guise, such as that learning must proceed from the simple to the complex, or that concrete operations with objects must precede abstract thought about them.

In Piaget's system the teacher will find, to his surprise, that motivation is assumed to be intrinsic. He will read almost nothing about the role of the teacher in stimulating interest or conveying a sense of standards. Readiness is assumed to be all important and the teacher's role seems to be mainly that of encouraging the child to discover things for himself and to exercise his cognitive abilities as they reach the appropriate point. The moral development of the child is sketched in Kantian terms, the child passing from a stage of heteronomy to a stage of autonomy. But nothing is said of the social conditions which make such a transition possible, or of the influences in early childhood that may prevent or distort it. On the subject of emotional development, or of more general forms of social development, Piaget has not yet spoken. From this account the teacher will get the general impression that the individual is rather like a Leibnizian monad, developing according to the laws of his nature, and spinning out categories and concepts from within as he explores the external world.

The teacher might be a more hard-headed person with high standards of scientific precision. He might therefore find Freudian theory too woolly in its terminology and too speculative and untested in its hypotheses. He might think that too much of Piaget was philosophy masquerading as empirical psychology and that the investigations were conducted with too little concern for experimental variables and on too few children. He might therefore turn hopefully to behaviourism and learning theory, whose main importance in psychology has been to establish psychology as a laboratory science. He will find here the old laws of association still going strong but applied to connections between movements instead of between ideas. He will find a great interest in the effect of motivation on learning. He will note that there has been a shift away from the old emphasis on extrinsic motivation and a willingness to admit intrinsic motivation. Indeed he may reflect somewhat sourly that plain curiosity is dressed up in a rather pretentious way as the 'drive to know' or the 'exploratory drive'. He may remark also on the revival of interest in transfer of training since it has been demonstrated that chimpanzees learn to learn. But he will wonder what most of the work done could possibly show about human learning in general. Indeed he might wonder what most of the experiments show about how animals actually learn things as distinct from how they may be induced to pick up things under very special conditions. He might concede that certain simple motor skills might be picked up by instrumental conditioning; he might grant that conditioning might account for certain phobias, addictions, and aversions. But as a hard-headed teacher he would surely remain incredulous about the relevance of most of the work done by learning theorists to what children have to learn in schools.

In a more liberal frame of mind such a teacher might reflect that the determination of behaviourists to confine themselves to observable data and to eschew introspective reports must severely limit what they can possibly investigate. If the inner life of man is banned from investigation, actions which necessarily involve intentions, emotions which necessarily involve appraisals of a situation, together with imagination, memory, perception, dreaming, and pain must all be ruled out as scientifically proper objects of investigation; for none of these phenomena can be described or identified without reference to consciousness. There is therefore precious little left of human behaviour to investigate. So the sterility of this approach to human learning is not surprising.

It may of course be the case that there are certain generalizations about extrinsic conditions covered by Thorndike's old laws of effect and exercise, which are relevant to learning, irrespective of what is learnt. But if behaviourist theory, incorporating such generalizations, is applied by some sort of analogy to the situation of human learning, certain other unpalatable features of the model may go with it. The teacher may be regarded as an external manipulator whose function is to 'shape the behaviour' of children to a prescribed pattern in the manner of a circus trainer teaching a seal some tricks. The child's view of the world may be neither here nor there. His relationships with his teacher may be looked at merely as a further set of experimental variables. Amongst processes of learning imitation of externally observed acts may feature, but not the introjection of sensed attitudes. The generalizations, e.g. about reinforcement, may be found to be valid, but the conceptual scheme in which they are incorporated makes it impossible to mark the moral features of the teaching situation. Indeed it is difficult to see how a consistent behaviourist can talk about moral relationships at all; for it is not acts as physical movements that are right or wrong, but actions incorporating specific intentions.

A teacher, who had made such a depressing pilgrimage in search of some sort of expertise about child development and human learning, could react in at least two ways. He might reflect, on the one hand, that these theories are complementary, not necessarily antagonistic to each other. The mistake is to adopt anything other than an eclectic approach to them. Piaget provides a most suggestive framework for cognitive development. He maps the stages of development of both theoretical and practical reason and relates this carefully to the acquisition of concepts necessary for scientific, mathematical and moral thinking. His account needs to be supplemented in the first place by more careful attention to historical, religious, and aesthetic modes of thought and to modes of thinking about individual people and societies. In the second place it needs to be supplemented by a Freudian type of theory which provides in the main a theory of passivity.[1] It explains distortions and lapses in thought, perception, remembering, and action. It deals with phenomena such as dreams, hysteria, and fantasy. It suggests explanations of various lapses from rationality which issue in forms of pathological thought and behaviour. A different level of mind operating in terms of wishes is postulated to account for such phenomena. These wishes, which are closely linked with the basic emotions of love, fear, and anger, have to be dealt with as the rational level of mind slowly develops. Freudian theory accounts both for the failure to develop rationality and for the disruption of rationality by the persistence of more infantile modes of awareness. Behaviourism, too, might be seen as contributing much to our understanding of general conditions of learning and of how simple reactions may be acquired.

On the other hand it might be concluded that there is little hope of men ever reaching agreement about any sort of conceptual scheme for ordering empirical findings about man and his development. Freudian theory, it might be suggested, is the work of a moralist who belongs to a persecuted race, a modern Stoic advocating a life of cautious prudence and control in a life situation which is bound to be fraught with conflict and frustration.[2] Behaviourism is essentially the product of a people

[1] See Peters, R. S., 'Emotions, Passivity and the Place of Freud's Theory in Psychology' in Wolman, B. B., and Nagel, E., *Scientific Psychology* (New York, Basic Books, 1965).

[2] See Rieff, P., *Freud, the Mind of the Moralist* (New York, Viking Press, 1959).

in which the distinction between the public and the private has become blurred and whose attitude to life is predominantly instrumental and materialistic. Piaget's theory represents a fusion of philosophy with a biologistic belief about self-development arising from the optimism of the nineteenth century. In other words it might be argued that all these conceptual schemes also conceal disguised valuations. Into alleged descriptions of human nature and its development are smuggled norms about the sort of creature a man should be. They enshrine not simply generalizations relevant to the development of a worth-while form of life but covertly prescribe its content.

4. THE POSSIBILITY OF A VALUE-FREE CONCEPT OF MAN

A strong case can therefore be made for saying that concepts of man are culture-bound and that they enshrine the valuations of those who propound them. It does not follow, however, from the fact that most concepts of man have been like this, that they must always be so. Indeed the fact that they have been so suggests higher level generalizations about man which may be true universally. Men are unique amongst animals in many ways, but perhaps one of the most important features of their life is that its form is influenced enormously by the concept which they have of themselves. Their concept of man is one of the most important and far-reaching threads in the fabric of the public tradition into which they are initiated. But it is not a constant in the thought of different societies. There are constants, perhaps, such as the need to eat, drink and sleep and eliminate. But the importance attached to these biological functions and their style and manner is determined by the varying social traditions. Built into these different traditions are different concepts of man—especially in respect of the differing categorizations of the individual's relation to society and to the natural world. Such differences in the concept of man are crucial in determining the application of principles of conduct.

Marx made this point graphically in his famous aphorism, 'It is not the consciousness of man that determines his existence—rather, it is his social existence that determines his consciousness.' This was a very important insight that any advocate of a more individualistic concept of man must take very seriously. Obviously, for instance, much of the argument about education and the development of mind advanced in Chapter II is drawn from the tradition of thought that ascribes central importance to man's social existence in the account of his consciousness. But Marx stressed this aspect of man's consciousness to the exclusion of the other equally important insight of the individualistic tradition, that privacy is the hall-mark of the mental, and that individuals can, within limits, make themselves by their choices. As a modern philosopher cryptically put the matter, 'The peculiarity of the soul is not that it is visible to none but that it is visible only to one.'[1] Marx touched on a limited aspect of this in his few and brief remarks about 'alienation'; but, in the main, problems to do with the privacy of the individual's consciousness and his responsibility for choice were obscured in the massive contours of a theory that regarded individuals and ideas as of minor importance, both from the point of view of the explanation of events and the explication of institutions. The Existentialists, on the other hand, have built a theory of human nature around the importance of individual decision and choice. Indeed Sartre's theory of human nature is almost a denial that the nature of man imposes any limitations on morality. Human nature, on this view, is more or less created by the exercise of choice. Men are what they make of themselves. If they think that they have a 'nature', which sets limits to this, they are engaged in deliberate deception to avoid the burden of responsibility; for 'choice' rears its head even in emotional reactions and in man's passivity to physical states.

It is not impossible, however, that a concept of man at a more abstract level, that takes account of insights such as these, might be developed. This would require sustained co-operation between psychologists, philosophers, and social scientists. At such a level the theories of thinkers such as Piaget, Freud, Marx, and Sartre might be found to be not completely incompatible; for they might incorporate important truths expressed in too concrete and particularized a form. For instance Freud's notorious Oedipus complex might incorporate an important generalization about the overriding importance of early learning in the sphere of social relationships; his theory of unconscious sexual wishes might be subsumed under a wider theory of passivity and undiscriminating awareness. Piaget, on the other hand, deals with the development of differentiated modes of thought and Sartre with decision and possible forms of self-deception. Marx focuses attention on the social determinants of thought and action.

[1] Wisdom, J., 'The Concept of Mind', *Proc. Aristotelian Soc.*, N.S. Vol. I, 1949–50, p. 195.

In educational theory such co-operation is absolutely essential; for philosophy can only contribute partially to the answering of any educational question. It may help to achieve more clarity about what forms of life are worth passing on, but it cannot determine how this task can be accomplished. It has been stressed, too, in this book that though philosophy can indicate how fundamental ethical principles involved in education might be justified, such principles cannot be determinately applied without a concept of man. The trouble, however, about most existing concepts of man is that they themselves covertly incorporate ethical valuations. The fundamental task, therefore, that remains to be tackled by those who wish to advance both educational and political theory is to get down to work in the philosophy of mind in conjunction with psychologists, social scientists, historians, and men of wide practical experience and shrewd judgment. The time has passed when philosophers could, with a clear conscience, spin theories of human nature out of their own observations and introspection.

PART THREE

EDUCATION AND SOCIAL CONTROL

CHAPTER IX

AUTHORITY AND EDUCATION

INTRODUCTION

It was maintained in Part One that education consists essentially in the initiation of members of a society into a form of life that is thought to be worth while. In Part Two an attempt was made to justify both the content of what is handed on and the manner in which it is distributed and adapted to individuals. Such initiation takes place, for the most part, in schools and colleges, and very little has yet been said about problems to do with social control within them. Even in a club, which people join voluntarily because of some common purpose which they wish to pursue, there are often acute problems of social control. Such problems are likely to be much more acute in schools, to which recruitment is not voluntary, and whose purposes the members do not fully understand until they are soon to leave—if they understand them even then. These problems of social control have been accentuated by the accelerated rate of social change with an increased gap and lack of understanding between the generations consequent on it, which has made it even more difficult for the young to identify themselves with the values which it is the business of schools and colleges to transmit.

Part Three will therefore be concerned basically with problems of social control; for, without a discussion of such problems, talk about education and about the justification of its matter and manner would be Utopian.

The most crucial concept for discussing social control in the school is that of 'authority'. A school is not an organization like a prison in which coercion is the main form of social control; neither is it like an industry in which control is exercised predominantly by economic sanctions and rewards. Its *raison d'être* is to transmit what a community values. It can approximate to a prison; the rat race in a society can also become so severe that the organization of a school can be distorted to reflect it. But these are both degenerate forms of a school. To get clearer about what is the appropriate form of social control in a school more has to be said about the key concept of 'authority'.

I. THE CONCEPT OF 'AUTHORITY'

The concept of authority is inseparably connected with a rule-governed form of life. It is only appropriately applied when there is a question of something thought, said, or done being correct or true. It is inseparable from the use of speech, symbolic gestures, and rituals by means of which verdicts, commands, and pronouncements, which lay down what is correct or true, are enunciated and vested with significance. 'Authority' thus presupposes some sort of normative order that has to be promulgated, maintained, and perpetuated. Legislators, judges, umpires, colonels, policemen and priests are typical figures of authority. There are procedural rules which give such people the right to decide, promulgate, judge, order and pronounce. They are thus authorized to lay down what the substantive rules are, apply them to particular cases, enforce them or announce them publicly perhaps with the appropriate rituals. In other words the concept of authority would be unintelligible unless we first had the concept of following rules with the built-in notion that there are correct or incorrect ways of doing things.

The converse, however, is not true. We can conceive of a society of highly moral beings living together amicably out of respect for the moral law and for each other as rational beings, without anyone being in authority, and without anyone being thought of as an authority. If, however, they had come into the world in the usual way, rather than arriving fully mature like angels, then they would probably have the concept of 'authority'; for they would, as children, have learnt what was correct and incorrect from parents and teachers, and from such psychological conditions they would have got the idea that there were some special people who knew about such matters. But, logically speaking, they could cease to apply this notion in adult life. If in such cases we talk of the 'authority' of tradition or of the moral law within, we are using the term 'authority' figuratively to speak of the backing which exists for the rules which they might live by. For 'authority' is not properly used in *all* spheres where there is an issue about what is correct or incorrect. It is only properly used in those situations in which decisions about what is correct or incorrect are reached by appealing to some source or 'auctor', or where certain people are thought to have peculiar insight into what is correct or true. 'Authority' therefore has its natural home in legal systems, armies, and religious communities. In such organizations special people are given the right to lay down what is correct in general, to apply rules to particular cases or to enforce them, or special people are thought to have peculiar insight into what is beyond the ken of ordinary mortals. Where there is an appeal to a special person as a source, originator, interpreter, or enforcer of rules the term 'authority' is properly used. This analysis of 'authority' has some kind of support from philology; for the original Latin word '*auctoritas*' denoted notions like those of 'producing', 'originating' and 'inventing' in the sphere of opinion, counsel, and command.

'Authority' is most in evidence in the sphere of social control where we have authority systems; we speak of those 'in authority' or of 'the authorities'. In this sphere it must be distinguished from power with which it is too often confused by political theorists and sociologists alike. 'Power' basically denotes ways in which an individual subjects others to his will by means of physical coercion (e.g. infliction of pain, restriction of movement), or by psychological coercion (e.g. withholding food, water, shelter, or access to means of attaining such necessities), or by the use of less dire forms of sanction and rewards (e.g. by manipulating access to material resources and rewards, sexual satisfaction, etc.), or by personal influences such as hypnotism or sexual attraction. Authority, on the other hand, involves the appeal to an impersonal normative order or value system which regulates behaviour basically because of acceptance of it on the part of those who comply. It operates because of understanding of and concern for what is intimated within a rule-governed form of life, which those in authority help to create and sustain. Authority, of course, may be and usually is supported by various forms of power. Behind the symbolic gestures of the policeman lies the coercive power which he can summon, or his hypnotic stare. But this is no reason for blurring the distinction between the two concepts.

Authority, however, is not confined to spheres of social control. We can speak of a person being *an* authority purely in the sphere of knowledge, e.g. on the Incas, on the history of Greece, or on the migration of birds. Such a person is assumed to have a right to pronounce on such matters because of his special competence, training, or insight. There is, however, a difference between authority in this sphere and in that of social control. In the sphere of social control the validity of, e.g., a law is determined by examining whether or not a rule was laid down by a person or body authorized to do it. The rule might be unwise or wicked, but its validity would not depend on appeals to the reasons implied by such appraisals; for as Hobbes put it, it is authority, not wisdom, that makes a law. Similarly the decision of a judge can only be annulled by that of a higher authority; it cannot be rendered null and void purely on account of its unreasonableness. In an authority system like an army the only legitimate way of challenging an order is to question a person's right to issue it. In the sphere of knowledge, however, the situation is very different. The ultimate appeal here is always to reasons, not to an 'auctor'. There are no umpires or constituted judges in the spheres of knowledge. Hence the incongruity of Charles II presiding as umpire over a circle-squaring debate in the seventeenth century. The pronouncements of any person who is *an* authority can always be challenged by appeals to evidence or grounds. He can always be mistaken. The authority of people who are treated as authorities in the sphere of knowledge derives from their likelihood of being right because of their special training or vantage point and because they have often been proved to be right before. Such authorities must always, therefore, be treated as provisional. Their status is rather like that of reliable witnesses in the case of perception. Nothing is ever *made* right because they say so, as it is in the sphere of law.

In the sphere of knowledge we talk of 'experts' as well as of 'authorities'. The difference lies in the aspect under which knowledge is viewed. If it is regarded as being instrumental to achieving some end, rather than pursued for its own sake, we tend to speak of the person as an 'expert'. Governments have experts to advise them on the implementation of various policies, whereas authorities are consulted when somebody simply wants to know something. 'Expertise' implies the application of knowledge, not just the possession of it. An expert swimmer or fencer is very different from an authority on these activities.

The teacher is an authority figure in both the above senses. He is put *in* authority to do a certain job for the community and to maintain social control in the school while he is doing it. He must also be *an* authority on some aspect of the culture of the community which he is employed to transmit. It is also expected that, to a certain extent, he will be an expert on the behaviour and development of the children over whom he is in authority, and on methods of teaching them. The complexities and conflicts deriving from such a complicated status will be explored later.

2. FORMAL AND ACTUAL AUTHORITY

In dealing with the concepts of equality and liberty in previous chapters it was found important to distinguish between the formal position defined in terms of normative rules and what actually happens. The same is true of 'authority'. Formally speaking a schoolmaster, for instance, can be in authority over a class; but in fact he may not be able to exercise authority over them. He has a right to give orders, but no one in fact obeys them. It may be the case, too, that an individual may emerge under certain social conditions whose commands come to be obeyed and decisions accepted even though he has no formal position in an authority structure. This happens usually when the personal qualities and abilities of the individual are peculiarly suited to the dominant purpose or need of a group, and when those of the formal leader are not. Or perhaps the emergent leader may represent a different system of values. Under ordinary circumstances the formal position is preserved and either there is a state of tension and dissatisfaction, or harmony is maintained by the individual who is formally in authority deferring to the effective leader of the group in judgment and delegating disciplinary and directive functions to him.

It is still a matter of speculation amongst social psychologists as to whether many generalizations can be made about the determinants of actual authority. Usually, of course, under stable social conditions, with legitimate rather than revolutionary leaders, the office makes the man. If he slips naturally into the role of a man in authority, people will obey the incarnation of the office. There are established expectations of the behaviour of office-holders and if an individual satisfies these expectations with reasonable competence there is a presumption in favour of his being effective. He must, of course, be committed to the purpose pursued by the group and must be knowledgeable and efficient in prosecuting it, i.e. he must have a modicum of expertise. If he has an 'air of authority' and behaves in a decisive way as if he expects to be obeyed or believed, such external signs of authority will increase his likelihood of actually exercising authority. He must also be shrewd and tactful in dealing with rivalries and tensions amongst members of the group. In brief his qualities must be such that he can exercise the most general functions of leadership so that he commands a degree of respect within his own group and presents an 'image' to the outside world of which they are not ashamed. Such generalizations about leadership, or the actual exercise of authority, apply to teachers as well as to anyone else who has to exercise authority over others.

Over and above these general qualities necessary for effective exercise of authority the specific qualities required will depend very much on the type of organization and the exigencies of the situation. Religious organizations, armies, and industrial groups require different gifts in their leaders. The conditions of peace as opposed to war, of full employment as opposed to unemployment, create needs which favour different types of men. Very often, too, the functions of leadership are split between two men who work together and whose gifts are complementary. The effective prophet such as Moses is usually supported by someone with more priestly qualities such as Aaron. Behind Elizabeth I stood Lord Burghley, beside Cromwell Ireton. Whether there are additional qualities of a more indeterminate sort that give some men power over others is more difficult to determine. Is anything specific intimated by expressions such as 'magnetic personality', 'hypnotic influence'? Are there some people who attract submission in the same sort of way as others attract sexual excitement? Freud suggested a kinship between being in love and being hypnotized.[1] To what extent does being a follower belong to the same family of concepts?

Speculations such as these can only be settled by delving deep into social psychology.[2] Of more philosophical relevance is the question of the ground of entitlement possessed by those who are in authority, irrespective of the empirical issues of whether or why they in fact exercise it. Max Weber is famous for his attempt to distinguish types of authority on the basis of answers to this question. He claimed that different authority systems can be distinguished by reference to the different grounds of legitimacy by which they are supported. In what he called a legal-rational system the claim to legitimacy rests on 'a belief in the "legality" of patterns of normative rules and the right of those elevated to authority under such rule to issue commands'.[3] This he distinguished from traditional authority 'resting on an established belief in the sanctity

[1] See Freud, S., *Group Psychology and the Analysis of the Ego* (London, Hogarth Press, 1921).

[2] See, for instance, Homans, G. C., *The Human Group* (London, Kegan Paul, 1951), Asch, S., *Social Psychology* (New York, Prentice Hall, 1952) and Krech, D., Crutchfield, R. S., and Bellachey, E., *Individual in Society* (New York, McGraw-Hill, 1962).

[3] Weber, M., *Theory of Economic and Social Organization* (Ed. Talcot Parsons, London, Hodge, 1947), pp. 300-1.

of immemorial traditions and the legitimacy of the status of those exercising authority under them'. Familiar figures of the first type of authority are a chairman of a committee in a modern business, a civil servant, or an umpire at cricket; of the second type a feudal lord, an eighteenth-century squire, or a Victorian father. Weber regarded the transition from traditional to legal-rational authority as the most important social change in the Western world. If we do not like it we call it the rise of bureaucracy.

The distinction between these two types of authority is very illuminating in the sphere of social control. Indeed the struggles in the sixteenth-seventeenth century in England can be represented very well in terms of the transition, at the political level, from traditional to legal-rational authority. The theory of government by consent was an attempt to rationalize the authority of the state. It ended, as do most such struggles in England, with a compromise. The rational device of appointing or electing a President or Lord Protector was rejected. Kingship was retained with its traditional basis of hereditary recruitment and its traditional rituals and adornments of authority. But the king was progressively stripped of rights to command and decide in all things that actually mattered, though the fiction of traditional rule was preserved by the formula which made governmental decisions the decisions of the king in parliament.

Weber argued, too, that with different grounds of legitimacy go different patterns of authority. A traditional ruler was a status figure to whom total deference was due. His staff was recruited on a basis of patronage and family connections. The spheres of competence were loosely defined and there was no fixed scale of remuneration. It was very much a matter of grace and favour. In rational authority, on the other hand, an office-holder is appointed to whom deference is due only in those spheres covered by his sphere of competence. A principal in the civil service can play cricket under the captaincy of one of his subordinates who is much better at cricket—an unthinkable situation in a traditional order. The officers are recruited strictly on a basis of competence for the job and their sphere of authority is strictly defined. They are paid regular salaries. It is too easy to forget the recency of the rationalization of authority in England. It was only in Gladstone's time that competitive examinations were introduced in the civil service.

This distinction of Weber's, then, is very illuminating for examining patterns of social control. But further complications are introduced when we turn to the sphere of knowledge, which is particularly important for a consideration of the place of authority in education; for in this sphere a person can emerge as *an* authority or as an expert without having been legally appointed and without inheriting some traditional type of status. Of course people—mainly teachers—are appointed to posts because they have shown themselves to be to some extent authorities in some sphere. There have been societies, too, where wisdom is confined by tradition to certain families or castes. But in the sphere of knowledge it is possible for people to emerge, like the Sophists, without legal appointment or tradition to back them, who come to be regarded as authorities. Needless to say, if such people are to be widely respected, there must be a tradition which accords importance to the sphere in which they make pronouncements. In some societies, too, there are collateral tests for eliminating charlatans and the mentally deranged. But nevertheless the basis of the entitlement of such oracles to pronounce is rather different; for they win for themselves a status which previously did not exist by their own achievements and proved credentials in the sphere of their choosing.

The direct connection between the competence, profundity, and training of an individual and the subject matter on which he emerges as an authority makes his position very similar to that of a person who emerges as a leader in the sphere of social control without ever having been appointed to an office or having inherited a status, e.g. in the sphere of war. Here again the personal qualities and competence of the individual must be directly related to some dominant purpose or need of a group. But these two types of self-generating authority are distinct. A prophet can emerge who is thought to be very wise; but like Luther or Bertrand Russell he may be ineffective on the executive side or tactless and lacking in shrewdness in co-ordinating his followers. On the other hand he may be like Pompey or Marius—very effective in prosecuting limited aims, a good manager of men, but without wisdom or grasp of larger objectives. It is only occasionally in the person of leaders like Pericles or Julius Caesar that the qualities necessary for being both an authority and for the actual exercise of authority over men go together. Both men combined vision of a political order, with expertise in implementing their vision and a personal magnetism which gave them authority over men.

In exceptional cases like these we are confronted by something approximating to what Weber called 'charismatic' authority. This rests on 'devotion to the specific and exceptional sanctity, heroism or exemplary character of an individual person, and of the normative patterns or order revealed or ordained by him'.[1] Weber was thinking primarily of outstanding religious or military leaders such as Jesus or Napoleon who erupt as revolutionaries into a traditional or legal-rational order and who command extremes of devotion on the part of their followers. He therefore pitched his account at rather a lofty level and the authority of such figures is decked with the trappings of vocation, signs and revelation. But the strand which runs through his account is the supreme importance of personal claims and characteristics. Such men are followed and believed because they are regarded as being not as other men. Success is therefore of the utmost importance to gaining such authority and keeping it. For until the normative order instituted by such men becomes either rationalized or traditionalized, it is only the personal qualities of the man and the success which derives from them that sustains him. This is obvious enough in the sphere of war. A legend grew up about Julius Caesar, for instance, because he never really lost a major battle.

The knowledge claim has, of course, to be in some practical sphere such as religion or politics, for such a charismatic figure to emerge. Then a person who is *an* authority becomes also *in* authority. This does not usually happen with authorities on theoretical matters, e.g. the migration of birds, unless they are in the teaching profession, where there is also a conflation of the notions of *in* authority and *an* authority.

In the teaching profession claims to knowledge are institutionalized by people being put in authority to transmit what has been discovered. A similar institutionalization happens, too, in the more mysterious realm of 'charisma' in which Weber was interested. But although Weber has much to say about the institutionalization of 'charisma', e.g. in the apostolic succession or choosing of the Dalai Lama, he was much more concerned with it as a source of revolutionary change. His interest was therefore mainly in those who erupt into a traditional or rational order and lay down a new normative pattern. But it surely is also the case that people possessing such qualities and claims are often those who actually exercise authority most effectively within a traditional or rational system, especially one like that of the Catholic Church where 'charisma' has been routinized.

The concept of 'charisma' conflates two notions which have here been distinguished, that of being *an* authority in some sphere which is of

---

[1] Weber, M., op. cit., p. 301.

concern to a group, e.g. religious values, and that of personal characteristics which enable people to exercise actual authority in the sphere of social control, which may include some kind of personal magnetism. Weber's stress on personal characteristics and success is important, but he does not sufficiently emphasize perhaps that rather different personal characteristics are demanded for the different spheres of authority, because of the different purposes of the enterprises. Revolutionary generals may have little in common with prophets. Furthermore he gives too little weight to the common form of life shared by leaders and followers alike which enables the latter to recognize success when they see it. Jesus, after all, was steeped in the traditional wisdom of the Jews; he provided new insights, but these were unintelligible apart from the tradition in which he had been nurtured and on which he spoke 'with authority' when still a boy. Weber's fascination for revolutionaries who might burst the bonds of bureaucracy resulted in a lack of interest in outstanding men who can prove inspiring leaders without being revolutionaries, provided that their insights and claims to knowledge are not too much at variance with the settled views of the organization to which they belong.

Authority, then, always presupposes the notion that something is right or correct.[1] It is usually a device for laying down what is right or correct, the right to which is accorded to specific people according to the two patterns outlined by Weber. But individuals can emerge who demonstrate by their ability to do or say what is appropriate that they have a right to be regarded as sources of wisdom or social control. If their insights are not too much at variance with the tradition in which they and their group have been nurtured, they make very effective leaders within a traditional or rational system. If, on the other hand, their insights are too revolutionary they may emerge as founders of new

[1] These further thoughts on charismatic authority owe much to Peter Winch's comments on my first attempt to get clear about the concept of authority in *Proc. Aristotelian Soc.* Suppl. Vol. XXXII, 1958. In his comments he attributed views to me which were quite contrary to my main thesis—e.g. his suggestion that I assimilated 'authority' to 'power'. But I agree, and agreed then, with his emphasis on the background of a rule-governed form of life which all talk of 'authority' presupposes. I still, however, do not want to make the sphere of 'authority' co-extensive with that of a right and wrong way of doing things, as Winch did. For within contexts where questions of rights and wrong are determined I think it important to contrast the recourse to authority with other methods of deciding what is right. Hence my stress on the connection between 'authority' and 'auctor', and the contrast which I make between morality and science, on the one hand, and spheres of regulation by authority on the other.

movements. It is often the case that people have magnetic personal qualities, with an ability to manage men, which assures them followers; but their claims to knowledge border on the dotty. They thus either emerge as leaders of outlandish sects or cults or they remain uneasily within an existing organization as cancerous cranks.

3. THE JUSTIFICATION OF AUTHORITY

That authority needs some sort of justification is a conviction that emerged into prominence only with the gradual crumbling of the old feudal order. Before that time the authority structure had been regarded as part of the order of things. The predominant social control had been that of tradition which prescribed a man's status and the roles which he had to play in the various areas of life. With the development of individualism and the new economic order, which was one of its main facets, life gradually became rather like a race, as Hobbes pictured it.[1] Individual effort, rather than traditional status, came increasingly to determine a man's place in the world.

It was not surprising, therefore, that under these conditions self-made men of the burgher and professional classes began to ask fundamental questions not only about who should rule but also about the justification of authority in general and the limits to which it could legitimately be extended.[2] Such questions were particularly pertinent at that time. For, as was argued in the previous chapter on 'Liberty', the realistic question to ask about any society is not whether there is social control, but what form it takes. With the advent of individualism the general tendency was for the old ties of tradition to be replaced by the strengthening and extension of the powers of the king. Those, therefore, who were very conscious of having shaken themselves free of the old shackles of a traditional order, were also very conscious of the possibilities inherent in the development of a new highly centralized form of social control, with statute law providing new and more efficient fetters to take their place. It was with good reason that Hobbes dubbed this new form of social organization *Leviathan*. But Hobbes' problem, like that of any other rational man at this period, was to catch the new monster with an adequate description which would make clear how the individual was situated with regard to it. Why should the individual, so

[1] See Hobbes, T., *English Works*, Vol., IV, p.53 (Molesworth, Ed.).

[2] See Oakeshott, M., *Rationalism in Politics* (London, Methuen, 1962), Ch. 1.

conscious of his newly-won position, obey its magistrates? What rights of the subject should be regarded as inviolate? On what conditions was rebellion justifiable?

These were all burning questions in the seventeenth century to which different theorists gave very different answers. It has been customary for political philosophers in recent times to pour scorn on these answers because they were couched in terms of 'contract' and 'consent', which presented misleading models of the actual situation in which the subject could be placed in relation to government. But, as often in 'minute philosophy', what is missed is what people have to say in spite of the way in which they say it, and the common presuppositions shared by those who argue in a similar idiom. The shared presuppositions, which united these disputants, were that institutions are alterable, that an authority structure is not part of the order of the world, and that authority itself is something that requires justification. All these disputants believed in rationality. Their view was that rational men could see that there were certain basic rules which were essential to social life which they called 'the law of nature'. But they also saw that men would be unlikely to live amicably in accordance with such rules, and that some form of authority was necessary to keep the peace or to protect the rights of individuals. What they differed about was the form and extent of the necessary authority.

It would be tedious and unnecessary to trace the different reasons put forward for the institution of authority, and for the limits that should be set to it. What was significant was the general agreement that authority was something that must be and could be justified. These philosophers provided the underlying rationale for the emergence of what Weber called legal-rational authority. Typically enough in England the trappings of traditional authority were preserved, but the functions and constitution of 'the king in parliament' were progressively rationalized. Many would argue that this process of rationalization still has not been carried far enough.

Whatever the merits of further rationalization at the political level it is manifestly the case that this process has not taken place with comparable smoothness in the home and in the school. I have elsewhere[1] defended the thesis that in the home both parents and children alike have grasped the point that a parent can no longer appeal to a traditional

[1] See Peters, R. S., *Authority, Responsibility and Education* (London, Allen & Unwin, 1959), Ch. 3.

status in order to justify his right to regulate the lives of his children. But this realization is too often accompanied by the flabby protestation that a parent has no rights in this respect at all—at least when children begin to reach the age of their almost inevitable rebellion. The proper reaction should not be the abandonment of the claim to authority but the rationalization of it in relation to the functions of the family and the age and responsibility of the children. The implications of this for the teacher will shortly be examined.

So far the discussion of the justification of authority has been dealt with more or less historically in relation to Weber's distinction between traditional and legal-rational authority. The rational case for it can be stated in more abstract terms as follows. Prima facie the institution of authority is an affront to a rational man because it runs counter to the presupposition in favour of freedom that was outlined in Chapter VII, and because it involves the institution of a system where what is to be done is not settled necessarily by an appeal to reasons, but by appeal to a man who may or may not have good reasons for what he lays down. The defence of such a system must be by reference to considerations deriving from the paradox of freedom,[1] or to considerations connected with the effective implementation of fairness (the rule of law, etc.), or to the principle of the consideration of interests, security being in the interest of every rational being. Political philosophers have given different weight to considerations deriving from these different fundamental principles. Hence their divergent views about the form and extent of authority. Hobbes, for instance, rested his case for authority almost entirely on considerations of security. Locke's case, which was much more a case for setting limits to authority, derived more from considerations connected with the safeguarding of rights from arbitrary interference and from his realization that without a system of law men, however rational, would tend to be prejudiced in their own favour in interpreting natural law and powerless to enforce it against aggressors.

The justification of authority in the sphere of social control is so obvious that it seems almost otiose to parade such reasons in public. Surely, it might be argued, men had always been well enough aware of the role of the state in providing conditions of security without people like Hobbes reminding them of it. *Salus populi suprema lex.* Was not Burke right when he exclaimed: 'One sure symptom of an ill-conducted state is the propensity of the people to resort to theories. . . . It is always

---

[1] See *supra.*, pp. 186–8.

to be lamented when men are driven to search into the foundations of commonwealth. . . .'? In a way he was right in his diagnosis though not necessarily in his conservative reactions to it. For people are led to probe into fundamental principles underlying the institution of authority only when an established way of conducting affairs is crumbling, or when some radical departure from an established practice is afoot. The attempt by the Stuarts to extend the sphere of the king's prerogative into areas traditionally covered by the Common Law was such a departure. To attack or defend such a departure fundamental questions had to be raised about the justification of authority. Hobbes' argument amounted virtually to saying that, as security was the sole reason for government, the king's prerogative, which traditionally covered matters to do with the security of the realm, must be extended indefinitely. There was no case for having an area marked out by the Common Law where the king could only proceed in accordance with precedents laid down by judges. Statute law must everywhere supersede Common Law, and the authority of the sovereign must be made absolute and unambiguous. Hobbes' opponents denied that security was the sole consideration. In recent times issues such as that of conscientious objection to compulsory military service and the Wolfenden Report, dealing with the treatment of homosexuals and prostitutes, have revived similar questions about the role of the state. The point is that particular issues such as these cannot properly be discussed without appeal to fundamental principles. A more profound and far-reaching point is that a traditional form of society has been replaced by one in which there is a widespread insistence that fundamental rights should be extended universally and that acts of government should be rationally discussed and defended. This cannot be done without raising fundamental questions about the purposes and limits of state action.

The rational case for authority in the sphere of social control is almost unanswerable, then, though all sorts of disagreements are possible about the weight to be given to different considerations deriving from different fundamental principles. The case for authority in the sphere of knowledge is, however, much weaker and it must be regarded at best as a provisional expedient. The difference, as has been explained before, is that in a legal system validity is determined by an appeal to authority whereas in matters of knowledge there is no such ultimate appeal. The findings of an obscure archaeology student can shatter the cherished theory of a great authority. In fields where it is appropriate to talk about knowledge there must be reasons which support the claim to know, and there must be public procedures for testing the reasons put forward. People must of course be brought up in the relevant tradition of thought and they must be trained to interpret evidence; but in the end nothing depends upon the appeal to particular men.

Nevertheless in every field of knowledge authorities emerge who have proved themselves by their record to be more likely to be right than most of their fellows. Their pronouncements are listened to with respect, though it is always admitted that they may turn out to be wrong. Indeed the history of thought is characterized mainly by the progressive falsification of pronouncements made by such authorities. The rational case for accepting such provisional authorities is twofold.

Firstly, ordinary people and governments have to make use of what knowledge is available in the conduct of affairs. Though they know that economists are often wrong in their predictions of trends and that psychologists are too often mistaken in their pronouncements about the probable results of treating children in one way rather than another, they have no real alternative to consulting such experts. For once a stock of knowledge begins to be built up the issue is not whether a man should tackle his tasks with or without some theoretical assumptions about what is likely to happen; it is rather whether his assumptions should be well established or not. He must therefore, if he is rational, avail himself of the best that is going. As under modern conditions no man can hope to be very knowledgeable in more than one or two spheres, he must necessarily avail himself as best he can of expert opinion. This means consulting the relevant authorities.

Secondly, knowledge can only be handed on and developed if institutions are devised for this purpose. If such institutions are to be organized on rational grounds, this means ensuring that those who are authorities on various matters are given the opportunity to instruct others and to take part in the administration of the affairs of their institutions. Those who are authorities must be put in positions of authority at a level which is consistent with the principle of public accountability.[1] For if laymen are given too much authority in academic institutions, the development of knowledge may be distorted by too much concern for what is of immediate use. And so we arrive at the appropriate point for considering the role of authority in education.

[1] See Ch. XI, Sec. 5(a).

4. THE FORMAL AUTHORITY OF THE TEACHER

Schools are institutions whose overriding aim should be that of education which, as was argued in Part One, involves the initiation of the young into a worth-while form of life. This involves activities and forms of thought and awareness which are regarded as intrinsically valuable (see Chapter V); it involves modes of conduct that are morally justifiable (see Chapters IV, VI, VII), together with their political derivatives, i.e. behaviour associated with 'good citizenship'; it involves manners, decency in dress and speech, cleanliness, etc., which are part and parcel of an approved form of life. It also involves skills such as reading and writing which are necessary conditions for such a form of life. These aims may be pursued with more or less accent on individual 'self-realization' within such a form of life, depending on the emphasis given to fraternity or to respect for persons (see Chapter VIII). Thus schools and colleges share with churches, research institutions, and various voluntary associations the function of preserving and transmitting the ultimate values of a society. This function is not entirely conservative in an 'open society'. For, as has been argued before, in such a society the values reside not simply in a content or body of knowledge and skills which is transmitted; they reside also in the principles of procedure and forms of thought that enable such a body of knowledge to develop and to be adapted to new circumstances.

Nevertheless societies cannot be perpetuated unless many menial and instrumental tasks are also performed and vast numbers of people are also trained in them. The Athenian way of life was made possible, to a large extent, by the slaves and metics who performed such functions. In a modern industrial society all such tasks have to be undertaken by citizens; for many of them training is essential. The school, therefore, has also an instrumental function in training and selecting people for such tasks. Good schools and colleges attempt to train people in such a way that they are educated as well. For most of the more prized jobs in society further training is necessary after leaving school. If, as in England at the moment, there is a shortage of places in such institutions, the school will have to act very much as a selective agency. A proliferation of examinations may militate against its efforts at education.

The teacher, therefore, has a dual role. He should be put in authority, in a modern legal-rational society, because he has established himself according to agreed criteria, as an authority on some aspects of the culture of the community. His job is to initiate others into what is regarded as worth while in itself. On the other hand he is also appointed to train people for some occupation and to act as an agent of selection in the competition for jobs and for higher education. Both these tasks require a specific expertise; for whether simple skills are to be taught or forms of knowledge and awareness to be handed on, there are always problems of teaching method. Authorities on subjects are not necessarily good teachers or knowledgeable about teaching methods. Skilled workers are often extremely inarticulate when it comes to initiating others. So teachers require a special expertise, whatever their role.

Different emphasis is given to these different aspects of the teacher's role in different countries. In the USA,[1] for instance, the school-teacher shares with other public functionaries a depressed status in comparison with that which he enjoys in Great Britain or France. This is partly due to the superior status accorded to business and wealth, partly to the social origins of teachers, and partly to their level of education. The notion of the teacher being 'an authority' on some aspect of the culture of his community has very limited application, though a high level of expertise in handing on the culture is expected. Schooling ever since the early days of the face-to-face democracy of the Founding Fathers has been regarded as the responsibility of the local community. Teachers are 'hired', often with precarious tenure, to promote ends which the parents consider that they know almost as much about as the teachers. Teachers are required to conform closely to the norms of the local community both in and out of school. They are at the mercy of local school boards who decide matters of salary, curriculum and courses. As most of the financing of the schools is a local responsibility as well, prominent businessmen in the local community have a large say in educational matters. The consequence is that the instrumental function of the school is very much stressed. Indeed education generally, even at university level, is thought of in predominantly instrumental terms. There is an emphasis on training in skills necessary for business.

In the realm of the ultimate values of the community there is an emphasis on socialization, on developing citizens who are dedicated to the American way of life. This makes sense in a country that has had to integrate so many immigrants. Because, too, Colleges of Education in

[1] See Baron, G., 'The Social Background to Teaching in the United States: An English Assessment' in *British Journal of Educational Studies*, May 1956.

which most American teachers are trained are set apart from universities and are rather despised by them, the notion that a school-teacher is an authority on something is one that is difficult to sustain. Furthermore, as there is plenty of room at the top in higher education, and as the country has abundant material resources, there is not so much pressure towards specialization and academic achievement at high school level. They lack the equivalent of the English sixth form. There is therefore not so much need for American school-teachers to be authorities on their subjects, irrespective of the various influences which militate against their being thought to be this. What is expected of them, however, is that they should be experts, to a certain extent, on methodology. They may be thought to be as other men in respect of their knowledge of their culture. But in respect of knowledge of children and how the culture can be transmitted to them they are expected to be much more knowledgeable. The demand is that they should be experts on means rather than authorities on ends.

In England, on the other hand, the finance and control of education is not entrusted to the local community and the teacher is never thought of as being 'hired' by it. The 'image' of the secondary school teacher is based largely on that of the teacher in grammar schools and public schools, most of whom have university degrees. The teacher, like the parson, was traditionally part of the Establishment. He was expected to know about history and Horace, just as the parson was expected to know the Scriptures. Because of this, and because of the high level of academic achievement in these institutions, the teacher is expected to be an authority on something—a more robust, if cruder, reflection of the university lecturer. Indeed it is not infrequent for sixth-form masters to take posts in universities, and there is a tradition that university dons are suitable people to be headmasters of public schools.

This introduces the next significant difference—the great authority of the English headmaster. He is traditionally the person to whom the English parent hands over his child to be initiated into matters beyond the parent's ken. The degree of autonomy accorded to headmasters, at every level in the school system in England, over matters to do with curriculum, syllabus, discipline and school organization is astonishing.[1] It is also entirely up to him how much he consults his staff and whether he tolerates a Parent-Teacher Association which may ask awkward

[1] See Baron, G., 'Some Aspects of the "Headmaster Tradition"' in University of Leeds Institute of Education *Research and Studies*, June 1965.

questions about the running of the school. This authority of the head-master rubs off to a considerable extent on to his staff. In so far as such a teacher thinks that he has a task, in addition to the development of academic excellence, he would probably place much more emphasis on the training of character than on vocational training or on anything as nebulous as 'the British way of life'. And by this he would probably mean rather high level virtues such as integrity, perseverance, courage, and fairness, rather than the values of a particular social group.

The teacher at the primary level does not enjoy quite the same status, in spite of the halo effect of the status of the secondary school teacher. Traditionally the old elementary school teacher was thought of as equipping rather inferior children with the basic skills necessary for performing menial tasks and with 'gentling the masses' so that they would be reasonably contented with their lot. This tradition dies hard in spite of the democratization of English education and the many exciting developments in the primary schools which require highly trained and intelligent teachers to implement. This difference in status is exacer-bated by poor pay and by the fact that most such teachers are trained in Colleges of Education, which are still outside the universities. It is crucial to the future of teachers trained in such colleges whether their colleges eventually come completely within the university orbit or stay outside it.[1] If they remain outside, teachers who are trained there are unlikely to improve their status within the community.

It is increasingly being realized that the teacher cannot perform his task adequately unless he is to a certain extent an expert on the psycho-logy of children and on their development, as well as being an authority on some subject. This is of particular importance at the primary stage because the minds of children at this age work very differently from those of adults and because they change rapidly as they pass through different stages. Developments, too, in the understanding of teaching subjects, such as mathematics and science in the primary school, reveal the necessity for teachers to understand the fundamentals of these subjects; they have suffered too long from teachers who have combined a rule of thumb 'method' with only the most elementary knowledge of the subject itself. Hence the absurdity of the view, so widely current, that it is the not too intelligent teachers who should staff the primary schools. It is also being realized that the problems which children have in learning cannot be understood adequately on the basis of their performance in a school

[1] See *supra*, Appendix to Part One, Section 3.

environment. Much more has to be understood about the homes which they come from and about the subtle social pressures which shape their lives. A teacher has therefore to develop a sociological dimension to the understanding of his task.

There is the added fact, too, that the public are becoming much more concerned about education than ever before and much more knowledge-able about it. The teacher can no longer rely on his traditional authority and on a combination of common sense and common room conversation, if he is to hold his own against vociferous and intelligent parents and against every kind of expert, who is advising him what ought to be done about schools and children. A working knowledge of psychology and sociology, as well as of subjects to teach, is becoming as essential to a teacher as a knowledge of physiology and anatomy is to a doctor. The teacher used to be regarded by tradition as an authority in England. With the passing of the traditional forms of authority, his authority, like that of anyone else, has to be rationalized if he is to have any in the com-munity. If he still wishes to be thought of as an authority rather than as someone put in authority to perform a predominantly instrumental task for society, he has to demonstrate that he is an authority on something. He can no longer rely on tradition to legitimatize his claim.

In the past those who have trained primary school teachers have been well aware of the necessity of expertise in method and understanding of children but have, perhaps, been a bit cavalier in their attitude to 'sub-jects'. At the secondary school level, by contrast, there has always been a tendency to think that it is enough to be an authority on a subject; methodology and a knowledge of children can be picked up on the spot. A graduate has been allowed the status of qualified teacher without any period of training. This bifurcation of the teaching profession has been accentuated by the fact that those graduates who trained as teachers did an extra year in a university department of education, which might have almost no connection with Colleges of Education, where non-graduates did their training. It is to be hoped that the need for *all* teachers to be, to a certain extent, both authorities on some subject and experts on methods of teaching, and on children, will become increasingly realized and that the authority of teachers will increasingly be rationally related to their understanding of matters to do with the curriculum and with children.

This different emphasis on the role of the teacher as an authority or as an expert has assumed that his basic concern is for education and that he is assumed by society to be working at this. Unfortunately this presents rather too rosy a picture of the actual state of affairs in England; for there are deep-stated factors which work against many teachers actually being able to devote themselves to their task in this way. These are the bureaucratic function of the teacher as an agent of selection, with the consequent stress on examinations, and the necessity for considerable time to be devoted to 'resocialization' because of cultural deprivation in homes and primary schools.[1] Expertise is, of course, required for the proper exercise of these subordinate roles. The danger is that just another dimension to the teacher's expertise is added, e.g. that of sociology to the exclusion of the emphasis on his role as an authority. Will these subsidiary roles, and the expertise required to discharge them, militate against the tendency for teachers to be thought of, to a certain extent, as authorities on the ultimate values of a community? Will it assist them to be regarded not only as custodians of a community's culture, but also as those who pass on forms of thought and awareness by means of which these values can be adapted and challenged as conditions change? Are they to be thought of as more mundane versions of those whom Weber envisaged as perpetuating the 'charisma' in a society once it had become institutionalized? In other words are they to be regarded as provisional authorities on the ends of a community who initiate others into a worth-while form of life? Or are they to be thought of only as experts on the means of transmitting such a culture, and on training citizens in useful occupations for the state?

This, of course, is not an either-or type of choice. As has been stressed many times, every modern state must train and select for necessary occupations. This can be done in a way which makes training the focus for education. Also, whatever his role, a teacher nowadays must increasingly be, to a certain extent, an expert on teaching methods, child development, forms of learning, and the social background of children. But the question is whether a teacher is also put *in* authority because, to a certain extent, he is regarded as *an* authority of a provisional sort on what a community values. Objective evidence of whether this sort of status is accorded to him will be found, on the one hand, by looking at the institutional connections in a society between the universities and the teaching profession. They will be found, on the other hand, by studying the content of teacher training with special reference to the

[1] See Appendix to Part One, Section 4(*b*).

time spent firstly on academic subjects and secondly on philosophy of education and the history of educational ideas as distinct from on methodology and the ancillary sciences of psychology and sociology.

The suggestion is not that teachers should be regarded as philosopher kings; rather that the stress placed in their training on critical and historical examination of the aims of education is an indication of the seriousness with which they are regarded as custodians of culture and as sources of change and challenge. Both sociology and psychology can also, of course, be taught liberally as sciences concerned with man's recent reflections on himself. They surely nowadays contribute very much to the outlook of an educated man. But there is a regrettable tendency in some quarters to look on them too instrumentally as *merely* further dimensions to the teacher's expertise.

5. THE ACTUAL AUTHORITY OF THE TEACHER

It is one thing for a teacher to have some status as 'an authority' in the community; it is quite another for him to exercise this form of authority effectively in a school. To start with, though it is hoped that he has been appointed fairly according to relevant criteria, the pupils have had no say in it; so there is not the element of consent to his authority which there is about many public appointments. Also the pupils have been compelled to attend school and the teacher's task may well be that of initiating them into something in which they are not initially interested, and which may not be endowed with significance by parental backing. Or they may be hostile to it precisely because their parents, against whom they are rebelling, set so much store by it. So the task is not straightforward like that of a person elected by a community to occupy a specific office. What then is the appropriate approach to it?

The task is basically to get the pupils to identify themselves with the aims of the school, to share the teacher's concern for what is being handed on. For a school is not like a concentration camp to whose aims the inmates must for ever be hostile. It follows that coercive techniques are unlikely to be successful; for they tend to alienate those who suffer from them from those who inflict them. The required identification is, therefore, unlikely to take place. Instrumental techniques are less likely to alienate pupils. If the teacher can relate what he has to pass on to some extrinsic interest which they may have, or to some vocational considerations, that may get them started. So also may marks and competitive examinations. But the trouble about the use of such extrinsic interests is that what is passed on may be distorted and a thoroughly instrumental attitude may be picked up by the pupils. They may learn some history or mathematics; but they may learn also that things are only worth working at if they are of some obvious use. They may fail to appreciate the intrinsic values inherent in what they are working at; they may acquire facts that they will soon forget and competences that may soon fall into disuse. On the other hand they may be got working at something by such lures and come gradually to appreciate it for its own sake. It is difficult to generalize about such matters without a solid body of evidence—which does not exist.

(a) The teacher as an authority

A more appropriate approach for a teacher is to behave as becomes a person who is an authority on something, to be true to his calling. A person who is genuinely an authority about something invests it with an aura. His enthusiasm for his chosen activity or form of awareness and his mastery of its intricacies lures others to be initiated into its mysteries. A teacher, therefore, must convey the notion that he is engaged on an enterprise of the human spirit which is not a matter just of transient titillation. Behind all such spheres of knowledge and skill stands the notion that there is a right and a wrong way of doing things, that some things are true and others false, and that it matters desperately what is done or said. A sense of curiosity and wonderment must be conveyed about questions which give the activity its point, together with a passion for precision in accepting or rejecting answers to them. In other words what is intrinsic to the activities and forms of awareness must be vividly intimated without arrogance. As soon as pupils begin to be infected with the excitement, to identify themselves with the quest, question and answer and other forms of encouragement can help to lead them on. The methods used will depend upon what is being taught; art requires different techniques from history.

Traditionally the solemnity of such encounters was marked by teachers wearing gowns. Books were produced in such a way that they could be thought of as possessions for ever. Other ritualistic devices marked out the special importance of the development of mind. There may still be much to be said for such external signs; for they convey insensibly the importance of what is being passed on and may aid the process of initiation. Obviously this kind of atmosphere has to be conveyed differently, depending on what is being taught. Every enterprise must develop its own appropriate rituals. The importance of such rituals is that they convey atmosphere; they link the past with the present and mark the value of what is being passed on without anything being explicitly stated.

What is being argued is that, psychologically speaking, some kind of identification has to take place between teacher and pupils so that the pupil takes into himself the values of the teacher. He must come to feel that what is being studied is important and that it matters whether the appropriate standards are attained. This is enormously helped by the tradition and 'tone' of school; for then the process of identification is strengthened and legitimatized by peer-group pressures. Ritualistic devices aid this process by intimating symbolically the significance of what is being transmitted, and hence by influencing sentiments. Lessons are obviously not quite the same as initiation ceremonies; but they are certainly most effective when they share some of their atmosphere.

But, of course, rituals and attachments to teachers are at best extrinsic aids which may facilitate the task of the teacher. They intimate, at second hand, as it were, that something of interest and of value is at stake; they may thus provide an atmosphere which may permit the teacher to get his pupils to enjoy first-hand experience of what is so marked out. If all goes well intrinsic motivations will develop—perhaps a passion to discover what is true or to create something that is elegant or beautiful or to perform some skill with precision and mastery. The acid test is the extent to which the pupils go on when the pressures are off and the teacher is no longer present. Has the teacher managed to set activities going in the minds of others that will eventually transform their interests and their view of the world? Or has he been more like a hypnotist who induces temporary changes in others only while they are directly under his influence?

The dangers immanent in this situation are obvious enough. In the discussion of 'charisma'[1] it was stressed that Weber conflated two distinct notions under this concept. One was that of having special claims to knowledge, the other was that of outstanding personal qualities including, perhaps, some kind of personal magnetism. There are dangers deriving from both aspects of 'charisma' which must be discussed in turn.

The first danger is that of those who are authorities becoming

[1] See *supra*, pp. 244–7.

authoritarian. It has already been argued that in the sphere of knowledge no one can be regarded as more than a provisional authority. Nothing is ever right or true just because an individual, however learned, says so; this depends ultimately on facts which are independent of persons, and on public procedures for discovering and assessing them. There is thus always what D. H. Lawrence called 'the holy ground' which stands between teacher and taught, to which the ultimate appeal must always be made.[1] The teacher has dwelt for a long time in it and is familiar with its contours; he has also been trained in the procedures of a discipline which are necessary for its appreciation and exploration. If, for instance, he is a scientist he will not only be familiar with scientific theories and knowledgeable about scientific facts; he will also be trained in scientific method by means of which such theories can be tested. His task as a teacher is not only to convey the importance and excitement of science and to display gradually how the world looks when revealed by the searchlight of scientific theories; it is also to initiate others into the procedures by means of which such assumptions, which include his own, can be assessed. The danger is that he will use his superior vantage point to dogmatize and pontificate. By so doing he may win disciples but he will betray his calling. For what matters is not what any individual thinks, but what is true. A teacher who does not equip his pupils with the rudimentary tools to discover this is substituting indoctrination for teaching. Paradoxically enough a teacher must both be an authority and teach in such a way that pupils become capable of showing him where he is wrong. The teacher is an agent of change and challenge as well as of cultural conservation.

This is tantamount to maintaining that the business of a teacher is to teach, not merely to instruct and certainly not to indoctrinate. As was indicated in Chapter I, Section 4, 'teaching' involves the passing on of knowledge, skills, or modes of conduct in such a way that the learner is brought to understand and evaluate the underlying rationale for what is presented to him. Indoctrination, on the other hand, involves either merely the inculcation of beliefs or the addition of a rationale which discourages the evaluation of beliefs, e.g. the appeal to authority as a backing. In the early stages of education, however, teaching in a strict sense may be impossible; for there may be very little possibility of getting children to grasp the reason why of things. They may have first to learn that metals expand when heated, or that electric wires are

[1] See *supra*, Ch. II, Sec. 2.

dangerous, without being able to understand why; similarly in the moral sphere they have to learn that certain things are wrong, such as lying or breaking promises, without grasping fully the reason why they are wrong. There is a place here for instruction as a preliminary to teaching proper. Such instruction would degenerate into indoctrination if it were done in such a way as to discourage the probing into principles at a later stage when the child's mental development was ripe for it. A child will tend to believe what an authority figure tells him; but if the person in authority instructs him in an authoritarian or doctrinaire manner this may make it very difficult for the child to pass from reliance on authorities to the acquisition of the underlying form of thought or awareness.

The danger of becoming doctrinaire and authoritarian is enhanced if the teacher possesses personal characteristics which incline others to follow him almost irrespective of where he leads them. Schools and youth movements abound with such Pied Pipers. On a staff they are a bane or a boon depending on their competence in their field and on their proclivity to employ their personal qualities for the right sort of ends. There are many who enjoy the feeling of power which such qualities give them over children. They thus tend to keep children in perpetual subservience to them and become jealous if they develop other attach-ments. They may be a disruptive influence because their control over children is so powerful that they are tempted to make their own rules or to relax school rules on impulse.

On the other hand a teacher possessed of such qualities may harness them sensibly to his aims as a teacher. He may be a rational type of man whose success depends largely on his drive, competence, and humility, and on his acute perception of what is going on in a class-room. But may-be he also has something extra which attracts people—an inner intensity, perhaps, which enhances his command of his subject and his outward air of authority. He can be well aware of what is happening and can wean his pupils away from fascination for him to fascination for the enter-prise to which he is trying to get them to commit themselves. A paradigm of a similar situation is that of Freud's discovery of transference. When he and Breuer were collaborating Breuer found after a time that a woman patient was in love with him. He was so shocked that he discontinued the treatment and went off for a second honeymoon with his wife![1] Freud, on the other hand, gritted his teeth and carried on. He discovered that

[1] See Jones, E., *Sigmund Freud, Life and Works* (London, Hogarth Press, 1954), Vol. I, pp. 246–7.

this was a phase through which most patients pass. He used their attachment to him to wean them towards the discovery of what was real and worth while.

(b) The teacher in authority

The teacher's task is complicated to a varying degree by the necessity of preserving conditions of order which are necessary conditions of its performance. Traditionally the image of the teacher is one of a forbidding figure who subjugates his charges by aggressive orders and coercive techniques, like a prison warder or an army sergeant. The inefficacy and indignity of this way of preserving the order appropriate to learning were rightly challenged. Unfortunately, however, it has been replaced in some quarters by that of the benign child-minder who keeps in the background and manipulates children by appealing to their interests. The teacher, in other words, has identified himself with the attitudes of a consumer-orientated society. The techniques of the supermarket have succeeded those of the prison.

What has happened in this well-meaning retreat from the use of authority is that the exercise of authority in general has become identified with a particularly repressive form of it. What is needed is not the abandonment of authority but its rationalization as a form of social control. The most typical device which is appropriate to control by authority, rather than by power or persuasion, is the giving of orders or commands, and the making of requests. Roughly speaking commands are the sorts of regulatory utterances for which no reason needs to be given. They are usually uttered in a characteristic tone of voice by people explicitly given a right to control behaviour in this sort of way. If people obey them *as* commands, rather than react to them as noxious stimuli, they must have been initiated into a form of life in which this type of regulation is an accepted convention. They function in an auditory dimension rather like the arms of a policeman in a visual one. In certain situations, when rapid and unambiguous direction is essential, the rational case for such a form of control is overwhelming. It would be extremely difficult to manage on a battlefield, or even on a football field, without them.

To many the giving of commands represents some kind of indignity. But whether it is so or not depends surely on the spirit and situation in which they are given. They are obviously inappropriate in personal relationships, which almost by definition are those lacking the structure of formal status and role. In status relationships the dignity or indignity of a command will depend upon whether it is required by the nature of the situation or whether it arises merely from the whim of a man. Some who are placed in authority delight in the right which it affords them to bend others to their will; or, perhaps, they bolster up the feeling of importance, which their status gives them, by exercising unnecessarily one of its more overt prerogatives. But commands need not be status-orientated in this sort of way; they can be orientated strictly to the task in hand.

If commands are task-orientated rather than status-orientated they are a thoroughly rational device for controlling and directing situations where unambiguous directions or prohibitions are obviously necessary. But to function as commands they must sound like them and be accompanied by the gestures appropriate to authoritative utterances; there must also be some acceptance of the value of the task on the part of pupils. Without this commands mark the point at which authority begins to degenerate into power. In a good teaching situation requests are usually all that is required to structure the situation. Indeed, once a good lesson is under way, its intrinsic interest should sustain it without much need of such props. Many might think that this form of social control was out of place with young children. But even at this early age the interesting study done by Miss Gardner and Miss Cass reveals the frequency with which good teachers use commands in controlling a class-room situation.[1]

Commands, of course, are not the only form of explicit social control which can avert recourse to coercion, threats, bribes and other extrinsic incentives. There are requests, which are a more polite form of command. There are also moral and prudential appeals, which are more becoming for a teacher, moral education being part of his task. In this sphere too his advice, exhortation, praise, or condemnation, can be status- or situation-orientated. He can commit himself to the class-room equivalent of that appalling domestic illogicality: 'I'm your father, and I say that you ought not to smoke. And that's why you ought not to smoke.' Or he can present reasons which are proper reasons for doing what he advises, e.g. that smoking is a danger to health. It is a further question, however, whether he makes children's doing what there are good reasons for doing dependent on their acceptance of such reasons. A teacher, for instance, may tell a boy that it is stupid and wrong to put

[1] See Gardner, D. E. M. and Cass, J., *The Role of the Teacher in the Infant and Nursery School* (Oxford, Pergamon Press, 1965), pp. 102–15.

objects on railway lines to see what happens to them when a train goes over them, But if he sees the boy doing it, is he going to let the matter rest there? It is a nice point to determine what matters can be left purely to moral persuasion and what matters must be subject to authoritative regulation as well. Natually he hopes that moral persuasion will do the trick; but often he is only too well aware that authority will have to be exercised if the moral appeal proves abortive. As boys get older the need for external control diminishes. Self-discipline takes the place of a discipline that is externally imposed. Constraints become internalized. But this would never happen unless they were first externally imposed; for the inner structure of the mind mirrors the outer structure of public traditions and institutions. The inner voice of conscience echoes the outer voice of the parent and teacher. So those who are in authority over children must provide a pattern out of which the boy can eventually develop his own style of self-regulation. Their authority is necessary for another generation to learn to live without authority. This is not likely to happen unless their exercise of authority becomes rationalized and task-orientated; for the young will rightly rebel against the irrational expressions of a traditional status. In brief, teachers and parents have to learn to be in authority without being authoritarian.

CHAPTER X

PUNISHMENT AND DISCIPLINE

INTRODUCTION

Although, ideally speaking, children should come to school eager to be initiated into the mysteries of civilization in fact many of them do not. It was argued in the last chapter that, confronted with this situation, the teacher should act in this situation as becomes a person who is an authority on something rather than have recourse straightaway to bribery, coaxing, or coercion. This sort of atmosphere helps identification with the teacher, who can gradually foster commitment to the values which he is trying to hand on. In so far as he has to rely on additional methods for ensuring the conditions necessary for learning it was argued that there are some, e.g. rituals and requests, which are peculiarly appropriate to the situation, if they are orientated towards the task in hand.

Nevertheless even the most inspiring, stimulating, and competent teachers sometimes come across pupils who will not submit to the discipline of the learning situation. Or a class is inherited from another teacher in which no tradition of discipline has been established. On occasions such as these authority on its own may be ineffective; it may have to be backed by power in order to maintain or bring about those minimum conditions of order without which progress in learning is not possible. This naturally introduces the question of punishment.

To speak of 'the question' of punishment is, in a way, to take the first step towards perpetuating the confusion with which most discussions of punishment are bedevilled. On the one hand it is argued that punishment is either wicked or inappropriate, crime being a form of social disease for which its perpetrators cannot be held responsible. On the other hand irate women get up in public places and demand the re-introduction of flogging because society is treating adolescents too softly. It is commonly thought that there are three different 'theories' of punishment. There is first the retributive theory, which believes in 'an eye for an eye and a tooth for a tooth' and is an inhuman relic of a barbarous age. Then there is the 'deterrent' theory which is a bit more civilized and the 'reformative' theory which is the most progressive and enlightened of all. To a large extent these discussions continue because of a failure to distinguish different questions about punishment. It may well be, too, that once these different questions have been distinguished, the so-called 'theories' may not appear to be incompatible with each other precisely because they provide answers to different questions.[1]

The first question that must be asked about punishment is that of the meaning of 'punishment'. How is it to be distinguished from 'revenge', 'discipline', 'deterrence', and 'reform'? Secondly the question of justification must be faced. What reasons are there for punishment? These first two questions are philosophical questions. Thirdly the possible forms of punishment must be examined. What type of sanction should be attached *in general* to breaches of rules? This is the legislator's question. Finally there is the judge's question—what punishment should be given for a particular breach of a rule? The rest of this chapter will consist in examining these four questions with special reference to the educational situation.

I. THE MEANING OF 'PUNISHMENT'

In a school situation a proclivity to punish people is often confused with discipline; but this is to confuse one way of preserving discipline with discipline itself. 'Discipline', etymologically speaking, is rooted in a learning situation; it conveys the notion of submission to rules or some kind of order. The rules may be those of what is learnt, e.g. the rules of grammar or of morals; they may be those of the method of learning, e.g. rules of practice and training; or they may be more general rules necessary for something to be learnt, e.g. rules relating to silence, posture, and diet. Such rules may be externally imposed by someone in authority or imposed by the learner on himself. Whenever we think about rules or a system of order from the point of view of their impress on a mind or minds it is appropriate to talk of 'discipline'. 'Discipline' is thus a very general notion which is connected with conforming to rules.

'Punishment' on the other hand is a much more specific notion which

[1] For more detailed treatment of these questions than is possible in this chapter see Benn, S. I., and Peters, R. S., *Social Principles and the Democratic State* (London, Allen & Unwin, 1958), Chs. 8, 9, and Hart, H. A. L., 'Prolegomenon to the Principles of Punishment' in *Proceedings of the Aristotelian Society*, Vol. LX, 1959–60.

is usually only appropriate when there has been a breach of rules. It involves the intentional infliction of pain or of something unpleasant on someone who has committed such a breach of rules. The pain also must be inflicted by someone who is in authority, who has a right to act in this way. Otherwise, it would be impossible to distinguish 'punishment' from 'revenge'. People in authority can, of course, inflict pain on people at whim. But this would be called 'spite' unless it were inflicted as a consequence of a breach of rules on the part of the sufferer. Similarly a person in authority might give a person £5 as a consequence of his breaking a rule. But unless this were regarded as painful or at least unpleasant for the recipient it could not be counted as a case of 'punishment'. In other words at least the three criteria of (i) intentional infliction of pain (ii) by someone in authority (iii) on a person as a consequence of a breach of rules on his part, must be satisfied if we are to call something a case of 'punishment'. There are, as is usual in such cases, examples that can be produced which do not satisfy all criteria. For instance there is a colloquialism which is used about boxers taking a lot of punishment from their opponents, in which only the first condition is present. But this is a metaphorical use which is peripheral to the central uses of the term.

In so far as the different 'theories' of punishment are answers to questions about the meaning of 'punishment', only the retributive theory is a possible one. There is no conceptual connection between 'punishment' and notions like those of 'deterrence', 'prevention' and 'reform'. For people can be punished without being prevented from repeating the offence, and without being made any better. It is also a further question whether they themselves or anyone else is deterred from committing the offence by punishment. But 'punishment' *must* involve 'retribution'; for 'retribution' implies doing something to someone in return for what he has done. It may involve something pleasant as in the case of gratitude or reward; or it may involve something unpleasant as in the case of punishment. Punishment in other words is one type of retributive transaction. Punishment, therefore, must be retributive—by definition.

In a school situation there are some things that are often called 'punishment' which are not strictly cases of it. Suppose, for instance, that a boy does not do his homework properly and is told to do it again. This is external discipline rather than punishment. It involves the use of command to make sure that some practice or preparation is undergone. There would be no intentional infliction of pain. There might, of course, be some blaming or shaming in addition to the command; but this would come in the category of moral exhortation rather than of punishment. If, however, the boy was caned or deprived of some privilege, this would be punishment. For something unpleasant would be intentionally inflicted as a consequence of the back-sliding. It might be the case, of course, that the required piece of work might be regarded as an unpleasant waste of time by the boy. But that would be neither here nor there. The teacher presumably would not be prescribing it because it was so regarded.

2. THE JUSTIFICATION OF PUNISHMENT

Punishment, then, is retributive by definition. It is part of the meaning of the term that it must involve pain or unpleasantness and that it must be as a consequence of an offence. But definitions, as has been pointed out before, settle no substantial questions. A teacher, confronted with a broken window in the class-room and a universal protestation of innocence on the part of the class, might say that he was going to punish the whole class by keeping them in. If it was pointed out to him that he could not be 'punishing' them until he had established guilt, he might well reply: 'I don't care whether you call it "punishment" or not. The fact is I'm going to keep you in.'

The point is that a normative relationship is built into the concept of 'punishment'. It is not a law of nature that if people commit offences pain is inflicted on them. This happens regularly only because men have instituted legal systems which ordain that offenders will have pain inflicted on them. People brought up under such systems therefore tend to make this retributive relationship hold. But the question has to be faced by rational men whether it is appropriate both that pain should be inflicted when a rule is broken and that it should necessarily be inflicted on and only on the person who has broken the rule. How can these normative demands built into the concept of 'punishment' be justified? It is one thing to understand what is meant by 'punishment'; it is quite another to give good reasons why punishment should exist.

The answer given to this question will depend, of course, on the general ethical theory which a man adopts. Such theories were discussed in Part Two of this book—especially in Chapter III. Briefly an intuitionist will adopt a retributivist theory as an answer to this question. He will say, in effect, that it is morally fitting that those who commit offences should have pain inflicted on them. There is an intuition of desert here. It would be morally outrageous if, generally speaking, wicked men flourished like the bay-tree. Those who do not see this are morally blind. The basic objection to this point of view is that of its arbitrariness and lack of objectivity.[1] There are many, e.g. Bentham, who do not see this connection as a self-evident one. He argued that pain is evil and that punishment is necessarily a 'mischief' because it involves the infliction of pain. How can it therefore be self-evident that it ought to be inflicted?

There are others, e.g. Westermarck,[2] who hold that punishment is the expression of a retributive emotion. It has therefore some kind of natural basis in the species and its self-evidence is connected with this. The objections to this view are obvious enough; they derive from objections to all such moral sense or emotivist theories.[3] Firstly such a theory only provides an explanation, not a justification. Even if punishment is the expression of a 'natural' reaction, men are subject to many natural reactions which they have to learn to inhibit. A moral judgment cannot be justified merely by an appeal to a generalization about man. Secondly there is the fallacy involved in the attempt to explicate judgments by reference to emotions. It was argued that emotions such as disapproval can only be explicated by reference to the appraisal which constitutes their cognitive core.

The most promising justification of punishment is that provided by the Utilitarians who argued that, though the infliction of pain is *prima facie* a mischief because pain is evil, a small amount of pain inflicted on offenders is less of an evil than the larger amount of pain which would be caused by the refusal to attach sanctions to socially important rules. Deterrence and prevention are therefore the basic reasons for punishment. For a Utilitarian the less sanctions have to be resorted to the better, because of the pain involved. It is the threat of punishment, as well as its actual infliction, that should deter. Some might object that sanctions do not in fact deter the people likely to commit the relevant offence. This might be true of particular sanctions, e.g. the death penalty. But it would be preposterous to argue that it is true of sanctions in general. To establish such a thesis the criminal law would have to be suspended for a period. Would anyone, reflecting on the probable con-

[1] See Ch. III, Sec. 3.

[2] See Westermarck, E., *Ethical Relativity* (London, Kegan Paul, 1932).

[3] See Ch. III, Sec. 4.

sequences, advocate such an experiment, men being what they are and many goods being in very short supply? A more fundamental objection to Utilitarianism is to ask how the axiom that pain is evil can be established. This can only be dealt with by an extension of arguments which were briefly sketched in Chapters V and VI.

A much more subtle objection to Utilitarianism is to point out that a case in terms of deterrence has only been made out for the infliction of pain; it still remains to be shown why pain should be inflicted on those who have committed the offences. And 'punishment' implies the infliction of pain on the guilty. A much more effective form of deterrence might be the taking of hostages or some kind of collective penalty. Teachers often have recourse to this when they keep a whole form in or deprive everyone of some privilege when they are unable to discover the culprit. What the boys say generally is that this is not fair. And, of course, they are dead right. For inflicting pain is a discriminatory act against a person or group of persons. This can only be justified if the person or persons have put themselves in a category which makes them different from others and so relevant recipients of such discriminatory treatment.[1] The relevant criterion of recruitment to such a category is by the voluntary commission of some kind of offence, or at least being involved in some way in it as an accomplice. Without such a connection it is a case of unfairness or of different treatment in an important matter without a relevant distinction being shown. But why should a Utilitarian, who only believes in punishment as a deterrent, be bothered with fairness?

Bentham argued that being fair in this way was in general a more efficient method of deterrence. But it would not take much ingenuity to produce cases in which there would be a clear choice between being fair on the one hand, and the more effective avoidance of pain on the other. This raises the general question of the status of the principle of fairness in a Utilitarian system, which would take us too far afield to discuss. In this book it has been argued that both fairness and the consideration of interests are fundamental principles of a rational morality and that they are therefore logically independent of each other. In some situations, therefore, these principles may conflict and a choice has to be made about the relative weight to be attached to them. Is the school-master in the above case to give more weight to fairness or to the common interests of all in sustaining the rule of law?

[1] See Ch. IV, Sec. i.

Of course on a Utilitarian view, or on any view which makes the consideration of interests a fundamental principle, deterrence is not the only reason for punishment. There is also prevention, which involves in some way isolating the offender so that he cannot trouble the community in this way. A case, too, could be made for reformation if it could be established that people are actually made better by being punished. It may be the case that prisoners can be treated constructively while they are being punished, so that they emerge from prison as better people. But this does not show that it is the punishment that has produced the required effect. Indeed this might have been produced in spite of, rather than because of, the conditions necessary for punishment. The case for reform is surely not as a reason for punishing people. Indeed it is often argued that the need to punish militates against constructive measures that can be taken in the sphere of reform. The basic case for punishment is surely in terms of deterrence and prevention. But given that punishment is necessary for these reasons, it is desirable to arrange the conditions of punishment in such a way that there is some possibility of a person being reformed *while* he is being punished, i.e. while restrictions are being put on his liberty.

It is often argued that when one is dealing with children a much stronger case can be made for reform as a reason for punishment than at the adult level. Many adolescents live in a world of fantasy and, it is argued, that the 'sharp shock' involved in punishment may bring them to their senses and help to establish them in socially more desirable forms of conduct. There is also the point that, in a school situation, the fact that education is the main business of the school lends weight to considerations connected with reform. For 'education' is like 'reform' in that it implies some change for the better. Anything therefore that goes on in a school must be viewed primarily under this sort of aspect. The question therefore has to be asked whether punishing children is likely to make them better.

'Better', of course, needs further analysis. Better in what respect? Education differs from reform in that it does not convey the same suggestion of bringing a person up to a standard from which he has lapsed. It is largely a matter of guiding children towards standards that they never dreamt of. It is highly dubious whether punishment helps much in this. In the sphere of school-work, for instance, is a boy likely to develop a love for mathematics if he is punished for getting his sums wrong or for omitting to do them? Of course he may be required to do them again correctly or to make up what he has failed to do. But this, as has already been argued, is discipline rather than punishment. Punishment involves some infliction of pain which is extrinsic to the neglected or mismanaged task. Is there any good evidence to support the view that such punishments improve performance? Disapproval and censure may to a certain extent; but actual punishment is a very different matter. Needless to say rewards and praise for tasks reasonably done are much more likely to improve performance than punishment and blame for tasks badly done. For they are more likely to aid identification with the teacher and hence commitment to the normative order of the school. Punishment is one of the most potent devices for bringing about estrangement. In the sphere of school work, then, the case for punishment as an aid to education seems pretty weak. This, however, is an empirical matter and evidence might be produced which demonstrates its beneficial effect. Even this, however, should be treated with caution; for it might demonstrate only the effect on learning an isolated task over a short period, not the long-term effects of such treatment.

There is perhaps a much stronger case for punishment in the sphere of the general rules of a school than in the sphere of school work. But the case in this sphere is much stronger on grounds of deterrence than on grounds of the moral improvement of the individual punished. It is necessary to distinguish at least three distinct types of situation where the issue of punishment might be raised. The first is in relation to breaches of those conditions of order which are necessary for an educational activity to proceed. This is usually called class-room discipline. The second is in relation to breaches of rules that are regarded in the community as a whole, as well as in the school, as being morally important and/or legally prohibited, e.g. stealing, lying, injury to the person, damage to property, breaking promises. The third is in relation to rules that are only of local importance for the smooth running of the school, e.g. not running in narrow corridors, signing out if absent for a meal, etc.

The presumption is that in these areas rules will not be insisted on purely for the sake of having rules. Either they are justifiable by reference to fundamental moral principles or they are clearly necessary for the particular purpose in hand or to avoid the inconveniences with which institutions are beset if they lack them. It is to be hoped, too, that the tradition of the school and the authority of the teachers, together with

S

273

moral exhortation, will be in the main sufficient to preserve this fabric of order. But there usually has to be a system of punishments in the background to act as deterrents. Such punishments have to be unpleasant and they have to be predictable. The more predictable they are, the less unpleasant they need be.

It is important to grasp that the case for such punishments does not depend on the probability that they will benefit the individual punished. Their justification is that they are necessary for preserving the system of order which is necessary for educational activities to proceed. The teacher may therefore be in a dilemma; for he may have to insist on punishing an individual as a deterrent or (e.g. when he sends him out of the room) as a preventive measure; but he may know that this will do no good to the individual punished. He therefore has to tackle the problem on two fronts. He has to implement the threatened sanction without partiality; but he also has to do all he can to get to know and understand the individual offender. He has to act both as judge and as probation officer. He has somehow to convey to the boy that he is on his side to a certain extent, that he is not unsympathetic to him as a fellow human being. He has, too, to devise some way of treating him that leaves open the possibility of reparation and of re-establishing himself in the community. Respect for law must be implemented with respect for persons. But it cannot be superseded by it. Institutions cannot be run as if they are nothing more than a complex concatenation of personal relationships.

It might be argued, on the other hand, that such punishments do not serve purely as deterrent or preventive measures; they sometimes assist in moral education. They help to mark out what is right and wrong and, if the teacher is careful to explain the reasons for the rules which are being enforced, they can help to stamp in desirable habits which will later make a solid foundation for a rational moral code. Again, whether punishment often has this effect on individuals is an empirical question. Most of the precise work done by psychologists in this area is on conditioning animals, a situation which is only faintly analogous. More direct evidence of a less carefully controlled sort, e.g. on methods of child rearing, seems to lend little support to the view that punishment proper has beneficial effects on the character-development of children.[1] There is evidence 'that punitive aggression by the parent leads to aggression by

[1] See Sears, R. R., Maccoby, E., and Levin, H., *Patterns of Child Rearing* (Evanston, Row, Peterson & Co., 1957).

the child, but no evidence that it leads to moral learning'.[1] Discipline, or the firm insistence on standards, combined with disapproval of departures from them and praise for compliance, is quite another matter. Probably the tie of affection with parents is more important than the actual techniques employed.[2]

These generalizations relate, however, to young children and to forms of training that are reasonably systematic. It does not follow from such studies that isolated punishments of the 'sharp shock' variety may not have beneficial results, not because they act systematically as negative reinforcers in the inhibition of types of undesirable conduct, but because they may bring adolescents to their senses and help them to grasp the consequences of their actions. Many adolescents who are prone to delinquency live in a world of fantasy and act impulsively in a mildly hallucinated state. Often isolation, or having to appear before a court and suffering all the consequences of such a public display of authority backed by coercion, has a very sobering effect. Certainly the threat of punishment deters adolescents. Indeed the famous Hartshorne and May Character-Development inquiry suggested that realistic punishment in the immediate situation is the most important variable in eliciting cheating or honesty.[3] Moral conduct in adolescence seems to be closely correlated with intelligence and with the general conceptual development of the child, including a grasp of social realities.[4] 'Sharp shocks' of this sort may function in a beneficial way by focusing awareness on social realities. Of course the boy may only become rather more prudent as a result. But is not prudence a virtue?

Too often in secondary schools the teacher is in another sort of dilemma which is created by the type of 'education' that is purveyed and by the prevailing tradition of the school and of the parents towards punishment. An unimaginative curriculum, severe streaming, and frequent examinations may foster no desire to learn. The children may have been so brought up that they think that adults only mean business when they resort to violence. This is the only sort of 'authority' that they understand. A teacher, therefore, who refuses to resort to the most

[1] See Kohlberg, L., 'Moral Development and Identification' in *Child Psychology*, NSSE Year-book, LXII, Part I, 1963, p. 303.

[2] See Kohlberg, L., op. cit., p. 302.

[3] Hartshorne, H., and May, M. A., *Studies in the Nature of Character:* Vol. I, *Studies in Deceit* (New York, Macmillan, 1928).

[4] See Kohlberg, L., op. cit. pp. 320–5.

repressive forms of coercion may have acute problems with discipline unless he is a spell-binder or has considerable histrionic gifts. What is he then to do? If he is going to teach at all he may have to do quite a bit of whacking or send boys to the head for more majestic treatment. If he does not he may be derided by pupils, by parents and by the rest of the staff. Yet he knows that such techniques probably do no good at all to the offenders and serve simply to alienate the boys further from genuine education. The long-term answer, of course, is to do something radical about schools where such conditions prevail. Since the Newsom Report the public are much more widely aware of this blot on our educational system.[1] But with a shortage of teachers and shortage of money for education such measures will take a long time. In the meantime many teachers are in an unenviable practical dilemma of which no philosopher can provide a satisfactory resolution.

3. THE FORM OF PUNISHMENT

The form which punishment should take will depend upon what reasons there are thought to be for punishing people. A retributivist will therefore argue that the form of punishment should be determined by looking backwards to the offence and making 'the punishment fit the crime'. Apart from the objections already mentioned to the type of justification underlying this demand there are two further difficulties inherent in it. The first is a practical one. How is this 'fittingness' of punishment to crime to be determined. 'An eye for an eye and a tooth for a tooth' sounds straightforward. Presumably, too, the death penalty fits murder and the confiscation of property fits theft—if the thief is possessed of any. But what 'fits' arson, rape, or public obscenity? How are these sorts of sums to be worked out? The prospect is even more daunting than that of implementing Bentham's calculus of pleasure. If it is answered that what is meant is that serious offences should be matched by serious punishments and trivial ones by trivial punishments, then what is meant by 'serious' and 'trivial'? Could these notions be applied to offences without bringing in utilitarian considerations of what people would be prepared to do to prevent others from committing them? Reference to such preventive or deterrent considerations may not, of course, be part of the meaning of 'serious' and 'trivial'. That is not being maintained. What

[1] *Half Our Future.* A report of the Central Advisory Council for Education (England). (HMSO 1963).

is being argued is that it would be difficult to apply these notions in concrete circumstances unless account was taken of what people in general would be prepared to tolerate.

Anyone who accepts some kind of utilitarian position about the reasons for punishment looks forward to the effects of different types of penalties in fixing a scale. He has in mind particularly the type of penalty which will be sufficient to deter people from committing a given type of offence; for he hopes that the threat of punishment will be sufficient to save frequent recourse to it. If the threat were completely effective, then the death penalty could do for all offences; for there would be no occasion even to inflict it. Since, however, no detection system is perfect, and since there will always be some who will chance their arm or act with insufficient thought for probable consequences, some punishments will have actually to be inflicted if the threat is to remain effective. A scale of possible penalties for each type of crime has therefore to be progressively arrived at, which will be sufficient to prevent too much damage to the community, without inflicting an intolerable amount of suffering on detected offenders. Statistics can help a community to arrive at the required adjustment, although a difficult moral choice is always involved. For the suffering of a few offenders has to be balanced against the probable harm to the community if their suffering was greatly reduced. In some cases 'preventive detention' is prescribed, e.g. for hardened criminals, not so much because of its deterrent effect on others but in order to remove a potential source of harm from the community.

It was argued that at the adult level it is difficult to regard reform as a reason for punishing people. Rather it is something that there are good reasons for attempting while a person is being punished, i.e. while restrictions are being placed on his liberty. If, however, reformative considerations are paramount, though it is optimistic to expect that the form of punishment will do much to bring about reform, it is important to ensure that the form of punishment, e.g. the conditions of detention, do not manifestly militate against the efforts of getting offenders to give a new direction to their lives. No one, of course, can *make* anyone else better. That is something that must grow gradually from within. But physical conditions and methods of treatment can aid or hinder such development.

At the school level, however, because it is necessarily an improvement type of situation, and because the punishment meted out is seldom of a very drastic sort, the case for considering the form of punishment from the point of view of its reformative effect is stronger. In effect this amounts to looking at most punishments from the point of view of whether they do much harm to the individual who is being punished. No teacher, of course, starts from scratch in a school in deciding on types of punishment. What he may or may not do is usually laid down by the head. The education authority, too, may forbid corporal punishment. He may be in a school where there is a complicated system of house-marks in operation, or where there is a formalized detention system. In other words it is usually a case of taking his pick from a number of alternatives that form part of the tradition of the school.

Of the usual forms of punishment the cane is probably the most effective as a deterrent. It is also probably the form of punishment which is likely to do most harm to the individual if used often. At best its reformative value will fall in the 'sharp shock' category. Its consequences to the individual are so unlikely to be beneficial that it is to be regarded very much as an ultimate deterrent. If it is regarded as this it is also much more likely to be effective *as* a deterrent. As was pointed out before, in some schools the tradition of the community may make it the only really effective deterrent.

Keeping children in after school is also an effective deterrent. They hate it—and so does the teacher who has to supervise them. There is also the problem of what to do with them when they are so detained. It becomes a farcical situation, and one that is very difficult to manage, if nothing constructive is done. Yet the conditions are scarcely ideal for doing much of educational value. Deprivation of privileges is another effective deterrent that is unlikely to do much damage to the offender. But it is not always easy to find a privilege that does not have repercussions with other boys or other members of staff. Many teachers attempt to devise forms of community service which 'fit the crime' in the sense that they make reparations to the community for the damage done by the offence, e.g. when property is badly treated. Usually, however, such 'service' requires a lot of time spent on supervision. It is questionable, too, whether the right attitude to community service is created by such enforced effort. But, if carefully chosen, this form of punishment may offer a genuine chance for reparation and for re-establishment in the community. It is, needless to say, peculiarly appropriate in cases of moral offences that obviously damage the community.

The effectiveness of such punishments in moral education depends largely on the extent to which they bring home imaginatively the consequences of actions as they affect other people. The truth of the matter is that punishment in a school is at best a necessary nuisance. It is necessary as a deterrent, but its positive educational value is dubious. Education cannot go on unless minimum conditions of order obtain, and punishment may on occasions be necessary in order to ensure such conditions. An experienced teacher knows well enough the sorts of incidents that are likely to promote disorder and will anticipate and avoid them. Under normal conditions enthusiasm for the enterprise, combined with imaginative techniques of presentation and efficient class management will avert the need for punishment. Boredom is one of the most potent causes of disorder. Authority there must be and an insistence on standards. There must also be, needless to say, a real understanding of and liking for children. The good teacher is always, as it were, 'out there' in the class room, not wrapped up in his own involuted musings. He is aware of everything that is going on and the children sense vividly his perception of them as well as his grasp of his subject matter. Humour is a great catalyst in a classroom; for if people can laugh together they step out of the self-reference cast by age, sex, and position. They feel that they are participants in a shared enterprise rather than spectators at a demonstration.

As was argued in the last chapter involvement in the enterprise is the key to an educational situation. Punishment produces estrangement. It separates teacher from taught and evokes hostility to the 'holy ground' that stands between them. It should only be used when the stamping of feet or the braying of asses makes all talk of such 'holy ground' a mockery. If the teacher has to turn himself even temporarily into a policeman it takes time to re-establish the atmosphere of the academy.

Some schools, of course, are in such a sorry state that there is little more that can be done than to have policemen in to stop riots, caretakers to keep the place clean, doctors and dentists to look after physical health, and psychiatrically trained teachers to care for the 'mental health' of the inmates and to do something about providing the 'socialization' which they are so obviously lacking. The conditions of schooling and the attitudes of the inmates make talk of 'education' almost as out of place as a fashion parade on a dung-hill. Teaching in such 'blackboard jungle' types of institutions requires special gifts and probably special training. It is more like a commando operation than an educational exercise; for the problem is basically that of establishing conditions for normal education to take place. Even so it is remarkable what can be achieved by sympathetic and hard-headed teachers with the most unlikely material in appalling circumstances.[1] Education is so much a matter of confidence and enthusiasm; words like 'tone' and 'spirit' are necessary to convey the feeling of the contagious atmosphere in which it can take root and spread. But there are some school environments which ensure that this contagion will not spread very far.[2]

4. PUNISHMENT FOR PARTICULAR OFFENCES

In Section 2, when the dilemma of the teacher was dwelt upon, who has to weigh the deterrent effect of punishment against its probable effect on the individual punished, the point was made that he has to show impartiality in preserving the rule of law but, at the same time, do something to establish a relationship with the individual punished which will mitigate the estrangement which is often created or perpetuated by punishment. This really raises the judge's question as distinct from the philosopher's and legislator's questions which have been considered to date. A judge or a school-master has a range of penalties from which he can select the appropriate one. Often mitigating circumstances or excuses are produced which may incline him towards leniency. What is the rationale behind the acceptance or rejection of such pleas?

It is important, first of all, to distinguish justificatory pleas from others which are put forward as excuses. For instance a person may plead that he killed someone in self-defence. This is quite different from pleading that he killed someone by accident. In English law neither are regarded as cases of criminal homicide, but the conditions which put them outside this category of offence are very different. In the first type of case what is done is not necessarily regarded as deplorable; in the second case what is done is regarded as deplorable, but the psychological conditions under which it was done may exonerate the agent. The latter type of plea is for absence of 'mens rea'; it is tantamount to saying that in a full sense the agent did not do what he has been described as doing. The act did not issue from his 'will' either because he was non-culpably

[1] See, for instance, Farley, R., *Secondary Modern Discipline* (London, Adams & Black, 1960).

[2] See Partridge, J., *Middle School* (London, Gollancz, 1965) for the description of such an example.

ignorant of some or other crucial fact relating to his action (i.e. it was unintentional), or because he lacked the relevant form of muscular control (i.e. it was involuntary) or because he was subject to forms of coercion or threat which no reasonable man could be expected to withstand. Acts in these categories would not be regarded as either morally culpable or legally punishable. If the plea could be sustained it would be reasonable to say in such cases that the agent was not responsible for his action.

Such exonerating conditions must be distinguished from mitigating circumstances. These refer to conditions which are thought not to exonerate people from blame or punishment but which are put forward to support a plea for leniency. Examples would be actions done under strong temptation or provocation, when a man's mental balance is temporarily disturbed. In cases such as these it might be reasonably said that a person's responsibility for his action was diminished.[1]

Two major questions are raised by such cases, both of which must be tackled briefly in general and then as they apply to the special case of children at school. The first is that of the possible extension of such pleas to *all* actions on the grounds that since human actions must, like everything else in nature, be subject to law, they are therefore all 'determined' and hence there are no actions for which human beings can be held responsible. Secondly there is the question of the justification for exoneration and for leniency in cases where a plea of extenuating circumstances can be sustained. How are such exceptional cases related to the general reasons for punishment?

(a) The 'elimination' of responsibility

The case for the elimination of the notion of responsibility altogether is advanced on two main types of ground. The first is that of the actual difficulty in practice of determining absence of 'mens rea'. In English law, as typified by the McNaghten rules, there has been a concentration on cognitive factors. In pleas of 'guilty but insane' it had to be established that the offender was suffering from a defect of reason of such a kind that he did not know what he was doing or that what he was doing was wrong. This is often very difficult to determine. But it has been further complicated by the more recent admission that a man may have know-

---

[1] See Hart, H. A. L., 'The Ascription of Responsibility and Rights' in *Proc. Aristotelian Soc.*, Vol. LXIX, 1948-9. Reprinted in Flew, A. G. N., *Logic and Language*, First Series (Oxford, Blackwell, 1952).

ledge of this sort but still lack the capacity to refrain from doing what he knows to be wrong or illegal. Extension of the pleas of coercion and duress to cover inner compulsions and defects of will makes the practical difficulty of establishing responsibility even more difficult than it used to be when the emphasis was on purely cognitive conditions. For how could it be conclusively established that an individual under temptation or provocation could have abstained from doing what he in fact did? Whatever else Lady Wootton accomplished in her chapter on 'Mental Disorder and the Problem of Moral and Criminal Responsibility'[1] she at least brought out the difficulties inherent in formulating and applying criteria for 'diminished' responsibility. There is also the development in law of the admission of cases of 'strict liability' where it is no defence to plead that the accused neither intended the act nor could have avoided doing it by the exercise of reasonable care.[2] Examples are possessing an altered passport, selling adulterated milk, dangerous driving. It is argued that if 'strict liability' can be admitted in some cases, it can be admitted in all. The approach to punishment should not be complicated by trying to investigate such recondite matters. Rather there should be more concentration on arranging 'treatment' which can be shown statistically to have beneficial effects.

This attack on the notion of responsibility is usually bolstered up by some pronouncements on the subject of determinism, it being assumed that the demonstration that human behaviour is 'caused' establishes also that men can never help doing what they do. If, therefore, on general grounds, the distinction between 'can help' and 'can't help' is otiose, there is little point in delving around to unearth recondite conditions which are merely insignificant details within the vast system of cause and effect.

This is not an appropriate occasion for a full discussion of the immensely complex cluster of problems centring round the concept of determinism in human affairs.[3] Only a few points can be made which

[1] See Wootton, B., *Social Science and Social Pathology* (London, Allen & Unwin, 1959), Ch. VIII.

[2] See Hart, H. A. L., 'Prolegomenon to the Principles of Punishment' in *Proc. Aristotelian Soc.*, LX, 1959–60, p. 19.

[3] For popular discussion of these issues see Peters, R. S., *Authority, Responsibility and Education* (London, Allen & Unwin, 1959), Part II. For fuller treatment see Benn, S. I., and Peters, R. S., *Social Principles and the Democratic State* (London, Allen & Unwin, 1959), Ch. 9. Pears D. F. (ed.), *Freedom and the Will* (London, Macmillan, 1963) and Strawson, P. F., *Freedom and Resentment*, Proc. British Academy, Vol. XLVIII (London, Oxford University Press, 1962).

are relevant to the topic of responsibility. Firstly the concepts of causal explicability and of unavoidability, which are often merged together under that of 'determinism', need to be distinguished. There is no necessary coincidence between them either; for at a common sense level there is a perfectly good explanation for something like swatting a fly on the window, which is also something that one could refrain from doing if one wished. It is not like jumping when sitting on a red-hot poker. Also knowledge of why one does certain things that one would like to avoid, e.g. being critical of one's critics, is often a necessary condition of being able to avoid it. The suggestion that unravelling causal factors demonstrates unavoidability may well derive plausibility from the generalization of certain unusual cases, e.g. post-hypnotic suggestion, the alleged facts of maternal deprivation, etc., in which certain types of causal conditions can be correlated with syndromes of a compulsive or unavoidable type.

This introduces the second point which is the need to distinguish different types of 'causes' which are appealed to in the explanation of behaviour. By this is meant not just the distinction between necessary and sufficient conditions, which is a very important one, causal explanation proper requiring at least sufficient conditions, but also between different types of conditions that are appealed to in the explanation of different types of behaviour. A lapse in speech may be explained by appeal to physiology; an 'unintentional' error in speech may be explained by postulating an unconscious wish; but the use of French rather than English to an *au pair* girl can perhaps only be explained in terms of a man's grasp of the situation and his desire to communicate— or to impress her by his command of the language. The phenomena of human behaviour are so diverse that different types of explanation, employing different families of concepts, are required to do justice to them.

No one has yet demonstrated that explanations given in terms of these logically different types of concept are reducible to each other or that one is deducible from the other.[1] Most of the things that we do, as distinct from things that happen to us, are explained in terms of a model in which an individual is postulated who is conscious of the situation in which he is acting, of means to ends and of rules governing the appro-

---

[1] See Hamlyn, D. W., 'Causality and Human Behaviour' in *Proc. Aristotelian Soc.*, Supp. Vol. XXXVIII, 1964, and Taylor, C., *The Explanation of Behaviour* (London, Kegan Paul, 1963).

priateness both of means and ends. Within this model concepts such as those of 'intention', 'deliberation', 'foresight', 'decision', 'choice', etc., have their appropriate place, and can count as 'causes' of actions just as a movement can count as a 'cause' of other movements in a sphere in which a mechanical model may be appropriate, e.g. in explaining an eye-blink.

We have recourse to such a model when we explain anyone's behaviour within a structured situation, e.g. on a committee, in an hotel, on a golf-links, in a laboratory. We are well aware that there are things that we cannot explain in this way, e.g. dreams, deliria, hallucinations. We are also aware that within the context of actions and performances there are slips, lapses, and mistakes which we describe as 'accidental', 'unintentional' and 'involuntary' which cannot be explained in this way either. One of Freud's great contributions to psychological theory was to suggest that such happenings are not inexplicable. He developed a special theory to explain both these 'parapraxes' and other phenomena such as dreams, hysteria, delusions, etc.[1] which also require a different sort of explanation. As a matter of fact he attempted to state fairly precisely the conditions under which his special explanations might hold.[2] The fact that there are borderline cases, that some actions may be overdetermined,[3] and that it is often difficult to decide to which category a given piece of behaviour belongs, does not invalidate the general theoretical importance of the distinction.

In brief, recourse to the doctrine of determinism does not help because within this doctrine different forms of causal explanation have to be distinguished. Involuntary and unintentional behaviour and states of mind in respect of which we are passive require a different type of explanation from straightforward actions and performances. They also have a different physiological basis. So the rough and ready criteria employed by lawyers have a solid underpinning in psychological theory.

The practical importance of these distinctions is as far-reaching as their theoretical importance. To quote Hart: 'Human society is a society

[1] See Peters, R. S., 'Emotions, Passivity and the Place of Freud's Theory in Psychology' in Wolman, B., and Nagel, E., *Scientific Psychology* (New York, Basic Books, 1965).

[2] See Freud, S., *The Psycho-pathology of Everyday Life* (London, Ernest Benn, 1914), pp. 192–3.

[3] See Peters, R. S., *The Concept of Motivation* (London, Kegan Paul, 1958), Ch. 3.

of persons; and persons do not view themselves or each other merely as so many bodies moving in ways which are sometimes harmful and have to be prevented or altered. Instead persons interpret each other's movements as manifestations of intention and choices, and these subjective factors are often more important to their social relations than the movements by which they are manifested or their effects. If one person hits another, the person struck does not think of the other as just a cause of pain to him; for it is of crucial importance to him whether the blow was deliberate or involuntary. If the blow was light but deliberate, it has a significance for the person struck quite different from an accidental, much heavier blow. No doubt the moral judgments to be passed are among the things affected by this crucial distinction; but this is perhaps the least important thing so affected. If you strike me, the judgment that the blow was deliberate will elicit fear, indignation, anger, resentment: these are not voluntary responses; but the same judgment will enter into deliberations about my future voluntary conduct towards you and will colour all my social relations with you. Shall I be your friend or enemy? Offer soothing words or return the blow? All this will be different if the blow is not voluntary. This is how human nature in society actually is and as yet we have no power to alter it.'[1] What has to be shown is that this system of descriptions, which seems to serve us perfectly well in ordinary life and which has taken us centuries to evolve, has no proper application. This cannot be established by pointing out that there are border-line cases where we are not quite sure what to say. This happens with all attempts at categorization. A more sensible alternative to Lady Wootton's programme would be to develop psychological theory in such a way that much more attention was paid to such important distinctions.[2] There is also presupposed in Hart's account the principle of respect for persons which, it has been argued, is what a rational person must accept in his dealings with other moral agents. Once this is abandoned there is no bar to manipulating others as we think fit. Lady Wootton senses the unpalatable ethical consequences of her position in her uneasy remarks about 'existing notions of morality'.[3] It is a pity that she did not pursue her qualms a bit further.

[1] See Hart, H. A. L., *Punishment and the Elimination of Responsibility* (London, Athlone Press, 1962), pp. 29–30.

[2] See Austin, J. L., 'A Plea for Excuses' in *Proc. Aristotelian Soc.*, Vol. LVII, 1956–7.

[3] Op. cit., pp. 253, 254.

(b) The justification of retaining responsibility

The main reason behind this attempt to eliminate the concept of responsibility is the well-meaning desire to direct attention towards the reformative rather than to the retributive aspects of punishment. Indeed, as Hart points out, the issues tend to be discussed rather as if there was no middle road between the denunciations of judges, which are redolent with retribution, and the Erewhonian visions of representatives of nineteenth-century scientism such as Lady Wootton. What has to be shown is a justification for making something depend on such distinctions which is not based on intuition. Such a justification can be provided by appealing to the fundamental principles discussed previously in Part Two of this book.

There is, first of all, a justification in terms of fairness. Whether a man is going to be punished in the accepted sense or subjected to some kind of remedial 'treatment', he is certainly being discriminated against. The only relevant ground for such distinction in treatment is the difference due to his having *put himself* in the category liable to punishment or 'treatment'. If pleas, starting with unintentional commission of an act, and ending with cases of mitigating circumstances, are not countenanced, it is palpably the case that individuals are being treated the same in respect of being discriminated against, when there are relevant differences between them. If 'strict liability' were insisted on in all cases then a man would be just as liable for what he did by mistake or by accident as for what he did on purpose. No doubt the 'treatment' accorded to him, to be determined by psychologists or social scientists, would be different. But the affront to the notion of fairness would be severe.

Severe also would be the affront to the principle of liberty. The presumption in favour of letting a man direct his own life and be free, if he so decides, to break the law, knowing the probable consequences of his action, would be rendered abortive by the constant possibility of his being held liable for all sorts of things which he might do by mistake or by accident. The values of self-restraint and of autonomy would also be down-graded. For our system ensures that a person who controls his impulses and keeps to the law is rewarded by being exonerated on the occasions when accidents or mistakes occur. But if men were merely 'treated' when they broke the law, there would be no such implicit reward. Indeed it is illogical for anyone who adopts a consistent 'treatment' position to wait for an offence. Psychiatric social workers should be scouring the land looking for likely candidates for 'treatment' before the law is broken. The 'treatment' position really depends upon sacrificing both liberty and fairness to an over-riding regard for the interests of the weaker-brethren. It is paternalism dressed up in a lab-coat. The importance of making such distinctions could also be defended in terms of deterrence. If the principal object of punishment is deterrence it can only be effective in the case of deliberate acts. Accordingly if the judge waives punishment when such a plea has been sustained, then the effectiveness of the deterrent is not necessarily impaired. It would be, on utilitarian grounds, a pointless mischief to make people suffer for any but deliberate offences.

In the case of extenuating circumstances a utilitarian would be more careful about leniency. He would want to know more about the nature of the condition in relation to which a threat was ineffective. In this respect some sorts of extenuating circumstances might be very different from others. 'Crimes of passion', for instance, might be decreased by severe threats whereas stealing 'for affection' might not. In such cases fairness might pull in an opposite direction to deterrence. Behind all such questions, too, is the problem of the weight to be attached to the deterrent as distinct from purely reformative considerations which has been touched on before. It is encouraging to note that Lady Wootton regards this as the 'fundamental dilemma of penal reform which the currently fashionable psychiatric methods of dealing with criminals refuse to acknowledge'.[1]

(c) The situation of children

The question now arises as to how relevant this discussion is to the question of punishing children in school. Obviously enough it opens up larger issues to do with the age of criminal responsibility and the state's methods of treating juvenile offenders.[2] But this in itself would provide enough material for another whole book. All that can be done here is to contrast and compare the position of the judge sentencing a particular offender with that of the school-master dealing with a particular culprit.

The first difference is that though the rules of a school approximate to the rule of law as, to a large extent, they are issued by those in authority and enforced by sanctions, their moral significance will be much more stressed; for the school is an educational institution and one of its main

[1] Op. cit., p. 337.

[2] See, for instance, *Report of the Committee on Children and Young Persons* (HMSO, October 1960), pp. 30–2.

287

functions is moral education. This means that much more attention will be paid to the question of motive than is usual in administering a legal system proper. Anything approaching 'strict liability' would be completely out of place; for one of the important aspects of moral education is the development of praiseworthy motives as distinct from externally imposed conformity.

Secondly the rule of law will not be seen purely as a system of deterrents protecting the community and enabling education to proceed; its educational value in developing the individual's ability to choose, restrain himself, and develop as an autonomous being will also be stressed (see Chapter VII, Section 5). This cannot be done if there is no reward for rule-following and if no exceptions are made in the frequent cases of unintentional, involuntary and accidental breaches of rules.

Thirdly, as was argued before, the teacher is in the position of the judge and the probation officer combined. He can both administer rules impartially and follow up his necessary punishments so that he can mitigate the conflict between the deterrent and reformative aspects of punishment. He has far more opportunities open to him for ingenuity and imaginative treatment than is open to any judge, and his knowledge of the individual offender puts him in a far more advantageous position for devising suitable forms of reparation.

Fourthly, there is the obvious point that knowledge of right and wrong and the ability to control impulses develop slowly and there are great individual differences in the rate of development. An infant has no knowledge of right and wrong and very imperfect control over his impulses and bodily movements. He cannot forsee the future and has no notion of the long-term consequences of his actions. He is prone to overmastering fear and anger which deflect him in pursuing his purposes. Even at a later age, when a child has quite a developed sense of right and wrong, it can be reasonably argued that he is so susceptible to peer-group pressure that it is only the very unusual and independent child who can stand out against his peers and refuse to do what he knows to be wrong. At an early age this type of pressure comes very near to coercion which is an accepted plea for diminished responsibility. Any teacher must therefore be very chary in expecting the same standards of behaviour from children at different ages whose strength of character may be undeveloped in relation to their cognitive development.

All this is true and must obviously influence very much the approach of any discerning teacher to children. He must have a good grasp not only of stages of moral development but also an insight into the position of individual children in relation to such stages. But behind all such understanding there is the question of respect for persons which is very much at stake when matters to do with extenuating circumstances and the age of responsibility are under discussion. The presumption in dealing with adults is that they are rational beings in the sense that they know the difference between right and wrong, that they can deliberate and adjust their actions in the light of the consideration of consequences, that they have a view about what their interests are and will resent interference with their attempts to implement this. There are, of course, some people who are regarded as 'patients' rather than 'agents' because this is permanently not true of them; others, through temptation or provocation, may be overcome by some overmastering impulse so that this is temporarily not true of them. We treat them temporarily as 'patients' and usually make allowances when it comes to punishment. But when do children reach the stage when we can treat them fully as persons? There is no magical age at which a sudden transformation takes place. Neither does the transformation occur by magic. It will only occur if children are treated progressively as if they are persons, and if they can identify with adults who have learnt to be persons and to treat others as such. They learn, surely, to be persons by being encouraged to plan their lives and to discover what is worth-while in spheres that are within their experience and competence, under a stable system of rules that guarantees a predictable environment. Gradually their sphere of discretion is widened as their experience and knowledge of right and wrong increases and their competence and control over themselves and their environment is enhanced. They do not learn this either by being conditioned like performing seals or by being allowed simply to do what they want.

To make many generalizations about how they do learn this would be very rash; for this is a region of moral education which has not been mapped in any precise manner. But one generalization might be made which falls under the general presumption that social beliefs alter social realities, and that people's behaviour depends to a large extent on the concept which they have of themselves. It is that the ability to exercise self-restraint and to behave autonomously depends to a large extent on the conviction that men are responsible for their actions. Once this presumption, which is the linch-pin of our legal system and of our approach to adolescents in schools, is surrendered, men may in fact come increasingly to behave like other-directed, manipulated puppets. It would be a pity if the form of life which we have developed, in which liberty and respect for persons are highly prized, was jeopardized by a malaise engendered by an imperfect understanding of the nuances which it contains.

CHAPTER XI

DEMOCRACY AND EDUCATION

INTRODUCTION

That education should be 'democratic' no one in a democracy would seriously dispute. This would be the equivalent of announcing in the Middle Ages that all education should be Christian. But what such an announcement would commit anyone to is far from clear. This is partly because of the vagueness which all such general terms of commendation must have if they are to fulfil their function of reminding a people of their ultimate valuations. It is also because of different interpretations which it is possible to give of the predication of 'democratic' to 'education'.

This could mean, first of all, that the educational system of a community should be democratically distributed and organized, whatever interpretation is given to 'democratic'. A system, for instance, which neglected the education of half the population or about whose organization 'the people' had no say would commonly be thought to be 'undemocratic'. Alternatively it might suggest that the organization of schools themselves should be 'democratic'. In other words a plea might be being made for the rights of the inmates, staff and pupils alike, to some say in the running of their institution. An English public school, run on highly autocratic lines, might be said to be 'undemocratic' in this respect. Alternatively the announcement might be drawing attention to the desirability of the content of education being democratic. The school's part in training citizens in the skills and attitudes appropriate for membership in a democratic community might be being stressed. Needless to say a school system might be 'democratic' in one or two of these ways but not in all. In dealing, therefore, with democracy and education it is necessary to treat separately at least these three possible interpretations. It is necessary also to consider carefully both the meaning and the justification of democracy in general, before considering its possible applications to education. This must now be tackled.

1. THE MEANING OF 'DEMOCRACY'

Democracy is usually thought of as a specific form of social control. It would be reasonable to expect therefore that the concept itself would intimate what was distinctive about it. The Greek word δημοκρατία suggested a system in which 'the people' did 'the ruling'; but who 'the people' might be, and what 'the ruling' might amount to, is far from clear when the notion becomes applied outside its natural home in the Greek city-states.

To start with, 'the people' to Greek political theorists meant 'the poor people' as opposed to the rich. But slaves and metics (resident aliens) were excluded. We would think that a system in which 'the people', roughly defined in this way, did the ruling was 'undemocratic'. The Greek theorists called government by consent, without any such reference to class, 'polity'. 'Ruling', too, is a highly ambiguous notion. Legislative, administrative, judicial, and executive functions have to be distinguished; 'the people' may have a share in some of these functions but not in all. The Athenians went as far towards popular participation at every level as anyone ever has.[1] All citizens had a right to attend and speak at the Assembly which met every month and which was the supreme legislative body. Its main administrative committee of 500, the Boule, was chosen by lot, 50 from each of the ten Athenian tribes. Each group of 50 formed a 'prytany' and each prytany formed an executive committee of the Boule for one-tenth of the year. One man was chosen by ballot to be chairman for each day. He presided over the meeting of the Assembly, if there was one, and was the titular head of the state for that day.

The administration of justice was also conducted in this extremely 'democratic' way. There were no permanent judges or barristers. There was a jury chosen by lot from the Assembly which merely had a presiding chairman. Parties conducted their own case. The one sphere which was not left in this way to amateurs and to the hazard of the ballot was that of war. Though all citizens were liable to military service, the ten Strategoi (generals or admirals) were elected annually, and re-election was normal for successful occupants of the office. It was through his occupancy of this office, as well as through his personal authority in the Assembly, that Pericles led Athens for so long. It was this that led

[1] See Kitto, H. F., *The Greeks* (Harmondsworth, Penguin Books, 1951), pp. 124–35.

Thucydides to remark that Athens was in theory a democracy, but in fact ruled by the leading citizen. It was this supremely important concession to professionalism that, no doubt, prompted Pericles to go no further than claiming, in his panegyric on the Athenian way of life, that, though not everyone was capable of initiating policy, everyone was competent to judge upon it.

This versatility and involvement in every level of government, of which Pericles was particularly proud, and which Socrates and Plato so scathingly attacked, is possible in a small face-to-face community such as that of Periclean Athens. The notion of 'the people ruling' has here a concrete and exciting application. Rousseau, writing in the eighteenth century, attempted to revive some such interpretation of 'the sovereignty of the people' in the small cantons of Switzerland. But what application can these notions have once large nation-states have developed, together with a permanent civil service and judiciary and a standing army and police force? Democracy under such conditions must become 'representative'. An Athenian would have regarded such a device as anathema in the sphere of legislation. Rousseau, in the same spirit, attacked the logical absurdity inherent in the suggestion that 'the people' could ever transfer their 'sovereignty' to such a representative body, and shrewdly pointed to the tendency of such bodies to develop their own corporate interests, which often run counter to those of 'the people', whom they are alleged to represent. There is the problem, too, of the relationship between the legislative and administrative functions of the state. Rousseau held that the 'sovereignty of the people' was only manifest in the legislative decisions of the people meeting in assembly. The administrative and executive details could be safely delegated to 'government'.[1] But as the pronouncement of 'the people', which revealed their 'General Will', must, of necessity, be very general, most of the crucial decisions would not in fact be those of 'the people', though they could be ratified and challenged in a popular assembly.

Is anything much then to be made of the notion of 'the rule of the people' once a state has become too large for its citizens to meet in a legislative assembly? Certainly the concept of 'sovereignty' is best dispensed with if anything is to be made of the concept of 'democracy'. It is essentially a legal notion which emerged into prominence when legal systems were in an ambiguous position at the time when Statute Law was emerging to challenge the place occupied by Common Law.

[1] See Rousseau, J. J., *The Social Contract*, Book III.

This led to incoherence in the structure of legal authority; for a legal system must have a supreme principle of procedure by reference to which the validity of law is determined.[1] In Great Britain this 'sovereign principle' came to be that whatever laws are passed by the king in Parliament must be accepted as valid by the Courts. It has nothing to do with 'the people'. It might be objected that nowadays Parliament must be elected by 'the people'; so after all the people are 'sovereign' in a democracy. But it is a law of Parliament that determines both this and what constitutes 'the people' for electoral purposes. Laws of Parliament also determine what are to count as valid election procedures.

Suppose it were then argued that 'the sovereignty of the people' is an empty shibboleth as a *de jure* notion but depicts dramatically a political situation in which, as a matter of fact, the people exercise final authority in the sense that their will is ultimately obeyed. But what is to be made of the notion of 'the people's will'? An individual can be said to have a will in that he deliberates about something, decides upon what he wants to do, and resolutely takes steps to implement this. A like-minded group, such as a group of farmers, might also rather figuratively be said to have a 'will' in the sense that they agree about some policy of common concern and resolutely pursue it. But can 'the people' be said to have a will in any intelligible sense such as this? Perhaps in a national emergency, when they are all united in the face of a common danger. But it is only on very rare occasions that 'the people' have a 'will' in this sense. Also Communist countries, which those in the West would not admit to be 'democratic', would claim that the people are 'sovereign' in this sense. And certainly they seem to be much more united in their pursuit of what they take to be their common interest.

Any such attempts to make concrete sense of concepts such as those of 'the will' or 'rule' of the people are doomed to failure if some kind of substantive interpretation is placed upon them. By this is meant the attempt to interpret them as if they referred to some existing consensus or common interest shared by all 'the people' which is implemented by government. The same must be said about the notion of government by the 'consent' of the people which is another catchword in the ideology of democracy. If 'consent' is meant to refer either to some explicit commitment on the part of the individual citizen or even to some vaguely sensed consensus about acts of government, then it is impossible to give

[1] See Benn, S. I., and Peters, R. S., *Social Principles and the Democratic State* (London, Allen & Unwin, 1959), Chs. XII and XV.

much concrete interpretation to the concept. We do not settle whether government is 'by consent of the people' by consulting public opinion polls. Indeed, if we did it would probably have been found that there was 'government by consent' in Nazi Germany. When, therefore, would government not be by consent, unless there was a state of rebellion or of mass emigration?

The proper alternative to treating these notions as substantive ones is to treat them as procedural. Then concrete interpretation can be given to them and it becomes possible to distinguish democracies from other sorts of government. What is implied is some established procedure by means of which the individuals who suffer from state action can be consulted and can bring their desires and opinions to bear on it. The 'will of the people' then indicates what has been decided by means of such procedures. This may not be what most of the people in fact want. But that is neither here nor there; for 'the will of the people' refers not to what goes on in any particular minds, but to a decision reached by agreed procedures such as the 'conventions of the constitution' in Great Britain. What these procedures should be is a further question. It might be possible, for instance, to have a democratic state run by a permanent civil service who had to use the device of a referendum to ascertain the wishes of the majority on any important issue. The coming of computers and of television make this a possible system of government and perfectly 'democratic'. Whether it would be as desirable as representative government is a further question. Similarly there is nothing which would make a procedural decision to accept a bare majority, a two-thirds majority, or unanimity, as being the 'essence' of any democratic procedure. The advantages of all such alternative procedures would have to be discussed on their merits. The concept of 'democracy' does not unambiguously entail any one of them.

In brief, when the concept of 'democracy' is applied generally to political institutions rather than confined to its natural home in the Greek city-state, very little can be spun out of it in the way of institutional provisions. What is intimated is some general requirement that there should be some kind of procedure for consulting citizens of a state about state action and policy. But this does not take us very far if we are to consider the relationship between 'democracy' and education. Is there then any other approach which can help to enrich this rather abstract explication of a concept?

2. THE PRESUPPOSITIONS OF THE DEMOCRAT

Terms like 'consent' and 'the sovereignty of the people' have to be understood in the context in which they emerge; a too formal approach to them often misses the important presuppositions that lie behind their emergence. They have a concrete historical context; they are much more like Bradley's concrete universals than Plato's 'forms'. Those, like Locke, who made much of 'the consent of the people', were speaking from within a tradition in which the king was required to summon Parliament for 'advice and consent' when he wished to impose taxes, which affected the right to property. The fiction was that 'the consent of the people' to taxation was given through their elected representatives. Sir Edward Coke, within the same tradition, maintained, understandably enough, that 'Prerogative is part of the law, but "sovereign power" is no parliamentary word. . . . Magna Carta is such a fellow that he will have no "sovereign".' A way of conducting political affairs had grown up in which explicit principles gradually emerged out of established practices with which rulers had of necessity to come to terms if they wished to rule effectively. The practices in embryonic form went back certainly as far as Magna Carta; they expressed the independent spirit of the English and were embedded in the tradition of the common law which maintained that in matters touching the subject's rights the king's power was limited by precedents which made explicit the customs of the people.[1] Because England was an island the king could only demand a standing navy for the defence of the realm, which was the sphere of his prerogative, not a standing army; and a navy is of little use in bringing recalcitrant subjects to heel. The Stuarts found to their cost, when it came to a show-down in the Civil War, that they were confronted not just with the New Model Army, but with subjects who controlled most of the means of equipping such an army. Also the king could never count on the undivided loyalty of the aristocracy. Class solidarity has never taken very deep root in England. Some kind of political system which was consistent with such stubborn traditions and diverse interests was therefore the only appropriate one. This meant toleration of conflicting opinions and it also meant discussion. The word parliament, coming from the French 'parlement', bore witness to this admission that effective government could only be by discussion. Elizabeth I was very sensitive

[1] For further explication of these matters see Peters, R. S., *Hobbes* (Harmondsworth, Penguin Books, 1956), Ch. 9.

to these traditions and very realistic in accommodating to them; the Stuarts, coming from Scotland, were not. Their appeal to the Divine Right of kings was alien and deeply offensive. These traditions were, of course, taken overseas to America by the Puritans where they developed a life of their own in a new and stimulating environment.

In Chapter IX the process by means of which traditional authority was progressively rationalized was briefly touched upon. But rationalistic ideas, popularized by lawyers such as Grotius, took root in England only because they gave expression at an abstract level to principles which were already immanent in the practices which proved such a stumbling block to autocratic advance. The appeal to 'natural law', 'natural rights', and to the 'social contract' between government and governed made sense to those who had always acted on the assumption that the king's judges only interpreted a 'fundamental law' that was there to discover, and which gave protection to their concrete rights, e.g. to property, and who were accustomed to being consulted for 'advice and consent' by the king. These abstract notions derived their distinctive interpretation from these existing practices—quite a different interpretation from the ones they received in France where there was no such deep-rooted tradition of individual liberty and of limitations on government.

Because of these traditions the Anglo-American conception of democracy has never envisaged 'the consent of the people' as authorizing a government, however elected, to do whatever is necessary for the promotion of the common good. In this respect Rousseau's—or Robespierre's—conception of popular government as an expression of the 'General Will' of the people is quite alien. If the presuppositions of Anglo-American democracy were to be formulated in an abstract way they would probably be something like this: first of all the theory of 'consent' and all the accompanying trappings of 'natural right' and 'contract' took root fundamentally as moralized or rationalized versions of practices which developed as *limitations* on any government whatsoever. Locke's fundamental tenet was that no man 'can be subjected to the political power of another, without his own consent'. Colonel Rainborough put the position much more forcibly in 1647 when he proclaimed 'Every man that is to live under a government ought first by his own consent to put himself under that government; and . . . the poorest man in England is not at all bound in a strict sense to that government that he hath not had a voice to put himself under.' The presuppositions underlying such demands are that government is at best a necessary expedient and that acceptance of it is conditional. Authority is necessary; but it must be constituted in such a way that it does not unduly oppress the individual. It is subject to moral appraisal and must be hedged round with safeguards for the subject. The American constitution, one of the greatest monuments to rationality in the history of man, represents an elaborate attempt to provide effective government within a system of checks and balances that were meant to safeguard the rights of individuals, and of minorities, against the possible tyranny of both the executive and the popular assembly.

This rational and conditional acceptance of authority implies an even more fundamental point, which is the commitment to reason and the denial of any ultimate authority on political matters. All political decisions are moral decisions 'writ large'. By that is meant that though, like educational decisions, they involve complex matters of fact about which experts must be consulted, they always involve moral judgments as well. And the making of moral judgments, as has been argued throughout this book, are within the scope of any rational man; they are not the prerogative of the gifted few. If Plato were right and the form of a good society were only discernible by a few specially trained philosophers, then the benevolent paternalism which he advocated would be the only appropriate form of government. Similarly if the classical Utilitarians were right, if 'happiness' were the only possible end of right conduct and of legislation, and if means of producing happiness were calculable, then all political decisions would become technical decisions and could be handed over to specially equipped social scientists with computers to do the necessary sums. The necessity of discussion and of governments having to defend their policies in public bears witness not simply to the independence and outspokenness of a race of individuals who are determined not to be pushed around without protest; it is also an implicit recognition of the cardinal fact that there are vital aspects of political decisions which are matters of judgment, not of computation. With problems of this sort the only appropriate manner of proceeding is to work towards 'solutions' by adjustment and discussion.

This does not imply moral anarchy, however. Without some kind of consensus such discussion would be impossible. The consensus is provided by the fundamental principles of morality which were explicated in Chapters IV to VIII of this book. These fundamental principles of fairness, liberty, the consideration of interests, and respect for persons were defended as being presupposed in the determination to settle things by reason. They are all of a procedural rather than of a substantive character. They thus provide a procedural framework of principles within which substantive solutions can be sought to both moral and political problems. They are thus presupposed in the Anglo-American version of the democratic 'way of life' which amounts to the determination to settle political matters by recourse to reasonable discussion rather than by recourse to force or arbitrary fiat. It has been argued that this way of conducting political affairs emerged gradually in the practices of our remote ancestors. The Anglo-American conception of 'democracy' is to be understood by reference to principles which have to be interpreted in the light of these practices; it cannot be spun out of the purely abstract concept of 'the rule of the people'.

3. INSTITUTIONAL AND PSYCHOLOGICAL REQUIREMENTS

It was argued in Section 1 that notions like 'the will of the people' and 'the consent of the people' must be interpreted in procedural rather than in substantive terms. In Section 2 it was argued that these notions were immanent in a tradition which demanded limits to government. With the rationalization of authority this approach to government came to be defended by appeals to moral principles, e.g. 'natural law' and 'natural rights', rather than to precedents, e.g. the frequent occasions on which monarchs had avowed their intention of honouring Magna Carta. Political obligation became a particular sort of moral obligation rather than simply an established system of practices. The question, however, is whether any particular political procedures are required by this moralization of political authority. It was argued that 'democracy' entails nothing as specific as procedures such as the election of representatives rather than the constant use of the referendum. But are no political procedures implied by the moral principles which are written into the determination to settle matters, if possible, by the appeal to reason?

(a) Procedures immanent in institutions
Surely the basic requirement is the procedure intimated by 'advice and consent'. Governments found that, of necessity, they could only rule by accommodating themselves to the demands of the major interests of the realm; the governed claimed that limits must be set by right to the king's prerogative. The procedure underlying the compromise reached was that of making provision for considering the interests of the governed.

299

And such provision must be concrete, not notional. J. S. Mill put this point very well when he said: 'The rights and interests of every or any person are only secure from being disregarded when the person interested is himself able, and habitually disposed, to stand up for them. . . . We need not suppose that when power resides in an exclusive class, that class will knowingly and deliberately sacrifice the other classes to themselves: it suffices that, in the absence of its natural defenders, the interest of the excluded is always in danger of being overlooked, and, when looked at, is seen with very different eyes from those of the persons whom it directly concerns.'[1] Those who maintained that there would be no justice without representation were suggesting one obvious device for implementing this cardinal political procedure made explicit by Mill. Whether the election of representatives or constant recourse to a referendum would prove the more effective device is a matter for detailed discussion. But both devices would be ways of institutionalizing this cardinal political procedure.

Of course, historically speaking, the view that every adult citizen should have a right to be consulted in some way took a long time to emerge. In the seventeenth century, for instance, Colonel Rainborough envisaged a universal franchise whereas Locke thought in terms only of the 'consent' of property owners. But historically speaking most general principles of this sort have first been fought for and established on a limited front by a particular section of the community before becoming generalized to all. Rousseau was so intent on ensuring that this principle should be universally implemented, without risk to the individual being misrepresented, that he claimed that there could be no proper democracy without every citizen attending the legislative assembly. Only this would ensure that the sovereign 'neither has nor can have any interest contrary to theirs'. But he also held that such a sovereign assembly was itself the measure of moral obligation and hence 'need give no guarantee to its subjects'. 'The General Will is always right and always tends to the public advantage.' In such claims for the General Will Rousseau not only showed a degree of *naïveté* about the type of consensus attained in deliberative assemblies; he also confused a form of authority and method of arriving at decisions, which are morally acceptable to a rational man, with the criteria of morality. He made the connection between moral principles and political procedures too tight. But what is quite clear is that without some concrete institutional device for implementing

[1] Mill, J. S., *Representative Government* (Everyman ed.), pp. 208–9.

consultation, the fundamental moral principles of the impartial consideration of interests and respect for persons could apply only in the private, not in the public realm.

The next general type of institutional requirement must be for some concrete safeguards for the public expression of opinion. For without such safeguards any formal procedure of consultation would be abortive. Individuals and groups having interests would have little chance of formulating and stating their claims and bringing pressure to bear on government unless they were guaranteed freedom of expression and association—subject of course to the sorts of conditions touched upon in Chapter VII. Toleration developed in this country as one of the basic conditions necessary for conducting our political life. It presupposed not indifference but an intense concern about opinions. Legal safeguards emerged to set a formal seal upon a tradition which had developed partly out of necessity and partly out of principle. Without it talk of consultation would be vacuous. Needless to say it is the sort of institutional provision required by the fundamental moral principle of liberty.

Finally there must be some procedure of public accountability. It would be absurd to develop an elaborate system for consulting the people on matters of public policy without also providing institutional procedures for governments to be taken to task for incompetence, or replaced if their conduct of affairs is unsatisfactory. The great virtue of democracy as a form of government is that governments can be changed without revolution. There are many methods of ensuring public accountability whose merits would have to be discussed in detail. But no system of government could be called 'democratic' without some institutional provision of this sort. This is probably the basic political procedure behind the more exalted notion of 'the sovereignty of the people'.

(b) The habits of a people

It has been stressed throughout this chapter that ideas like 'government by consent' arise within a tradition of political activity and are to be understood not simply as abstract ideas but also as concrete universals. To quote Oakeshott: '. . . Locke's *Second Treatise of Civil Government*, read in American and in France in the eighteenth century as a statement of abstract principles to be put into practice, was regarded there as a preface to political activity. But so far from being a preface, it had all the marks of a postscript, and its power to guide derived from its roots in actual political experience. Here, set down in abstract terms, is a brief conspectus of the manner in which Englishmen were accustomed to go about the business of attending to their arrangements—a brilliant abridgement of the political habits of Englishmen.'[1] This is a slightly one-sided picture of Locke's *Second Treatise*, but it makes the main point, the indispensability of a background to the understanding of political concepts. Oakeshott also argues brilliantly that such systems of ideas can only be applied intelligently and effectively by those who have been brought up in this tradition of behaviour. Locke's ideas took root in America because Englishmen went with them to give them concrete interpretation. In France they never took root effectively. When such a system of ideas is shipped abroad as an 'ideology' it is always hazardous. A better method is when 'the workmen travel with the tools—the method which made the British Empire. But it is a slow and costly method. And, particularly with men in a hurry, *l'homme à programme* with his abridgement wins every time; his slogans enchant, while the resident magistrate is seen only as a sign of servility.'[2]

A precondition, therefore, of a 'democratic' system of government being more than a set of slogans is that a people should have had some relevant experience by reference to which they can apply its abstract principles. It is one thing to formulate principles clearly, and another to justify them, as has been constantly reiterated in this book. But it is still another thing to *apply* moral principles intelligently to concrete circumstances. It is in this area of the application of abstract principles that Oakeshott's writings are particularly pertinent. The consequences of this for 'education for democracy' are not difficult to deduce.

Another precondition of the democratic way of life is that there should be a large measure of consensus at the level of procedural principles. In justifying the principles of fairness, liberty, the consideration of interests, and respect for persons appeal was constantly made to the abstract notion of a man determined to conduct his life by reason, who must seek the co-operation of others in working out what there are reasons for doing. If the democratic way of life is to be a reality, there must in fact be a large number of people who are committed in fact to such a way of conducting their affairs. Otherwise discussion would degenerate into propaganda or abuse, and men would treat those who did not agree with

[1] Oakeshott, M., 'Political Education' in *Rationalism in Politics* (London, Methuen, 1962), pp. 120–1.

[2] Oakeshott, M., op. cit., p. 122.

them as scoundrels or as lost souls in need of salvation. 'Institutions', says Popper, 'are like fortresses. They must be well-designed and manned.'[1] But men to man them do not grow up like mushrooms overnight. To train them is a vast educational undertaking. The life of reason is itself a tradition, the tradition of criticizing traditions,[2] into which a new generation has to be constantly initiated. Without an effective tradition of reasonableness and tolerance democratic institutions would be a formal façade.

There is a final psychological precondition of democracy which is somewhat more elusive. It is that of willingness to participate in public life. This is distinct from the other two psychological preconditions already mentioned; for it is not an unusual phenomenon to encounter members of democratic societies who are administratively competent and eminently reasonable, but who have a distaste for attending to public affairs. Perhaps they will turn up at a meeting if some vital right is threatened; perhaps they will reluctantly take on some office out of duty, if pressure is brought to bear upon them. But they lack that zest for public life which was so characteristic of the Athenians. What is missing is the feeling of fraternity. Their concern for their own interests and healthy feeling that government is a necessary nuisance may have led them to neglect an appropriate focus for the fraternal feeling.

If apathy towards public life becomes widespread democratic institutions are in danger. Rousseau perhaps went too far in trying to rekindle this love of the public life so characteristic of the Greeks. Certainly partly through his influence it permeated the French communes and led to disastrous disregard for the rights of individuals. Its modern counterpart in Communist China and in the USSR indicate clearly both its power and its possible excesses. By contrast the independent attitude of the English, and their distrust of this focus for fraternal feeling, seems eminently sane. But it too may have its excesses. The English are more a race of barrack-room lawyers than of shop-keepers. This tradition has ensured liberty but perhaps at the cost of fraternity. In the USA the balance is more even. Liberty itself is seen very much in terms of attendance at meetings in the neighbourhood and participation in local affairs. They have not the Englishman's confidence that public matters

[1] Popper, K. R., *The Open Society and Its Enemies* (London, Routledge, 1945), Vol. I, p. 126.

[2] See Popper, K. R., 'Towards a Rational Theory of Tradition' in *Conjectures and Refutations* (London, Kegan Paul, 1963).

can be safely left to politicians and civil servants most of the time. This is partly because of the deep-rooted distrust of government so characteristic of the Americans and partly because of the inferior status of politics compared with that of business. They have not the equivalent of the permanent top-ranking civil servant. A new lot comes in with a new President. This means that the American citizen feels much more strongly than his English counterpart the necessity of vigilance, of keeping a check on what the politicians are doing. Also, and perhaps even more important, is the merging of the distinction between the public and the private in the average USA township. They are generally a much more fraternal people. In America they have no walls to their gardens. The similarity, in this respect, between the USA and the USSR has often been noted.

4. THE JUSTIFICATION OF DEMOCRACY

Very little need be said about the justification of democracy; for the basic justification has already been given. As a way of life it represents an articulation in appropriate institutions of the fundamental principles of morality that were justified in Part Two of this book. Thus its ethical foundations have already been established. In Section 3(a) of this chapter it was argued that for this way of life to be publicly implemented at least three political procedures are necessary—those of the consultation of interested parties, of safeguards for freedom of discussion and assembly, and of public accountability. In what particular institutions these procedures are best enshrined is a matter for discussion in the light of contingent circumstances.

It is often said that democracy is an impracticable form of government because it demands of the ordinary citizen qualities which only the few can possess. It must, in the end, represent the views of the 20 per cent who understand what 20 per cent means. This is particularly true nowadays, when estimates of government policy depend upon an understanding of economics which is beyond the reach of most, and of military and diplomatic secrets that no responsible government would ever divulge in public. If democracies appear to work it is only because the *élite* are not too much hampered by having to make concessions to uninformed prejudices.

There is something in this criticism, but not much. To start with it rests upon a naïve view of what is required by the procedures of consultation and public accountability. In a representative system of government there is a tendency to interpret these procedures in terms of some fiction involving a substantive interpretation of notions such as 'the will of the people'. Those who are put in authority, be they members of Parliament or civil servants, are appointed to rule in the public interest; they are not necessarily delegates expressing either a sectional interest or 'the people's will'. As Burke put it: 'Your representative owes you, not his industry only, but his judgment; and he betrays, instead of serving you, if he sacrifices it to your opinion. . . . If government were a matter of will upon any side, yours, without question, ought to be superior. But government and legislation are matters of reason and of judgment, and not of inclination; and what sort of reason is that, in which the determination precedes the discussion; in which one set of men deliberate, and another decide; and where those who form the conclusion are perhaps three hundred miles distant from those who hear the arguments?'[1]

Anyone in authority knows perfectly well that the opinion of the ordinary man about the balance of payments or about the advisability of retaining some remote naval base is not worth much. He knows, too, that he himself has to rely on experts to advise him about all sorts of aspects of policy. His task is not simply to follow public opinion but also to help create it; he must use his authority in support of proposals put forward by people who know what they are talking about. And the public can generally judge the wisdom of policies when they are confronted with their actual outcome. As, however, the stuff of political decisions is the adjustment of interests, a ruler will be very foolish not to consult the major interests affected by any proposals. But concern for the public interest also requires that the interests of individuals and minorities, who cannot exert strong pressure, should not be disregarded. There are issues, too, like those connected with sexual morality and crime, where public policy must be determined more by general moral considerations rather than by expert knowledge. On these matters the conscience of the 'ordinary man' is often as sensitive as that of the ruler. One of the distressing features of modern democratic government is that rulers themselves are, perhaps, too much victims of the presuppositions of this criticism. The wide acceptance of the view that a government must have a 'mandate', and the fear of being thrown out at the next election, often cripple government at a time when political parties are

[1] Burke, E., 'Speech to the Electors of Bristol' 1774 in *Works* (Bohn ed.), Vol. I, pp. 446-7.

evenly matched. Many much needed reforms are not tackled either because there are no votes to be won by making them, or because votes will be lost if any government dares to tackle them. Present examples in England are the divorce laws and the anomalies connected with religious instruction in state schools.

Underlying this criticism, too, is perhaps the strange view that there could be some ideal government in which abstract notions of justice and of the consideration of interests are perfectly realized. This is a Utopian dream. To start with, as has been argued before, the very notion of government itself, implying the placing of some man in authority over others, is prima facie an affront to a rational man. It cannot, by its nature, be an ideal state of affairs; it is at best a necessary expedient. Given that there must be government the realistic question to ask is not whether democracy matches up to some fanciful ideal, but to consider soberly which state of affairs would be worst for a rational man. He must surely think, with Locke, that the worst state of affairs possible is 'to be subject to the inconstant, uncertain, unknown, arbitrary will of another man'. Starting with despotism he can work upwards through the possible forms of government and consider them soberly in terms of the potentialities for oppression and misery which they harbour. When he eventually comes to democracy he may be only too well aware of its frustrations, failings, and hypocrisies; but at least it need not represent such a threat to the individual as other forms of government. It may veer in that direction, if it becomes equated with majority rule, as de Tocqueville so clearly saw. But it need not. It has the supreme virtue that if particular occupants of office turn out to be even worse than expected—and why should it be thought that those who are anxious for office are likely to be angelic beings?—then at least they can be removed without a revolution.

A rational man can reflect, too, that a democracy in which authority is rationalized and in which consultation, safeguards on discussion and assembly, and public accountability are embedded in the practices of a people, represents the only form of political life which is consistent with the fundamental principles of morality. He may even come to enjoy some aspects of the public life which democracy makes possible. His feeling of fraternity may be focused on the striving for the public interest; he may even feel that doing what he can to preserve this thin crust of rationality is even more worth while than pursuing some more private interest. It would be impossible for him to feel in relation to the state as the Athenians felt about their πόλις; but at least in the life of some institution of a democratic sort he might feel some joy in participation. He might feel kinship with other rational beings, both living and dead, in tackling problems rather than parading prejudices. He will know, of course, that any thought of a final solution to them is absurd. Indeed he may realize that the very expedients which are adopted to cure present ills open up dimensions of difficulty undreamt of by his predecessors. But the point is to perpetuate the procedures for tackling problems, not to expect final solutions. The joy consists in travelling with others, not in arriving. Indeed what would count as arriving?

5. DEMOCRACY IN EDUCATION

What implications for education are there in this somewhat pedestrian and piecemeal account of democracy? As was pointed out in the introduction, 'democratic' can be predicated of education in at least three ways. These must now be briefly explored.

(a) The democratization of education

To say that education is not democratic may, first of all, be to condemn it for falling short of the general moral demands made on an educational system by those committed to the democratic way of life. Without education an individual in a modern industrial society is unlikely to be able to proceed very far in developing the particular aspect of a worthwhile form of life to which he is suited; also an educational system acts selectively in equipping citizens with skills and knowledge that are essential to the community's viability and development. From the point of view, therefore, both of the community and of the individual, a democrat would insist that education should be made available for all and that it should be fairly distributed. The implications of this were considered in Chapters IV, V and VI. He would also demand, as a rational being committed to liberty, as well as to fairness and the consideration of interests, that as much freedom of choice should be given to parents and to children as is consistent with the pursuit of objectives falling under the other two fundamental principles, and that all these principles should be implemented with respect for persons. As was made clear in Part Two the enunciation of such general principles is much more likely to command universal assent than proposals for their implementation in concrete circumstances. In this respect they resemble the pronouncements of Rousseau's General Will. But there is no need at this juncture to retrace the ground covered in Part Two.

Another highly debatable question is what institutional devices are appropriate for assuring procedures of consultation and public account-ability which, it was argued, are necessary for making the democratic way of life a reality? No one would dispute that, as education involves a vast expenditure of public money, those who are responsible for man-ning educational institutions should have to consult with those for whom they are run, and that they should be accountable to 'the public' for the way in which they discharge their responsibilities. But the question is at what level this should take place, and what degree of autonomy should be accorded to the teaching profession. In England, for instance, though universities are financed largely by the state, the universities themselves, through the device of the Universities Grant Committee, which acts as a buffer between the universities and the Department of Education and Science (formerly between the universities and the Treasury), enjoy a remarkable degree of autonomy. Colleges of education, on the other hand, are financially and administratively responsible to the local education authorities, or, if they are voluntary colleges, are largely responsible to the Department of Education and Science, and are con-stantly jibbing at the restrictions placed on them. From this point of view, however, their life is idyllic when compared with that of an Ameri-can high school which comes under the jurisdiction of a local school board.

There is very little of a general sort that can be said about this matter. Decisions must depend on at least three major factors in respect of which countries differ greatly. There is first of all the general pattern of democratic procedures prevalent in a country, which will obviously influence the way in which education is administered. It is very difficult, for instance, to compare the English system of accountability with that of America, in view of the fact that England is about the size of New York State, which obviously affects very much the issue of central as distinct from local responsibility. Also, as has already been pointed out, the attitudes towards government in the two countries differ markedly. Both these considerations will affect the willingness of parents to hand over their children to a state educational system without insisting on the right to a close scrutiny at a local level of what is being done.

Secondly, different educational institutions require different forms of control. Universities, with their emphasis on research, are very different from nursery schools and local Technical Colleges. Thirdly there is the important difference, already touched upon in Chapter IX, of the variable status accorded to the teacher in different countries. Is he thought of mainly as an authority on the ultimate values of a community? Or is he regarded mainly as a person 'hired' by the community to train citizens in useful skills and to select them efficiently for necessary occupations?

Obviously these three major variables make it almost impossible for anything of a general nature to be said about the form and level of public accountability. Discussion would have to be detailed and concrete within the context of an established set of institutions. It is no good demanding a centrally organized and controlled system, e.g. the French system, in the USA where the size of the country and the democratic traditions are so different. A philosopher could add his contribution to such a discussion, but enough has been said to show that no substantive 'solutions' can be deduced from philosophical considerations alone.

One general point, however, would follow from the stress placed in Chapter IX on the concept of the teacher as 'an authority', as the custodian of the quality of life of a community. That is that, under modern conditions of democracy, which some have even gone so far as to class as 'the rule of groups' rather than 'the rule of the people', teachers must make themselves much more effective as an organized pressure group on matters of general educational importance. At the moment the public are aware of their collective pressure only in the matter of salary negotiations.

It is often said that this means that teachers should make themselves more effectively into a 'profession'[1]—but what is meant by this? To the ordinary man being a member of a 'profession' means little more than earning a salary rather than a wage. But there surely must be more than this tenuous type of similarity between a doctor, dentist, and a barrister. Presumably members of professions are united also in having tasks which require specialist knowledge and a lengthy period of training. They must, too, have common standards of an ethical sort which are specific to their station and duties. They can be guilty of 'unprofessional conduct'. It is one thing for a university teacher to have an affair with his colleague's wife, but it is quite another thing for him to seduce one of his students. Members of a profession must therefore keep in active touch with the centres of teaching and research from which their specia-

[1] See Lieberman, M., *Education as a Profession* (Englewood Cliffs, New Jersey, Prentice Hall, 1956).

list knowledge emanates, and they must have effective machinery at both the local and the central level for keeping in touch with each other and for making and implementing their collective decisions. In regard to the first requirement teachers have a dual obligation. On the one hand they have to keep in touch with developments in the 'subjects' which they teach; on the other hand they have also to be *au fait* with developments in the 'methodological' aspects of their task, e.g. in educational philosophy, psychology, and sociology. The role-reversal involved in putting themselves from time to time into the situation of pupils once more should also increase their insight into problems of teaching. In regard to the second requirement they should meet in their local associations to discuss matters of common concern. In England Institutes of Education were set up following the McNair Report to provide institutional implementation of the first type of requirement. Teachers are coming to avail themselves increasingly of the facilities and opportunities afforded by Institutes for conferences, and various forms of in-service training on both a part-time and a full-time basis. In this way they are able to keep abreast of the development of knowledge, and there is a built-in source of change, development, and fresh ideas. There are signs, at least in some big urban areas, that the old hostility between hard-bitten practitioners on the job and starry-eyed idealists in Colleges of Education is beginning to be dissipated. But has a corresponding change taken place in teachers' associations? Are meetings well attended when anything other than salaries are under discussion? Are not teachers' associations infected with that general lukewarmness towards democratic participation which was mentioned earlier in this chapter? Certainly there seems to be a much greater sense of involvement in a common enterprise amongst American teachers. But in England generally, as was also mentioned before, the feeling of fraternity seems seldom attached to such common concerns at a local level.

(b) *The school as a democratic institution*

There has been a lot of talk since the time of John Dewey about the school as a democratic institution, but one suspects that few schools deserve such a title in any full-blown sense. And why should they? To start with, in England at any rate, the headmaster is appointed to do a job with very wide terms of reference and it is up to him how much of his authority he delegates. He is also responsible for the organization of a community of predominantly immature people. There are some matters, e.g. the curriculum, the competence of his staff, about which it would be quite inappropriate for him to consult pupils, let alone give them any powers of decision. It is important, therefore, that any discussion of democracy within the school should be prefaced by a realistic appraisal of what the formal position of the headmaster is.

Disillusionment with democracy is only too likely to develop if lip-service is paid to procedures, such as consultation and public accountability, while at the same time those taking part in them know full well that the headmaster is really making the important decisions. It is perfectly right and proper that he should be doing this on certain issues; that, after all, is implied by his being in authority. But in such cases the terms on which others are being consulted should be made clear. This applies in dealings both with staff and with pupils. Is this a situation where a meeting is summoned so that the headmaster may seek advice which perhaps he will not take? Or is it a meeting at which what is decided is what is going to be done? Those who have spent hours attending meetings in schools, colleges, and universities are only too familiar with the cynicism that can be bred if there is ambiguity on this cardinal point. Rationality requires not a haphazard summoning of retainers for 'advice and consent' but a structured situation in which people know where they stand.

Once this general point has been made the form and content of decision procedures becomes a very contingent matter. It depends very much on the age of the pupils, the substance of the decision to be made, and the tradition of the school. Any democratically minded headmaster will consult his staff about most things and provide as much scope as he can for corporate decision. He will encourage children to organize activities themselves with or without staff participation, depending on the nature of the activity and the age of the children.[1] He may institute a school council or parliament, depending on how worth while and effective he judges such a body can be, whose spheres of competence are necessarily bound to be very limited on crucial issues of school policy.

There is then the sphere of discipline and duties which have to be discharged on the community's behalf. The classic device for involving pupils in this has been the appointment of prefects. Indeed Arnold's idea, which has been widely adopted by public schools, is to leave disciplinary matters connected with residence, leisure and games, as

[1] For further details of the various possibilities see Ottaway, A. K. C., *Education and Society* (London, Kegan Paul, 3rd ed., 1962), Ch. IX.

distinct from lessons, almost entirely in the hands of prefects. In a boarding establishment this obviously makes much more sense than in a day-school. It is, however, commonly said nowadays that the institution of prefects is an outworn relic of a bygone and rather brutal era when older boys were encouraged to lord it over younger ones, whose turn to copy such undesirable attitudes would come when they themselves stepped into the shoes of their predecessors.

This type of criticism is sometimes justified; it depends very much on the concept of a prefect prevalent in a particular school. But critics of the prefect system do not usually have in mind the complete abolition of a system whereby senior pupils are given responsibility for various community activities and duties; what they have in mind is the rationalization of such an authority system. Office-holders should be appointed on a purely functional basis for limited periods with defined spheres of competence. There should be rotation in office and some system of public accountability. What is objected to is a system whereby senior pupils, because of their academic ability or prowess at games, are appointed to a status which gives them rather ridiculous privileges, e.g. being permitted to put their hands in their pockets, and entitles them to act rather like traditional squires in a parish of juveniles. Some such rationalized system is obviously necessary for getting various jobs done. If public endorsement is given, e.g. by a school council, for some of the rules which the officers have to enforce, then discipline is not entirely something which is externally imposed by the headmaster and staff. The value of such a system as a training ground, both for developing a rational attitude towards authority and for the actual exercise of it, is obvious enough. But that brings us to the final aspect of democratic education.

(c) Education for democracy

Nothing that goes on in a school can be looked at purely from the point of view of whether it is or is not consistent with the general principles of the adults who are responsible for it; there is also the question of its effect on children and the encouragement offered for the development of a way of life. Any school in a democratic society must therefore consider realistically what it can do to develop democratically minded citizens. The character of such citizens was outlined in Section 2 of this chapter, where it was explained how the democratic way of life, with its emphasis on discussion and the use of reason, developed out of practices which were gradually established.

The fundamental principles, of which an abstract type of justification was given in Part Two of this book, were implicit in these practices. They were gradually made explicit and defended in a more abstract way as the new tradition of rationalism took root, with its demand that nothing should be accepted simply because it is traditional. This did not mean necessarily a change in practices; it meant a different backing or 'ground of legitimacy' to revert to Weber's way of making this point. Most British works in ethics and political philosophy since the time of Hobbes have been attempts to produce a rationale of this way of life. Critics of such works often make the derisory comment that they are rather like shadow boxing; for the philosophers do not doubt that people ought to act justly, be tolerant, consider the interests of others, keep promises, and tell the truth, any more than they doubt that, in some sense, government ought to be by the consent of the people. What they argue about is how these principles can be justified. But on the view put forward in this book this is just what one would expect. For a democratic system can only work if there is a massive consensus at the level of fundamental principles.

It may be argued that the writings of Hegel, Marx, and the Existentialists are only explicable in the light of the *breakdown* of such a consensus. Hence the relativistic account of moral principles as merely reflections of historical or economic conditions, and the stress by Existentialists on individual decision. This may be true of Germany and France and might be a very important factor in explaining the failure of liberalism in these countries; but it certainly is not true of England and America. Of course there are acute disagreements about issues such as gambling, abortion and extra-marital sex relationships. But it is precisely because there is agreement about the procedural principles of fairness, tolerance and the consideration of interests, which provide a framework for such issues to be discussed, that we can afford to differ about lower-level matters where fundamental principles conflict. Such a consensus does not, of course, make these principles valid; that has not been argued. But it is necessary for making democracy more than a formal façade.

How then can schools contribute to initiating each fresh generation into this way of life? This is a vast topic comprising as it does the main substance of moral and political education. It would require a separate monograph to deal with it, and most of the issues would be psychological rather than philosophical. All that can be done in a brief space is to make one or two general remarks which will serve to link this topic with what has been touched upon before in this book.

The underlying idea of all such education must surely be that children should recapitulate in a brief span the more gradual development of their ancestors. They should be initiated into traditions in which the fundamental principles of reason are implicit. At first they will learn to act from others who know how to act, without understanding the reasons. Gradually they will come to grasp the principles underlying their actions, which make reasons relevant, and will be able to act with understanding and to adapt their practice to novel situations. They may also come to challenge some practices as being no longer rationally defensible.

In following this historical paradigm they will be doing, psychologically speaking, all that they can do in learning to live in a reasonable way. For in all education we are confronted by what I have elsewhere called the paradox of moral education.[1] The palace of reason has to be entered by the courtyard of habit. Even in a society where children are encouraged to develop as autonomous beings it is not till about the age of seven or eight that the notion begins to dawn, that rules are not transcendentally given as part of the social order, but that there are reasons for them.[2] They therefore have first to acquire a firm foundation of basic rules[3] in a manner which does not incapacitate them for rational rule-following at a later stage. How they learn to do this is a comparatively unexplored psychological question. But obviously their relationships with parents, teachers, and other authority figures has much to do with it. For like most difficult things in life moral conduct is probably acquired by some process of apprenticeship. If all goes well they will gradually come to grasp in a more explicit way the fundamental principles which provide the backing for the rules which have become almost second nature to them. There are, it has been argued, certain fundamental attitudes underlying this way of life—an overall concern for truth, respect for persons and a feeling of fraternity for others as persons. The contrast between reason and feeling is out of place; for feelings cannot exist without a cognitive core, and the reasonable man must have the appropriate attitudes to sustain him in his manner of life. There may well be a 'natural' basis for such rational attitudes in

[1] See Peters, R. S., 'The Paradox of Moral Education' in Niblett, W. R. (Ed.), *Moral Education in a Changing Society* (London, Faber, 1963).

[2] See Ch. VII, Sec. 5(*a*), on 'autonomy'.

[3] See Ch. VI, Sec. 3, on 'basic rules'.

curiosity and in sympathy for others; but how these become marked out as being of overriding importance, and how they become transformed by built-in standards such as those of relevance, consistency, and impartiality, is an unexplored problem in moral development. Piaget makes much of the fact of the development from the transcendental to the autonomous stage in moral development.[1] But the explanation of the fact, especially in relation to the motivational aspect of such development, is not forthcoming.

Many have argued that peer-group experience is as critical in learning to grasp fundamental principles such as those of fairness, tolerance and the consideration of interests, as is the relationship with authority figures in acquiring a firm foundation of basic rules. This may well be so. But those in authority can contribute much if they provide paradigm examples of reasonable behaviour, and if they help adolescents to accomplish one of the most difficult things of all—the development of a rational attitude towards authority. Any adolescent who has grown up in a fairly normal way must have an attitude towards authority which is to a certain extent ambivalent. On the one hand his attitude must be tinged with feelings of dependence, submissiveness, and perhaps admiration, which are precipitates of his early relationship with his parents; on the other hand there is also that hostility towards such figures which was first roused when they thwarted infantile desires for gratification, and which is kindled afresh when they stand in the way of the assertion of independence in adolescence. This spark of hostility is often fanned into a flame by a combination of peer-group pressure and parental intransigence or feebleness.

Teachers are therefore very often the focus of attitudes towards authority which they themselves have done little to deserve. They may be batting on a wicket which has been treated with candy-floss or trampled on by elephants. They have to learn, therefore, to develop a reasonably detached and uninvolved attitude towards hostile or clinging reactions towards themselves; for the reactions may be more towards what they represent than towards what they are. They must appreciate, too, that patterns of social control are different in families occupying different places in the socio-economic continuum. 'Middle-class' families tend to be much more prone to employ persuasion and to adapt their discipline to individuals; it is person-orientated rather than status-orientated. 'Working-class' families, on the other hand, tend to employ a

[1] See Piaget, J., *The Moral Judgment of the Child* (London, Kegan Paul, 1932).

much more status-orientated all-or-nothing method of control, in which commands and blows alternate with gusty expressions of affection. Teachers, who nowadays are predominantly recruited from a 'lower middle-class' background, may more often encounter problems with discipline if they teach children from a predominantly working-class area.

In Chapter IX the point was stressed that the teacher has to accept the fact that children may identify with him and that he must turn them outwards from an interest in him to an interest in what he is trying to teach. So, too, in the sphere of attitude training, the teacher must accept the fact that he may be regarded as a traditional status holder towards whom either total deference or defiance is due. He has to start from this attitude towards himself and work gradually towards developing a more rational attitude towards an office which he happens to occupy. He has to get children to grasp the point of having people in authority, and to learn to detach this from their like or dislike of the particular people whom they happen to find there.

About training in the manning of democratic institutions there is little to say that has not already been intimated. Much can be done by instruction, by the study of institutions and of their historical development, by visits to Parliament and to council meetings; but practical experience is of far more importance. People sometimes have the naïve illusion that others have a natural flair for contributing to discussions or fulfilling the responsibilities of an office; but of no activities is Aristotle's contention, that the things we have to learn to do we learn to do by doing them, more true than of political activity. Administration requires judgment above all things—judgment of people and judgment of priorities. This can only be learnt by practical experience, preferably under the tutelage of somebody who already has it. There is no way of formalizing it or reducing it to recipes. It is imparted on the job rather than learnt in lectures. A beginning can be made with this at school, if some members of staff have the wisdom and the patience to act in an advisory capacity on various committees and in connection with responsibilities undertaken by the pupils.

The willingness of children to participate in such democratic procedures, and to take on responsibilities, depends mainly on those intangible factors often referred to as the 'tone' or 'the social climate of the school'.[1] It depends also very much on the emergence of leaders. There

[1] See Ottaway, A. K. C., op. cit., Ch. IX, pp. 176–85.

are some such as Sir Karl Popper who argue that democrats should not be preoccupied with the problem of training leaders; for they will emerge all right. The proper preoccupation of the democrat should rather be to devise institutions to protect ourselves against them should they turn out to be too tyrannical.[1] This type of reaction is understandable in the light of the Nazi background against which Popper was writing. It was strengthened, too, by revelations by psychologists about 'the authoritarian personality' and about the unsavoury motives that many leaders seem to harbour. Given, too, the assumption that power tends to corrupt, a half-truth that many find impressive, the build-up against training leaders in a democracy begins to look pretty formidable.

This reaction, however, is really too undiscriminating. It fails, for a start, to distinguish different types of authority,[2] and to indicate the sort of rational leadership that is appropriate in a democracy. There can surely not be anything particularly objectionable about a reasonable, competent man, with a sense of public responsibility and a desire to work with others on some common task, being prepared to take office for a period, if he is appointed by properly constituted procedures with a clearly defined sphere of competence. Of course he may harbour strange motives for doing what he does. He may have a repressed desire to dominate or a yearning to demonstrate his virility. But what if he has? Any teacher may well have such hidden motives too, as well as latent homosexual tendencies or a reluctance to face a life amongst adults. The question is whether such motives distort or disrupt the discharge of his palpable duties. People can be judged only for their conscious intentions and for the competence and decency with which they discharge their duties. If we were all assessed by the state of our innermost souls, very few of us indeed would participate in public life.

There is also the point that experience has shown that one of the main things that can be done in this sphere of training is to transform the concept which a person has of his task. There is not much at such a late stage than can be done about people's innermost motives. Judgment they can only pick up on the job, together with various tricks of the trade, if they work in the company of more experienced people. But attitudes to the discharge of duties can be altered by a combination of experience and group discussion. This is surely one of the main values of super-

[1] See Popper, K. R., *The Open Society and Its Enemies* (London, Routledge, 1945), Vol. I, Ch. 7.

[2] See *supra*, Ch. IX.

vised teaching practice for teachers. Much along similar lines can be done with senior pupils at school towards developing a rational attitude towards the exercise of authority.

A rational attitude towards authority is not conveyed purely by the way in which an individual teacher advises a prefect or handles disciplinary problems with a class. It is conveyed more subtly in much more intangible ways. What chance, for instance, has an assistant master in encouraging such an attitude if he himself is treated in an authoritarian manner by the headmaster, often in front of the boys? If members of staff show little respect for persons in dealing with each other, there is little likelihood of children being so contra-suggestible that they will develop it. This 'social climate' of a school is probably much influenced also by rituals; for rituals are one of the most effective ways for intimating what is of ultimate value without explicitly stating it. In a school the ritualistic aspect of committees, councils, and prefect systems may be as important as the actual training which is provided in carrying out concrete responsibilities. The point has often been made in this book, that both in the sphere of education generally, and in that of moral education, children have to be initiated into forms of thought and behaviour, the rationale of which they cannot at first properly understand. And they have to be got on the inside of these forms of thought and behaviour before they can properly understand them. Rituals, as well as the use of authority, are a method by means of which the importance of a practice can be marked out and children made to feel that it is something in which they should participate. It is surely better than bribing them or goading them.

Rationalists often attack rituals because they lack instrumental value; they do little to promote any palpable purpose. This, of course, is just the point about them. If a practice has an obvious instrumental value, e.g. taking a train to work, there is no need for it to be ritualized. If, however, the point of a practice is difficult to discern because, perhaps, it is largely internal to it, then ritual both serves as a lure for those who are outside and also helps to revive and sustain the belief in it by those who are inside.[1] There are many whose cynicism about the actual working of Parliament has been tempered by participating in some of the

[1] For further discussion of the importance of rituals see Bernstein, B. B., Peters, R. S., and Elvin, H. L., 'Ritual in Education' in *Philosophical Transactions of the Royal Society*, Series B, 'Ritualization of Behaviour in Animals and Man', to be published in 1966 or 1967.

majesty of its rituals, most of which are steeped in historical significance. Such rituals help to unite the past with the future and to convey the sense of participation in a shared form of life. They do something to mitigate the feeling any rational being must have about the triviality and transience of his life upon earth. They do much, too, to develop that feeling of fraternity which is the life-blood of any effective institution.

Democracy is an extremely difficult way of life to sustain. The fundamental moral principles on which it rests—those of fairness, liberty, and the consideration of interests—are principles which are imposed on strong and primitive tendencies. Its emotional underpinning in respect for persons and a feeling of fraternity for others as persons is accessible only to rational men. It requires knowledge about and interest in public affairs on the part of its citizens, and a widespread willingness to work its institutions. It needs, as is often said, constant vigilance to prevent encroachments on the liberties of the individual, as well as institutional safeguards through which such vigilance can find expression. Men do not spring up like mushrooms to run its institutions; they have to be trained. But what more fitting focus could there be for the feeling of fraternity than that of contributing to such a form of life and training others to perpetuate it?

Perhaps in England we are suffering from a kind of malaise, which is accentuated by an overburdened economy. The conservative is afflicted with nostalgia for an age when England had an empire and when life—for the few at any rate—was more gracious. The progressive is disillusioned because he has realized that political panaceas seem prosaic if they are practicable enough to be implemented, and throw up yet another set of problems. Perhaps we are not sufficiently proud of that of which we have a right to be proud—the gradual evolution of a form of government that a rational man can accept. But acceptance is not enough; we have to learn to participate more actively in it with zest and humility. We may then shake off myths about our past and illusions about our future, and come to realize that the most worth-while features of political life are immanent in the institutions which we in fact have. Our problem is to convince ourselves of this as well as to convince our children.

INDEX OF PROPER NAMES

SUBJECT INDEX

INDEX

GEORGE ALLEN & UNWIN LTD

Head Office
40 Museum Street, London W.C.1
Telephone: 01-405-8577

Sales, Distribution and Accounts Departments
Park Lane, Hemel Hempstead, Herts.
Telephone: 0449 3244

Athens: 7 Stadiou Street, Athens 125
Auckland: P.O. Box 36013, Auckland 9
Barbados: P.O. Box 222, Bridgetown
Bombay: 103/5 Fort Street, Bombay 1
Calcutta: 285J Bepin Behari Ganguli Street, Calcutta 12
Dacca: Alico Building, 18 Motijheel, Dacca 2
Hornsby N.S.W: Cnr. Bridge Street and Jersey Street, 2077
Ibadan: P.O. Box 62
Johannesburg: P.O. Box 23134, Joubert Park
Karachi: Karachi Chambers, McLeod Road, Karachi 2
Lahore: 22 Falletis' Hotel, Egerton Road
Madras: 2/18 Mount Road, Madras 2
Manila: P.O. Box 157, Quezon City, D-502
Mexico: Serapio Rendom 125, Mexico 4, D.F.
Nairobi: P.O. Box 30583
New Delhi: 1/18B Asaf Ali Road, New Delhi 1
Ontario: 2330 Midland Avenue, Agincourt
Singapore: 2480-6 Orchard Road, Singapore 9
Sydney N.S.W. 2000: Bradbury House, 55 York Street
Tokyo: C.P.O. Box 2718, Tokyo 100-91

AUTHORITY, RESPONSIBILITY AND EDUCATION

R. S. PETERS

There is something called 'common-sense', on which the English have often prided themselves, which is alleged to remain steadfast in the face of extravagant theories and rapid change. Yet there can be little doubt that many intelligent and practical people find themselves bewildered in the face of many social problems today. From what sorts of moral basis are they to be approached? Can morality stand on its own feet or must it have religious backing? Have Freud and Marx shown that moral principles are merely the product of environment and upbringing and that men are not responsible for their beliefs and backslidings? What sort of authority should parents exercise over their children nowadays? What aims should educators have in a world of rapid change? Of what use is psychology to the teacher?

Dr Peters has collected together a variety of talks which he has given over the past three years, and is publishing them in the hope that they will contribute something towards the clear-headedness of common-sense people.

GEORGE ALLEN & UNWIN LTD